PRAISE FOR MU

"*Jailhouse Lawyers* is a must-read for everyone connected in any fashion to the criminal justice system. It illuminates a dark area seen by few and outlines the legal battles still waged from the 'hole' by the semantic warriors who inhabit it. The book plumbs the depth of man's inhumanity to man by exploring the ongoing legal attack by underground lawyers on an unfair legal system. Death-row prisoner Mumia Abu-Jamal, an award-winning journalist, once again demonstrates his courage in opposing the oppression of prison existence."

—Tony Serra

"Like the most powerful critics in our society—Herman Melville . . . to Eugene O'Neil—Mumia Abu-Jamal forces us to grapple with the most fundamental question facing this country: what does it profit a nation to conquer the whole world and lose its soul?"

—Cornel West

"His voice is vital and strong. . . . The power of his voice is rooted in his defiance of those determined to silence him. Magically, Mumia's words are clarified, purified by the toxic strata of resistance through which they must penetrate to reach us. Like blues. Like jazz."

—John Edgar Wideman

"Brilliant in its specificity and imperative, Mumia Abu-Jamal's work is about why multitudes of people don't overcome. It rings so true because he has not overcome."

—*LA Weekly*

"Abu-Jamal offers expert and well-reasoned commentary on the justice system. . . . His writings are dangerous."

—*Village Voice*

"Mumia refuses to allow his spirit to be broken by the forces of injustice; his language glows with an affirming flame."

—Jonathan Kozol

"Mumia is a dramatic example of how the criminal justice system can be brought to bear on someone who is African American, articulate, and involved in change in society. The system is threatened by someone like Mumia. A voice as strong and as truthful as his—the repression against him is intensified."

—Sister Helen Prejean,
author of *Dead Man Walking*

Jailhouse Lawyers

OTHER BOOKS BY MUMIA ABU-JAMAL

Live from Death Row
Death Blossoms
All Things Censored
Faith of Our Fathers
We Want Freedom

Jailhouse Lawyers

PRISONERS DEFENDING
PRISONERS V. THE U.S.A.

Mumia Abu-Jamal

Foreword by Angela Y. Davis

City Lights Books
San Francisco

Cover design: Pollen
Cover photo of Mumia Abu-Jamal © April Saul/*Philadephia Inquirer*
The cover photograph depicts a holding cell and is not an accurate
reflection of the small cell the author has been forced to occupy on
death row for the past twenty-seven years.

Library of Congress Cataloging-in-Publication Data
Abu-Jamal, Mumia.
  Jailhouse lawyers : prisoners defending prisoners v. the U.S.A. / by
Mumia Abu-Jamal ; introduction by Angela Davis.
      p. cm.
  ISBN-13: 978-0-87286-469-6
  ISBN-10: 0-87286-469-3
  1. Legal assistance to prisoners—United States. 2. Prisoners—Le-
gal status, laws, etc—United States. 3. Law—Study and teaching—
United States. I. Title.

  KF337.5.P7A78 2008
  344.7303'566—dc22
                                                2008020491

City Lights Books are published at the City Lights Bookstore,
261 Columbus Avenue, San Francisco, CA 94133.
www.citylights.com

CONTENTS

Acknowledgments *9*

Foreword by Angela Y. Davis *13*

Note from the U.K. Publisher *21*

Preface *27*

1. Learning the Law *35*

2. What "the Law" Is *51*

3. When Jailhouse Lawyers "Represent" *73*

4. What about Street Lawyers? *117*

5. The Jailhouse Lawyering of Mayberry *151*

6. A Woman's Work in State Hell *167*

7. The Ruiz Effect: How One Jailhouse Lawyer Made Change in Texas *185*

8. From "Social Prisoner" to Jailhouse Lawyer to Revolutionary: Ed Mead's Journey *191*

9. Jailhouse Lawyers on Jailhouse Lawyers *205*

10. The Best of the Best *217*

11. The Worst of the Worst *233*

12. The Social Role of Jailhouse Lawyers *243*

Afterword *249*

Appendix A *255*

Appendix B *260*

Endnotes *265*

Index *279*

About the Authors *288*

ACKNOWLEDGMENTS

This book, like any other, is not a solitary project, although it may seem so, given the domain of the writer.

Books have many mothers and fathers, and are often born of the slightest of suggestions offered on the wind.

First and foremost, however, one must give credit to those men and women who toil in the dungeons of Babylon as jailhouse lawyers, and who are often tossed into the hole for telling another prisoner how to file a writ or helping someone prepare a complaint.

Their work made this work possible.

I thank Delbert Africa (who first told me about jailhouse lawyers), Steve Evans, one of the first I ever met, and also express thanks to:

Frank Atwood
Amber Bray
George Rahsaan Brooks-Bey
Dejah Browne
Roger Buehl
Shaka Cinque aka Albert Woodfox
Matthew Clarke
Margaret Midge DeLuca
Jane Dorotik
Barry "Running Bear" Gibbs
Antoine Graham #203246
Richard Mayberry
David M. Reutter

Samuel C. Rutherford III
Iron Thunderhorse
Teresa Torricellas
Charles "The Dutchman" Van Dorsten
Herman Joshua Wallace
Robert Williams
Ronald "Chief Justice Fatburger" Williams
Ed Mead

These are some of the many jailhouse lawyers (even though some have rejected the name) who answered my questions and wrote with passion and purpose out into a silent world. I thank them for their correspondence.

There are many jailhouse lawyers who wish to remain anonymous, under the radar, because of their very well-founded fear of repression, the hole, or other means of restraint.

I thank them all for being excellent teachers and commend this work to their critique and comment.

The contributors/writers/editors of *Prison Legal News* and its continuing editor (although no longer a prisoner), Paul Wright, also have my thanks. These men and women perform unsung jobs in places where street lawyers fear to tread.

Thanks too to Global Women's Strike and one of its staunchest members, Selma James, who suggested that I do this book and then offered to edit and publish it, sight unseen, even before I had agreed to write it.

I am also quite thankful to my American publisher, City Lights Books, and its indefatigable Brooklynite editor, Greg Ruggiero (of Open Media fame), who took collect calls in the late hours of the night and early morn to help craft this work. His and City Lights' meticulous attention to detail have joined to make this a far better work.

The writer is also thankful for the invaluable support of Noelle Hanrahan and several staffers of the Prison Radio (P.O. Box 411074, San Francisco, CA, 94141), for helping make this process a success.

Thanks to Frances Goldin, agent extraordinaire, who helped bring this baby home to you, dear reader.

My wish is only to tell a story that has never been told before, enriching our understanding of the world's Prison-house of Nations—the USA.

With an estimated three million men, women, and juveniles in American prisons, there are three million stories to be told.

This is but one that I have the high honor of telling.

Mumia Abu-Jamal
Death Row, USA
January 2009

FOREWORD
By Angela Y. Davis

One of the most important public intellectuals of our time, Mumia Abu-Jamal has spent more than twenty-five years behind bars, the majority of that time on death row. He is supported by millions all over the planet, not only because of the egregious repression he has suffered at the hands of the state of Pennsylvania, but because he has used his abundant talents as a thinker and writer to expand our knowledge of the hidden world of jails, prisons, and death houses in which he has spent the last decades of his life. As a transformative thinker, he has always taken care to emphasize the connections between incarcerated lives and lives that unfold in the putative arenas of freedom.

As Mumia has repeatedly pointed out, those of us who live in the "free world" are not unaffected by the system of state violence that relies on imprisonment and capital punishment as pivotal strategies for ordering society. While those behind bars suffer the most direct effects of this system, its raced, gendered, and sexualized modes of violence bolster the institutions and ideologies that inform our lives on the outside. In all of his previous books, Mumia has urged us to reflect on this dialectic of freedom and unfreedom. He has asked us to think deeply about the racial and class disproportions in the application of capital punishment, rarely taking advantage of the opportunity to call upon people to save his own life, but rather using his writing to speak for the more than three thousand people who inhabit the state and federal death rows. Over the years, I have been especially impressed by the way his ideas have helped to link critiques of the death penalty with broader challenges to the expanding prison-industrial-complex. He has been particularly helpful to those of us—activists and scholars alike—who seek to associate death penalty abolitionism with prison abolitionism.

In this book, *Jailhouse Lawyers: Prisoners Defending Prisoners v. the U.S.A.*, Mumia Abu-Jamal introduces us to the valuable but exceedingly underappreciated contributions of prisoners who have learned how to use the law in defense of human rights. Jailhouse lawyers have challenged inhumane prison conditions, and even when they themselves have been unaware of this connection, they have implicitly followed the standards of such human rights instruments as the Standard Minimum Rules for the Treatment of Prisoners (1955), the International Covenant on Civil and Political Rights (1966), and the Convention Against Torture and Other Cruel, Inhuman or Degrading Treatment or Punishment (1984). Mumia argues that the passage of the Prison Litigation Reform Act (PLRA) is a violation of the Convention against Torture, for in ruling out psychological or mental injury as a basis through which to recover damages, such sexual coercion as that represented in the Abu Ghraib photographs, if perpetrated inside a U.S. prison, would not have constituted evidence for a lawsuit. If jailhouse lawyers are concerned with broader human rights issues, they also defend their fellow prisoners who face the wrath of the federal and state governments and the administrative apparatus of the prison. Mumia Abu-Jamal's reach in this remarkable book is broadly historical and analytical on the one hand and intimate and specific on the other.

We are fortunate to be offered this history of jailhouse

lawyers and this analysis of their legacies by one who can count himself among their ranks. Mumia's words in the opening section of the book about the general conditions that create trajectories leading prisoners to jailhouse law are compelling. He writes of a "deep, abiding disenchantment with lawyers that forces some people to become their own, and also to assist others. In every penitentiary, in every state of the U.S., there are men and women who have learned, through study and experience, and trial and error, the principles of the law."

Many of the jailhouse lawyers evoked in the pages of this book—including the author himself—were well educated before they entered prison. Studying the law was more a question of focusing their intellectual skills on a different object than of familiarizing themselves and becoming comfortable with the discipline of learning. But there are also those jailhouse lawyers who literally had to teach themselves to read and write before they set about learning the law. Mumia points to what was for me a startling revelation: jailhouse lawyers comprise the group most likely to be punished by the prison administration—more so than political prisoners, Black people, gang members, and gay prisoners. Whereas jailhouse lawyers are now punished by what Mumia calls "cover charges," historically they could be charged with internal violations for no other reason than that they used the law to challenge prison guards, prison regimes, and prison conditions.

The passage of the Prison Litigation Reform Act (PLRA)—understood by many to have saved the court from frivolous lawsuits by prisoners—was a pointed attack on the jailhouse lawyers Mumia sets out to defend in these pages. He successfully argues that many significant reforms in the prison system resulted directly from the intervention of jailhouse lawyers. Some readers may remember the scandals surrounding conditions in the Texas prison system. But they will not have known that the first decisive challenges to those conditions came from jailhouse lawyers. Mumia refers, for example, to David Ruiz, whose 1971 handwritten civil rights complaint against Texas prison conditions was initially thrown away by the prison administrator charged with having it notarized. As we learn, Ruiz rewrote the complaint and bypassed the prison administration by giving it to a lawyer, who handed it over to a federal judge. This case, *Ruiz v. Estelle*, was eventually merged with seven other cases originating with prisoners. They challenged double- and triple-celling and work regimes that incorporated the violence of plantation slavery.

Moreover, Texas, along with other southern prison systems, relied on what were known as "building tenders," i.e., armed prisoners acting as assistants to guards, for the governance of the institution. The largely white guards and building tenders poised against the majority Mexican- and African-American prisoners led to "abuse, corruption and officially sanctioned injustice." For those who assume that charitable legal organizations in the "free world" were always responsible for the prison lawsuits that led to significant change, Mumia reminds us that what is now known as "prison law" was pioneered by prisoners themselves. These lawyers behind bars practiced at the risk of punishment and even death. Ruiz himself was placed in the hole after filing this lawsuit against the warden. But, as Mumia points out, the state of Texas was eventually compelled to disestablish the building tender system and to curtail its overcrowding and the overt violence of its regimes. Such contemporary suits as the recent one brought in part by the Prison Law Office against the state of California, which focuses on overcrowded conditions and the lack of health care in California prisons, have been precisely enabled by the work of jailhouse lawyers—those who risked violence and even death in order to make their voices heard.

In light of the major transformations that have historically resulted from the work of jailhouse lawyers, it is not surprising that Mumia argues strenuously against the Prison Litigation Reform Act, whose proponents largely relied on the notion that litigation by prisoners needed to be curtailed because of their proclivity to submit frivolous lawsuits. One of the cases most often evoked as justification for the passage of the PLRA was mischaracterized as claiming cruel and unusual punishment because the prisoners received creamy instead of chunky peanut butter. This was not the entire story, which Mumia offers us as a powerful refutation of the underlying logic of the PLRA. Popular representations of prisoners as intrinsically litigious were linked, he points out, to representations of poor people as more eager to receive welfare payments than they were to work. Thus he connects the 1996 passage of the PLRA under the Clinton administration to the disestablishment of the welfare system, locating both of these developments within the context of rising neoliberalism.

Mumia Abu-Jamal's *Jailhouse Lawyers* is a persuasive refutation of the ideological underpinnings of the Prison Litigation Reform Act. The way he situates the PLRA historically—as an inheritance of the Black Codes, which were themselves descended from the slave codes—allows us to recognize the extent to which historical memories of slavery and racism are inscribed in the very structures of the prison system and have helped to produce the prison-industrial-complex. If slavery denied African and African-descended people the right to full legal personality and the practices of racialized second-tier citizenship institutionalized the inheritance of slavery, so in the twentieth and twenty-first centuries, prisoners find that the curtailment of their capacity to seek redress through the legal system preserves and reaffirms that inheritance.

Mumia's profiles include both men and women, both people of color and white people, with disparate motivations and often very different ways of identifying or not identifying themselves as jailhouse lawyers. Prisoners have challenged the law on its own terms in ways that recapitulate the grassroots organizing by ordinary people in the South that led eventually to the overturning of laws authorizing racial inferiority.

As Mumia points out, if there is increasing respect for the religious rights and practices of people behind bars, then it is largely due to the work of jailhouse lawyers. In the state of Pennsylvania, where Mumia himself is imprisoned, one extremely active jailhouse lawyer profiled in the book is Richard Mayberry, who initiated many important lawsuits, including the case known as *I.C.U. (Imprisoned Citizens' Union) v. Shapp*, which broadly addressed health, overcrowding, and other conditions of confinement in Pennsylvania prisons.

> The I.C.U. case ended in a settlement, which required an agreement by all parties. Mayberry served as class representative and signed on behalf of thousands of state prisoners, and a court-agreed settlement went into force, creating new rules that covered the

entire state system. The I.C.U. provisions became the foundation for every subsequent regulation that governed the entire state, and they lasted for decades, until the passage of the Prison Litigation Reform Act. (161)

Mumia not only offers accounts of cases and profiles of prison litigators who have had a lasting impact on the prison system in the United States, he also reveals the extent to which jailhouse lawyers provide legal assistance to their peers, both with respect to their cases and with respect to institution violations. In relation to the latter, outside lawyers are often actually prohibited from representing prisoners, whereas jailhouse lawyers are permitted to assist prisoners in their defense of institutional charges.

Whether the lawsuits generated by jailhouse lawyers are expansive in their reach, potentially affecting the lives of large numbers of prisoners, or whether they are specifically focused on the case of a single individual, they have indeed made an enormous difference. Mumia Abu-Jamal has once more enlightened us, he has once more offered us new ways of thinking about law, democracy, and power. He allows us to reflect upon the fact that transformational possibilities often emerge where we least expect them.

Free Mumia!

NOTE FROM THE U.K. PUBLISHER

This book came out of a visit with one of the most famous prisoners in the world and the most famous living Philadelphian. Mumia Abu-Jamal—Mumia, as he is known to millions—has been on death row for over a quarter of a century. In December 1981 he was arrested for killing a police officer who shot him as he ran to help his brother. Mumia was sentenced to death after a trial so flagrantly racist that Amnesty International dedicated an entire report to it, concluding:

> Based on its review of the trial transcript and other original documents, Amnesty International has determined that numerous aspects of this case clearly failed to meet minimum international standards safeguarding the fairness of legal proceedings. Amnesty International therefore believes that the interests of justice would best be served by the granting of a new trial to Mumia Abu-Jamal.[1]

Mumia and I had never met but I came well-recommended. He had high regard for my late husband, C. L. R. James, author of *The Black Jacobins*, a Marxist and organizer who advocated both class struggle and black autonomy. Niki Adams and I visited Mumia at the end of 2004, and despite the Plexiglas separating us from this handsome, handcuffed man,[2] we talked—from when we were let in at 9:00 a.m. until 3:30 p.m. when we had to leave him behind.

Mumia was remarkably well–informed; as a practicing

journalist he works hard to stay up to date. He hardly mentions his situation or his case. Helped by an optimistic and even temper, he keeps his eyes on the prize, tackling the mountain of work he sets himself. Few of us outside function that well.

When Mumia mentioned jailhouse lawyers, he was taken aback by our excitement. While prisoners everywhere are driven to become legal experts to defend themselves, we had not heard this expertise named and acknowledged. Niki coordinates a self-help legal service[3] in London; the low-income people she works with learn the law and insist on its application to win the justice that professional lawyers—Mumia calls them "street lawyers"—can't or won't fight for. Jailhouse lawyers, amazingly, were doing similar life-saving work, with immeasurably more constraints and fewer resources.

Before we left that afternoon, we had asked Mumia if he would consider writing a book about jailhouse lawyers. The first on this important subject, it would enable the public to glimpse a crucial aspect of the growing movement against the prison-industrial complex hidden by high walls and steel doors, one which Mumia knows inside out. (We later learned—not from him—that his own jailhouse lawyering had got him appointed vice president representing jailhouse lawyers of the National Lawyers Guild.)

A couple of months later, he wrote to say yes, he would do the book and agreed to work with us on it, despite an ocean between us.

At the time I knew nothing of what Mumia had to consider before agreeing to do this book. He has a heavy schedule. He writes books and articles. He phones weekly commentaries to the Prison Radio Project. He sends messages to movement events—showing solidarity with their causes and using his voice to transcend the barriers of prison walls. He needs to do a lot of reading, making careful notes and excerpts since he's allowed only seven books at a time in his cell which, he says, is "as large as your bathroom." Despite repression and restraints, Mumia Abu-Jamal is leading *his* life, not the one he planned for himself but not the one his persecutors planned for him either.

As I got to know him, I began to understand that Mumia personifies the best of the movement of the 1960s: committed, principled, loyal, and determined to win. He became a Black Panther at 14, when millions of young people in many parts of the world were creating communes and collectives. Panthers, under constant attack, couldn't choose as many white kids did to "turn on, tune in and drop out." Panther life was also collective but one of struggle and service: from legal defense to the breakfast program for children, to distributing bags of groceries to poor Black people. By their late teens, many of these young people were experienced political organizers. Some, like Chairman Fred Hampton Sr., who was killed by the government when he was 21, became distinguished political leaders. Mumia, a teenager, spoke at Hampton's Philadelphia memorial.

Mumia's journalistic mastery and consistency derive from this history, training, and an uncompromising commitment to change the world. This makes his journalism among the most radical and distinguished in the United States—a beacon during the benighted Bush years. The support movement, which has stayed the hand of the state against his execution, has grown worldwide because of who he is, a fighter free of machismo and self-indulgence.

These qualities inform every page of this book, which took shape despite petty and malicious prison restrictions. Telephone charges for prisoners are inflated to dollars per minute even as tariffs dwindle for the rest of us. Prisoners are denied access to computers—Mumia has yet to use one or go online. He must buy typewriter ribbons inhouse at inflated prison prices—ribbons reused until they become so lightly inked that the script can barely be read let alone scanned; each draft of the book needed retyping. City Lights Books and Mumia continued the editing process, resulting in the final version presented here.

Mumia uncovers what extraordinary lives of resistance some prisoners have created from need, imagination, and determination. Drawing on his experience, compassion, and extensive correspondence, he sketches portraits of great jailhouse lawyers focussed on beating justice out of the system. Often spurred by the need to repair the damage to their own cases inflicted by lazy and uncaring "street lawyers," Mumia describes how jailhouse lawyers learn the law, the precedents, the jargon, and mount a legal defense, often formidable. Despite great odds, they often—well, sometimes—win, and even win big. Other prisoners might then apply for their help, and some then get hooked into dedicating their time to this. In the process they carve out a life for themselves, a victory in itself.

Mumia doesn't neglect women, the least visible of the prison population. More than one jailhouse lawyer dedicates herself to justice for women prisoners. Compounding the tragedy of imprisonment, women often carry the heavy responsibility and guilt of being mothers.

No word was added or deleted without Mumia's express permission. He was always ready to consider another view. We debated (sometimes in long letters) the impact of jailhouse lawyers winning. Does it give the system credibility when after great effort you save a life? We concluded that not only does every life matter but that every victory strengthens and encourages our side.

As this book goes to press, an appeal on Mumia's behalf submitted by Robert R. Bryan, his committed lead attorney, is being considered by the U.S. Supreme Court. The key issue is that racism in jury selection kept some Black people off the jury, ensuring Mumia's conviction. If the Supreme Court accepts his appeal, Mumia will get the new trial he has fought for.

Racism in jury selection, central in thousands of cases of imprisoned women and men of color, including on death row, is a crucial aspect of racism in the United States. If you're Black you can now be elected president; but unless you're president, racism can still keep you off a jury; and if you're accused of a crime, racism can impose a jury likely to convict whatever the evidence. In confronting racism in jury selection, Mumia is doing cutting-edge justice work for many others.

One in every ninety-nine people in the United States, and one in every nine Black men between the ages of 20 and 34, are in prison.[4] We hope this book will contribute to changing that. It could also inspire another kind of collaboration. The book tells the story of how one jailhouse lawyer learned that legal action inside could be far more effective if it was reinforced by simultaneous actions outside. We see no reason why what jailhouse lawyers do should not be regularly supported in this way. That's for the future—though we hope not too far in the future.

At showings of *In Prison My Whole Life*, a new film about Mumia's case, audiences have been immediately engaged by him. His voice from death row, powerfully honest and compelling, is a force against the death penalty, but also against racism and sexism, exploitation and war. He speaks for internationalism, for movements, and for revolution. Mumia, our jailhouse lawyer, advocates to liberate us all from the social, political, and psychological prisons that hold us captive. Best of all, he introduces us to jailhouse lawyers who, like him, are determined to win.

Selma James
November 2008

PREFACE

I mean, c'mon—seriously! What in the hell *is* a "jailhouse lawyer"?

Depending on your station in life, the term is apt to evoke a variety of responses. Disbelief. Laughter. For some, perhaps confusion.

Jailhouse lawyer? The term implies a dissonance, a kind of contradiction in terms.

Yet, even if some shun the title, there are tens of thousands of men and women who actually are such a thing, and like most people, they are heir to all the winds of whim, good and bad, competent and incompetent, large-hearted and petty.

Years ago, before I entered the House of Death, I interviewed a man in Philadelphia's Holmesburg Prison who was quite opinionated on the subject. His name was Delbert Africa, a well-known member of the revolutionary MOVE organization, who soon would face a de facto life sentence in Pennsylvania's dungeons for being among nine people who had the temerity to survive a deadly police assault on their home and headquarters on August 8, 1978.[1]

Delbert Africa was an eloquent interviewee who spoke with a distinctive country accent, his conversation peppered with passion, reason, and commitment. He spoke disparagingly of jailhouse lawyers, and when I asked him why he felt this way, he responded, "Them dudes get in there, read alla them law books, and before you know it, they be crazy as hell!"

"What do you mean, *crazy?*" I asked.

"Well, they may not be crazy when they *get* here, but after a while, after a few months of reading that shit, they go down to City Hall, and when they see that them folks down there in City Hall, in the System, don't really *go* by that so-called law, well!—it plumb drives them dudes crazy!"

"Yeah, man, but why it drives 'em dudes crazy?"

"'Cuz they cain't believe that the System don't follow they own laws!"

"But why?" I continued.

"It drives they ass crazy 'cuz they cain't handle the fact that the System just make and break laws as it see fit! How many treaties they done signed with the Indians? Ain't a one of 'em they done kept! Some of 'em broke 'em befo' the ink was dry on 'em old treaties! Them the same folks who run this System today! If they couldn't keep a treaty with Indians when they first got here, what make you think they gonna keep they so-called law today, especially when it come to me and you, man?"

"Bro—I get that; I understand that. But what's up with them *crazy jailhouse lawyers*—I don't get that."

"They go crazy becuz, Mu, they really believe in the System, and this System always betray those that believe in it! *That's* what drive them out they minds, man. They cain't handle that. It literally drives them out they mind. I see 'em around here, walkin' 'round here dazed, crazy as a bedbug!"

It took me a while, but I got him. When he told me

those words, I was a *free* man—as free as a Black man can be in America—and working as a reporter and producer for a Philadelphia public radio station. When Delbert Africa broke it down for me, I had no idea that, years later, his words would take on such significance.

His words flew back to me like a pigeon to its coop when I was in the prison law library speaking with a younger man named Qadir who was on death row with me. Qadir was a prodigious legal researcher. He read criminal cases constantly and researched his own case to the nth degree. He knew the relevant case law, the pertinent statutes, and had tightly studied precedents that reflected on the issues in his case.

As he discussed the matter with me and showed me the case citations and excerpts from those cases to support his argument, he asked my opinion. I had been on death row longer than he had, so I ventured that he may have been correct in what the state court opinion said, but that alone wouldn't determine the outcome of his case. He was especially focused on the fact that his capital jury had surreptitiously broken sequestration—the court's order that the jury be separated from the public for fear of tampering—and was certain that because they crept out of their hotel rooms and partied with other hotel guests until dawn, a new trial would be granted.

Qadir was adamant.

"Look, Mu—here it is, right here, in black and white! A jury can't break their sequestration—it's a direct violation of a judge's order!"

"I hear you, Qadir—but, just 'cuz somethin' is written there in those books, don't mean the Supremes [shorthand for the Pennsylvania Supreme Court] gonna grant you relief."

"Yes, it do, Mu! It do! Here it is in black and white, man! They *gotta* grant me relief!"

"Qadir—"

"They *gotta*—it's right here!"

"Qadir—"

"Can't you see that, man? It's hornbook[2] law—they *gotta* give it up!"

"Qadir—Qadir! They do what they wanna do, man! Just 'cuz it says something in one case, they don't have to go by that case, man. I agree with you, that you got a damn good argument—and you should prevail—but I don't go for that 'gotta' rap."

"You wrong, Mu! You wrong! Here it is right here! They *gotta* give it to me! No ifs, ands, or buts! It's in black and white!"

Qadir would not, indeed, could not relent. Nothing I said could get through.

It would be months, perhaps a year, after our law library debate, that the Pennsylvania Supreme Court finally delivered its lengthy opinion. It affirmed both the convictions and the sentence of death. In dry, distanced legalese, the judges explained away the wayward jury. The defendant could not prove any prejudice derived from the jury's escape from the hotel during its sequestration.

Within days, Qadir was heard muttering and blathering stuff from his cell about "the Mothership" coming to pick him up, to fly him away from death row. It took days, perhaps weeks, for men around him to talk him down, to bring him around.

His mind, unable to accept the court's decision, had snapped. He was right on the legal precedents, but what did it matter?

✛ ✛ ✛

While I was being held at Huntingdon Prison in central Pennsylvania, a volunteer lawyer visited who wanted to assist me in a civil action, and we discussed the law.

He was giving me the drill, telling me his opinion on what the law was on First Amendment[3] issues, and I replied, "Man, the law ain't nothing but whatta judge *say* the law is."

The lawyer abruptly stopped his discourse and stared.

"What's wrong, man?"

"Uh—nothing . . . but why did you say that?"

"'Cuz that's what I see, man. You could have an issue, and it be on all fours with a issue in a case. You be right, and you know you right! The judge shoot you down. Now, what's the law? What's written in that law book, what's written in that case, or what the judge say?"

"In my first year of law school, that's exactly what my law school professor used to teach! I'm just surprised to hear you say almost the same things."

"Damn! And I didn't have to go to law school to learn that, huh?"

All across America, there are many men and women in county jails and state and federal prisons who are active, working jailhouse lawyers, but most of whom have never spent an hour in a law school class. They have learned, in their own way, what the "law" is, hard-won knowledge earned through years of experience in the fight.

This is the story of law learned not in the ivory towers of multibillion-dollar-endowed universities, surrounded by neatly kept lawns and served by the poor, who clean, sweep, and wash their cares away. It is law learned in the bowels of the slave ship, in the hidden, dank dungeons of America—the Prisonhouse of Nations.

It is law learned in a stew of bitterness, under the constant threat of violence, in places where millions of people live, but millions of others wish to ignore or forget.

It is law written with stubs of pencils or with four-inch-long, rubberized flex-pens, with grit, glimmerings of brilliance, and with clear knowledge that retaliation is right outside the cell door.

It is a different perspective on the law, written from the bottom, with a faint hope that a right may be wronged, an injustice redressed.

It is Hard Law. These are the stories from that voyage.

Mumia Abu-Jamal
Death Row, USA
January 2009

Jailhouse Lawyers

1

LEARNING THE LAW

How does an imprisoned person become a jailhouse lawyer?

There is no Jailhouse Lawyer University. There is no jailhouse bar exam. There are no associations that one is required to join.

Some actually study basic Anglo-American law through correspondence courses, which are usually rudimentary histories of legal development, legal theory, and broad legal principles. Such courses enable a student to function as a paralegal, or one who assists a lawyer in the performance of a lawyer's duties.

But we must consider the context. In most American prisons, where illiteracy is common, someone with paralegal skills can make quite an impact. Such abilities, combined with a modicum of common sense and research of relevant cases, can mean the difference between a winning case and a dud.

When some institutionally trained lawyers find their way into jail (after disbarment, of course), they sometimes function as jailhouse lawyers, but this is a rare occurrence.

Most are taught by other jailhouse lawyers, a method that hearkens back to the once-common practice of apprenticeship. For example, Abraham Lincoln, famed as a trial lawyer before becoming president, never attended a law school. He learned by watching, by studying legal treatises, and by doing.

While apprenticeship still obtains in several states of the Union (roughly six states, among them California and Vermont), it is not a common practice. Today's lawyers have usually studied three to four years at a law school approved by the American Bar Association, following four years of undergraduate education. While we may assume that such an extensive education equips people to function as lawyers, one who has had a lifetime of experience in the field might argue with such a view.

Former chief justice of the Supreme Court Warren Burger has described "our" legal profession as "sick." In Burger's view, the U.S. legal profession is marked by "incompetence, lack of training, misconduct, and bad manners. Ineptness, bungling, malpractice, and bad ethics can be observed in courthouses all over this country every day."[1]

If such was the view of one of the nation's leading judicial officers, the wonder is not that there are tens of thousands of jailhouse lawyers, but that there are not many more.

It is this deep, abiding disenchantment with lawyers that forces some people to represent themselves and also to assist others. In every penitentiary, in every state of the United States, there are men and women who have learned through study and experience, trial and error, the principles and practices of the law.

Many study case reports[2] from cover to cover, and by so doing learn not grand theories of law, but how actual litigants fare in real cases where life, liberty, and property are at stake. Instead of dealing with a single state, such reports often describe cases from broad regions of the United States, so students learn about cases and outcomes in various state court systems, providing further insight into how their state may be out of step in some respects. They frequently read through broad areas of the law, not limited merely to criminal issues but including civil law, divorce complaints and property disputes. Such studies enable good jailhouse lawyers to serve their clients in a variety of ways.

Because such students will never be trained as representatives of the state, as in most law schools, they become deeply committed advocates for those they assist and serve. Their clients are their associates, sometimes their friends, and they themselves are as confined as those they are assisting. Since both client and jailhouse lawyer are convicts, it isn't a stretch to say they identify with their clients, since they share an adversary. For both jailhouse lawyer and client, the state is that entity that stole their freedom and with which they must contend, and they are thus highly motivated to fight for those who enlist their help.

What follows are stories and firsthand accounts from the shadow world of jailhouse lawyers. These are stories of prisoners who use their time and mental energy to aid their often uneducated and illiterate fellow prisoners, for little more than a bag of coffee or a pouch of tobacco as pay.

Steve Evans

Steve was a slight, intense man, with a distinctive limp from his North Philadelphia days. With his curly hair and sharp features, he looked like an olive-skinned Puerto Rican. When he spoke, however, his accent was definitely North Philadelphia, with a taste of his family's native Virginia.

Because he refused to take a cellmate, he was placed in the "hole," the prison's disciplinary housing unit on B Block of the century-old Huntingdon State Prison. In the approximately seven years that he spent in the hole, he left his cell rarely, venturing to visit the so-called yard—it was actually a row of cages—perhaps twice in half a decade, while conducting the majority of his business by either rapping to people from his cell or writing notes to them.

He had two hard-and-fast rules that governed his practice: no snitches and no baby rapers. All other convicts could approach him for help and he would usually find time to work on their cases. He was also a teacher for younger men who aspired to become jailhouse lawyers. He worked incessantly.

He asked men around him to order cases from both the prison law library and from various courts (for example, the U.S. Supreme Court provided a limited number of free opinions of their cases). Steve therefore read constantly and, fueled by an ever-present cup of Maxwell House coffee and a potent drag of his hand-rolled Top cigarette, he would take time off to discuss cases with interested guys deep into the night.

His reputation reached far and wide; men knew that he could be trusted to write their writs or advise them on where and how to lodge an appeal, when no other person on earth seemed to care. Every so often, a guy would come back from court and announce that Steve's advice was correct; he had received a new hearing in his case, or sometimes a new trial. Steve seemed to take such news with genuine equanimity. If he obtained an ego boost from such news, it never showed. He seemed nonplussed about his considerable talents and brushed off praise like dandruff.

This seemed all the more remarkable in the context of prison's all-male milieu, where machismo often demands egotism.

Once, he was compared to another legendary jail-house lawyer, an older white guy named Mayberry who won more civil cases than most lawyers do in their entire careers. It is rare to open a case report that doesn't begin or end with Mayberry in the citation, or at least mention him in the text.

Steve demurred.

"I don't even compare with that dude, man. I mean, he has spent a lifetime in these joints, filing cases from here up to the Supreme Court. His stuff is in the casebooks, man. He done made more law than street lawyers."

When the speaker wouldn't accept his assessment, Steve went even further.

"Dig this—I can't even hold a jock strap to that dude, man. I might know this or that about the law—and at that, only criminal law—but this dude knows criminal law and civil law, back to front. I don't, man."

When the speaker once again protested, Steve politely closed the door.

"I ain't got no ego about this stuff, man. I will help a brother, but I'm also helping myself. I learn when I look at other cases, man. But I don't trip on it, man. I ain't got no ego about the law, man. That's *they* law; it ain't *our* law, dude.

"They make that shit up as they go along."

Such an assertion may sound shocking, but is it?

We, as Americans, believe that laws are decided by judges (or justices) of the courts. Essentially, judges say what the law is.

But history teaches us that it ain't always so. Let us briefly examine the case of *Santa Clara County v. Southern Pacific Railroad* (1886).[3] When California sought to tax the wealthy railroad companies, the companies went to court to defeat the challenge. The case went all the way to the Supreme Court, which, not surprisingly, ruled in favor of the rich.

What is remarkable isn't *that* they did it, but *how* they did it.

If one peruses the text of the opinion, one will find no reference to what is now regarded as its central holding: that corporations are *persons* within the meaning of the Fourteenth Amendment to the Constitution, and are thus entitled to full constitutional protections.

How can that be?

It seems that the court reporter, whose duties are to record the proceedings, introduce the opinion in the printed text, and then publish the official opinion, cited a remark made by the court's Chief Justice prior to oral arguments. In what are called the headnotes[4] to the case, chief court reporter J.C. Bancroft Davis wrote, "The defendant Corporations are persons within the intent of the clause in section I of the Fourteenth Amendment to the Constitution of the United States, which forbids a State to deny to any person within its jurisdiction the equal protection of the laws."[5]

But headnotes only serve as a convenient summary of the actual case. This recap is sometimes referred to as a syllabus. In any event, *they are not part of the case*. No judge or justice writes a headnote, nor is the court bound by any part of it.

Writing headnotes is the duty of the court reporter, who, while a court employee, is not a judicial officer.

Yet Davis' assertion became the law—and it stands to this very day. Now, to return to our deeply held belief that judges make laws, that's true—to a point. Perhaps it's truer to say that judges make such laws as their law clerks allow.

I say that because these law clerks, usually stellar twentysomething grads of the nation's most prestigious law schools, perform a dazzling array of judicial duties, so much so that such a credential virtually ensures one's future as a law professor or practitioner. Indeed, law clerks have a habit of being recycled in later life as Supreme Court justices (which makes sense, for haven't they already done the work?). Perhaps the best-known of recent years was the late Chief Justice William Rehnquist, who was a law clerk for Justice Robert Jackson of New York.

What do law clerks do? Former law clerk Edward Lazarus wrote a book about his experiences during what he termed the "dog days" of the court's term, March and April. He lists some of the duties of the law clerks:

> [D]rafting majority opinions, drafting dissents, drafting concurrences (opinions that agree with the result reached by the majority opinion but for somewhat different reasons), writing "bench memos" (which help a Justice prepare for a case the Court is about to hear), writing post-oral argument memos (which amend views set forth in bench memos), commenting on draft opinions, dissents, and concurrences circulated by other Chambers, recommending which new petitions for *certiorari* the Court should grant, and advising on emergency applications, often including last-minute requests for stays of execution.[6]

Given that insight, who really makes law?

There is a considerable distance between the offices of a court clerk and the prison cell, yet the vagaries of the clerk's duties visit profound consequences on the inmate. For many men in Huntingdon State Prison, that distance of class, space, and power was bridged by the intercession of a committed jailhouse lawyer.

Steve Evans taught what he learned about the law to as many men as he found were patient enough to study. There are now dozens of people all around the state who have learned from him.

The problem was, as much as he tried, Steve couldn't get anything really cooking on his own case. It's the bane of jailhouse lawyers. They seem to be able to help everybody but themselves. With his aggravated assault case—Steve said he shot a dude who was trying to shoot him—he couldn't buy a new trial. Yet, win or lose, he continued to try to get a good result. He fought as long and as hard as he could.

Steve never obtained the key to his own case, and maxed out—did the maximum sentence. As he prepared to leave Huntingdon Prison and return to his beloved family home in Virginia, he was served notice of a long-forgotten federal detainer—a legal order forbidding his release to anywhere but federal custody—and snatched straight into federal custody, where his fight for freedom began anew.

This was not to be. Disheartened by the turn of events, after nearly a decade of living in the hole, smoking—as he used to joke—"like a Cherokee," rarely exposed to fresh air or sunlight, Steve died of lung cancer while imprisoned in Lewisburg Federal Prison in Union County, Pennsylvania, near Bucknell University.

Before he died, one of his students, a remarkable

autodidact named Warren Henderson, would make his teacher proud—as well as break his heart.

Warren Henderson

Warren was a young man who came to Huntingdon after the ruinous street wars of the 1970s had raged like a tsunami through North Philadelphia. Like far too many coming from the city's decaying public schools, he was poorly educated and could barely read.

Locked in the hole for years, Warren found that the only companions he could count on (other than his "old-head" Steve) were books. So, through force of will, he taught himself to read. And once those strange black scribbles on paper began to make sense to his brain, he broke the bank of learning and reading.

He didn't just love reading, he loved books, and scoundrel that he was, he became what Steve jokingly called a "biblio-kleptomaniac"—a notorious book thief. Any book that came into his hands would be quickly and thoroughly devoured—and then would mysteriously disappear!

One day, returning from the yard, I glanced into his cell, only to find him sitting in the very center of the cell, with his feet tucked beneath him like a Zen monk. On the floor were four thick books, placed around him like cardinal points of a compass.

Having never seen such a sight before, I asked him what was he doing.

"I'm readin', Mu," he innocently answered, as if it were obvious to any slug with a brain.

"Four books—at one time?"

"Sure," he replied, with his distinctive high-octave voice, as if it should've been obvious to a dim-witted child.

"But, why . . . ?"

"I gotta get 'em read before the guards come in and take 'em!"

I recognized among the books one I sent him a few days before. It was *Miguel Mármol*, Salvadoran poet Roque Dalton's remarkable biography of the Latin American revolutionary. I began questioning Warren about the early chapters and he answered each question promptly and correctly.

He spoke about the other texts just as easily.

"But, Warren—how do you read four books at the same time?"

"I read one chapter from one book, then spin around to the next book, and then the next, until I finish them all."

"And you don't get mixed up or confused by switching from one book to the next—one storyline to the next?"

"Nope—it's fun that way! You don't do that?"

"Don't do that? I can't do that, man! Stuff'll get all jumbled up!"

"C'mon, Mu—stop playin', man."

Warren was serious. But I never saw the copy of *Mármol* again.

Warren would ship hundreds of books home to his mother. When I asked him about it, he said, "When I get home, I'ma start a community library, so kids in the 'hood can grow up readin' these books."

When Warren went home, however, he wouldn't get the chance to build his dream. He got into a conflict with another young man in the informal drug industry and was convicted of slaying the man. He was sentenced to life in October 1991. While awaiting trial, he was also charged with stabbing a man to death at the since-closed (and later reopened) Holmesburg Prison in Philadelphia.

Warren, well schooled by Steve Evans, acted as his own attorney at the murder trial where there was no shortage of jailhouse snitches. The jury was out for six hours before they returned with their verdict.

Not guilty.

Even the trial judge had to admit, "You did a good job representing yourself."

Warren calmly responded to the verdict, "It took a long time to prove my innocence."[7]

He had no GED.[8] He had no college degree. He had no law degree. But he had years of tutelage under Steve Evans, jailhouse lawyer. Evans's instructions doubtless saved him from death row.

Warren learned many things in the hundreds of books he swiped and read, among them a deep love of reading and a hunger for writing. He's written and self-published several books on his rough-and-tumble upbringing in North Philadelphia. His first work, published in 2005, was *City of Nightmares: BQ4775*, a book as raw and as original as its author.

Warren also read his share of law books. Through long years of reading, as well as enduring Steve's late-night lectures, Warren Henderson learned the law.

The Law of Jailhouse Lawyers

In prison as elsewhere, as we have seen, law is what the judge says it is. What published opinions claim, in all their legal niceties, matters little.

For jailhouse lawyers, one of the fundamental cases is *Johnson v. Avery*, a 1969 U.S. Supreme Court decision that rejected Tennessee's punishments against a prisoner who assisted another prisoner with his legal work.[9] Tennessee argued that the prisoner violated a prison regulation barring prisoners from functioning as jailhouse lawyers; he violated state law restricting the practice of law to those licensed to do so.

The Supreme Court determined that the central question was the availability and quality of legal assistance provided by Tennessee to those prisoners who needed it. The state allowed prisoners minimal assistance, sometimes limited to allowing prisoners to place phone calls to public defenders, and the court, finding this wanting, held that absent more adequate assistance, it could not penalize a prisoner jailhouse lawyer for giving his. In essence, the *Johnson v. Avery* decision recognized not the right of jailhouse lawyers to practice, but the right of their clients to have meaningful access to the courts. Nevertheless, it has become a kind of charter for jailhouse lawyers ever since.

Some states have attempted to institutionalize this practice by sending interested prisoners to paralegal courses and, when they graduate, hiring them as prison library assistants. This comes with quite a caveat, however, for some paralegals are strictly forbidden to assist prisoners in preparing or bringing a legal claim to court. They may provide case citations or copies of cases decided by a given court, but only if the borrower knows and cites the proper case numbers. Yet by restricting rather than expanding the right of the imprisoned to fight their case or to litigate a claim against the prison or the state, the state's initial aim is reached, albeit by other means.

Before *Johnson v. Avery*, jailhouse lawyers were routinely thrown into the hole for their writ-writing activities. In *Johnson's* wake, however, states across the country lost a series of cases brought by jailhouse lawyers who, as a direct consequence of their violation of prison regulations, had lost good time, or a cut in one's term, and other amenities. For example, in *Ayers v. Ciccone*, a federal court granted a writ of habeas corpus, ordered restoration of the petitioner's good time, and issued a permanent injunction against the enforcement of the regulation without a "reasonable alternative" that offered legal help to prisoners of the Missouri Medical Center.[10]

But a funny thing happened in the aftermath of *Johnson v. Avery*.

Prison administrators began using other reasons and pretexts to punish prisoners who were active jailhouse lawyers—especially those who were engaged in civil actions against the prison administration.

In 1991, a group of scholars, researchers, and activists headed by Mark S. Hamm conducted an extensive review of disciplinary actions occurring in prisons across the country. The study found that no segment of the modern American prison population—not Blacks nor gays nor AIDS patients nor gang members—outweighed jailhouse lawyers when it came to prisoners who were targeted by the prison administration for punishment.

In their report, "The Myth of Humane Imprisonment,"[11] the writers presented a telling tableau of the most frequently disciplined groups of prisoners:

Table 1[12]

Group	Percentage of sample
Jailhouse lawyers	62.1
Blacks	51.2
mentally ill	37.5
Gang members	32.7
Political prisoners	33.3
Hispanics	29.6
Homosexuals	24.0
Whites	20.1
AIDS patients	18.4
Physically handicapped	17.3
Asians	5.0

The report notes, "Respondents observed that guards and administrators had a standard practice of singling out jailhouse lawyers for discipline and retaliation for challenging the status quo." It is telling that those who, for the most part, are the most studious of prisoners, those who are most apt to use pen and paper—rather than, say, a "lock in a sock"—to address and resolve grievances, are the most targeted of all prison populations. It speaks volumes about the threats posed to the people who think and who work to transform the repressive power relations that exist in every prison in the United States.

While the Hamm report may not have met the standards of rigor required by academic journals, other studies, such as that undertaken in furtherance of the civil actions of *Ruiz v. Estelle*,[13] have certainly confirmed that prison discipline is disproportionately harsh on jailhouse lawyers.

Few people are better situated than jailhouse lawyers to observe the contradictions in society and, on occasion, to bring them forth into public view. For their services, for protecting the Constitution from violation, their institutional reward is often a bitter consignment to the depths of the hole. The reason is actually quite simple: unlike other groups in prisons, jailhouse lawyers, in helping to free other prisoners or reduce their sentences, act to challenge how the joint is run. Jailhouse lawyers force prisons to change their formal rules and regulations, especially when they are illogical or downright silly, and for this administrators unleash their disciplinary arsenal with special vehemence.

That is why in every hole, in every prison, you will find some jailhouse lawyers who are there on pretextual—and frequently false—disciplinary reports. Under U.S. constitutional law, it was no longer kosher to write them up for being a jailhouse lawyer. Other "cover charges" are inflicted instead.

That's the way the game is now played.

2

WHAT "THE LAW" IS

What *is* "the law"?

It really depends on who you ask.

Like Scripture, the law seems to be many things to many people.

The great French Enlightenment thinker Rousseau once opined, "Law is an invention of the strong to chain and rule the weak."[1]

In Marx's view, it is "the will of [one] class made into a law for all."[2]

Is law merely morality or the institutionalization of what we commonly view as right and wrong?

In the United States, where history evolves from the spectacle and national drama of slavery, law fails on the question of its internal morality. The words of North Carolina Supreme Court "Justice" Thomas Ruffin, spoken in 1829, leave no doubt as to the morality of his pro-slavery rulings: "The power of the master must be absolute, to render the submission of the slave perfect. . . . As a *principle of moral right, every person in his retirement must repudiate it.* But in the actual condition of things it must be so."[3]

Now, as then, the law continues to be an instrument of the powerful, morality be damned. For the weak, the powerless, the oppressed, the law is more often a hindrance than a help.

As early as the 1760s, the man now deemed the avatar of Western capitalism, Adam Smith (author of the economics classic, *An Inquiry into the Nature and Causes of the Wealth of Nations*, 1776), lectured openly on the role of the law, and whom it serves:

> Laws and governments may be considered in this and indeed in every case as a combination of the rich to oppress the poor, and preserve to themselves the inequality of the goods which would otherwise be soon destroyed by the attacks of the poor, who if not hindered by the government would soon reduce the others to an equality with themselves by open violence.[4]

No beating around the bush there! The law as that which "preserve[s] . . . inequality"? The voice of this apologist for capital seems more direct than that of his revolutionary adversary—Marx. It shows us, in this rare instance, how both sides of the class struggle may agree on what, in essence, the truth is, even in defense of opposing sides and differing interests.

For prisoners, it isn't necessary to philosophize about the law. The law is as real as steel and hard as brick. It is not a theory, nor an idea. It is grim reality. And while we are often told about the neutrality of the law, through discourses that claim equality, daily lives lived behind prison walls reveal quite another reality.

This is especially so for those prisoners who are conversant with the language of Black history, a language for which the law holds little mystery or awe. Students of this language, a language of the dispossessed, recognize that millions of people were held in brutal bondage—legally. That there were, indeed, separate laws for Africans in a land that proclaimed its founding principle to be freedom. The law that "preserve[d] inequality" reigned then, and has since only changed its outer garb, and occasionally its public discourse. Yet where it counts, it remains essentially the same.

The vicious, draconian Slave Codes that covered the South like a shroud reemerged in the aftermath of the U.S. Civil War in the form of Black Codes, which, as scholar-activist and former political prisoner Angela Y. Davis explains,

> . . . criminalized such behavior as vagrancy, breach of job contracts, absence from work, the possession of firearms, and insulting gestures or acts. . . . Replacing the Slave Codes of the previous era, the Black Codes simultaneously acknowledged and nullified black people's new juridical status as U.S. citizens. The racialization of specific crimes meant that according to state law, there were crimes for which only black people could be "duly convicted."[5]

Given this specific history, it is no surprise that its legacy has bled into the present age, and who can deny that the law is, in essence, a repressive instrument of the rulers to keep the ruled in line?[6] Jailhouse lawyers, especially when they successfully utilize the law as an instrument against their keepers, are upsetting this precarious social applecart. And as we have seen, there are serious costs to such an endeavor, even if it is a legal activity, since after all there is a formal law and an informal law. There is the written law and entirely another law that is practiced.

This schizophrenia lies at the very core of U.S. law. It was recognized over a century ago when a French researcher named Alexis de Tocqueville visited America to study its institutions and cultural life. In his classic work of 1835, *Democracy in America*, he recounted his curious conversation with a Pennsylvanian who boasted of American freedoms:

> I said one day to an inhabitant of Pennsylvania, "Be so good as to explain to me how it happens that in a state founded by Quakers, and celebrated for its toleration, free blacks are not allowed to exercise civil rights. They pay taxes: is it not fair that they should vote?"
>
> "You insult us," replied my informant, "if you imagine that our legislators could have committed so gross an act of injustice and intolerance."
>
> "What?! Then the blacks possess the right of voting in this country?"
>
> "Without the smallest doubt."
>
> "How comes it, then, that at the polling-booth this morning I did not perceive a single [N]egro in the whole meeting?"
>
> "This is not the fault of the law. The [N]egroes have an undisputed right of voting, but they voluntarily abstain from making their appearance."
>
> "A very pretty piece of modesty on their parts," rejoined I.
>
> "Why, the truth is that they are not disinclined to vote, but they are afraid of being mistreated: in this country the law is sometimes unable to maintain

its authority without the support of the majority.
But in this case the majority entertains very strong
prejudices against the blacks, and the magistrates are
unable to protect them in the exercise of their legal
privileges."

"What?! Then the majority claims the right not
only of making the laws, but of breaking the laws it
has made?"[7]

According to de Tocqueville's local informant, it was
indeed lawful for free Blacks to vote in early-nineteenth-
century Pennsylvania, though without the law's protection.
It is further telling of the capricious nature of the law that
two years after the publication of his work, Pennsylvania
stripped this very right from a "man of colour" during a
general statewide election.

William Fogg, described in the law books as a "free
Negro or mulatto," filed suit against county officials to
seek a ruling on his right to vote, since he met all of the
state's voting qualifications. In Luzerne County's Common
Pleas Court, the presiding judge gave the jury instructions
that appeared to concede the Black man's main claims, and
ordered them to issue a rare, directed verdict:

It is finally urged that a free [N]egro or mulatto is not
a citizen, within the meaning of the constitution and
laws of the United States and of the State of Pennsylvania, and therefore is not entitled to the right of
suffrage. This the court regards as the most important
point in the cause, and the question, as it is avowed on
the part of the plaintiff, which this suit was brought
to settle.

We know of no expression in the constitution or laws of the United States, nor in the constitution or laws of the state of Pennsylvania, which can legally be construed to prohibit free [N]egroes and mulattoes, who are otherwise qualified, from exercising the rights of an elector. The preamble to the act for the gradual abolition of slavery, passed on the 1st of March, 1790, breathes a spirit of piety and patriotism, and fully indicates an intention in the legislature to make the man of color a *freeman*.

As there is no dispute between the parties in relation to the facts of this case, and as the opinion of the court upon the points [of] law is decidedly with the plaintiff, the verdict of the jury must be in his favor.[8]

Attorneys for the county officials filed a writ of error in the Pennsylvania Supreme Court, which granted the writ and reversed the judgment of the lower court. The Byzantine processes by which it came to its decision and the basis upon which the court came to its finding must be seen to be believed.

Pennsylvania's Chief Justice John Bannister Gibson wrote the opinion for the court:

About the year 1795, as I have it from James Gibson, Esq., of the Philadelphia bar, the very point before us was ruled, by the high court of errors and appeals, against the right of [N]egro suffrage. Mr. Gibson declined an invitation to be concerned in the argument, and therefore, has no memorandum of the cause to direct us to the record. I have had the office search for it; but the papers had fallen into such disorder as to preclude a hope of its discovery. Most of them were imperfect, and many were lost or misplaced. But Mr. Gibson's remembrance of the decision is perfect, and entitled to full confidence. That the case was not reported, is probably owing to the fact that the judges gave no reasons; and the omission is the more to be regretted, as a report of it would have put the question at rest, and prevented much unpleasant excitement. Still the judgment is not the less authoritative as a precedent. Standing as the court of last resort, that tribunal bore the same relation to this court, that the Supreme Court does to the Common Pleas; and as its authority could not be questioned then, it cannot be questioned now.[9]

In this reading of the "law," a court transforms imperfect memory into legal precedent, and missing authority into perfect reason. The court's opinion, based on faulty memory, no records, a misreading of the state constitution, and a repealed statute, unanimously determined that "it is difficult to discover how the word freeman . . . could have been meant to comprehend a colored race."[10]

The Pennsylvania Supreme Court, interpreting the state constitution's assertion (in art. I, §3) that "in elections by the citizens, every FREEMAN of the age of twenty-one years, having resided in the state two years before the election, and having within that time paid a state county tax" shall thus be "eligible to vote," launched into an extended discussion of the meaning of "freeman" and denied that "the word freeman . . . could have been meant to comprehend a colored race."

The case was tried a generation before the ignoble *Dred Scott* decision—made by a U.S. Supreme Court composed of a majority of slaveholders—that had launched a war, and it came down to the same, narrow, uncivil ground: "[N]o colored race was a party to our social compact."[11] In the 1837 case *Hobbs v. Fogg*, Pennsylvania law made it illegal for Blacks to vote, even if one met all of the qualifications of taxes and property under the state's constitution.[12]

Essentially, the state's highest court made an exception to the claim that had sparked a revolution against England, "taxation without representation," for tax-paying Black Pennsylvanians continued to pay taxes, but by judicial edict they could not vote for their political representatives.

Nearly a century and a half after *Hobbs*, a Black revolutionary named John Africa would strike a similar chord when writing of late-twentieth-century Philadelphia that "the law was a weapon for the rich and a whippin' for the poor."[13]

If this was law, what of the outlaw?

For jailhouse lawyers, the law could sometimes be wielded as a weapon or a tool.

It took years of long, hard legal struggles to secure basic constitutional protections for religious practices, many of which were spearheaded in the 1960s and 1970s by Black Muslims, Native American activists, and Buddhists. When members of the Nation of Islam tried to practice their faith like other groups that were seen as more legitimate, prison administrators didn't hesitate to deny them religious practice rights. This of course forced courts to address the question of whether such a faith was a religion, and if so, whether states were required to provide rights of religious expression. One of the earlier Black Muslim cases was *Fulwood v. Clemmer*, which the federal court in Washington, D.C., decided thus:

> It is sufficient here to say that one concept of religion calls for a belief in an existence of a supreme being controlling the destiny of man. That concept of religion is met by the Muslims in that they believe in Allah as a supreme being and as the one true God. It follows, therefore, that the Muslim faith is a religion.[14]

A decade after *Fulwood*, a prison case would make its way to the U.S. Supreme Court wherein a man claimed the right to be able to freely practice his Buddhist faith. In the 1972 case *Cruz v. Beto*, the court decided a case that had been dismissed by lower courts.[15] The Supreme Court ruled in the Buddhist prisoner's favor, and it seemed that the door had inched open for Black Muslims as well. Indeed, *Cruz*'s progeny includes cases supporting religious practice rights of Native American traditional believers, as well as such nontraditional practices as Satanism, Wicca, and the like. However, it is ever problematic for a political body such as a court to determine what is and what is not religious, as may be seen in the 1981 case *Africa v. Pennsylvania*.[16] There, the federal appeals court used analogy to determine what was and what was not religious. In a nutshell, the court held that absent the indicia found in traditional faiths, such as hierarchy, buildings of worship, and denomination of a supreme being, for example, courts should decline to grant rights to religious practice. Given that *Africa* involved a claim raised by a member of the MOVE organization, it should be no surprise that the court was swayed by the revolutionary beliefs of the claimant, rather than a true concern over the adherent's religious beliefs. It is undeniable that throughout the world there are religions that are non-hierarchical, have no formal buildings (at least of brick or stone), and do not posit the existence of a supreme being, such as some forms of Buddhism.

That said, courts have tended to be more expansive of prisoners' rights claims in other contexts. In fact, cases have been brought challenging other prison conditions, regarding decent medical care, for example, as well as fair misconduct hearings, other First Amendment rights (e.g., free speech), and more. Some prisoners challenged unfair transfers to other prisons, unjust firings from jobs, or improper parole regulations. The 1960s and 1970s marked a wave of civil suits addressing a plethora of unjust conditions. These cases are legendary, recounting incidents of prison staffers filing false disciplinary charges, locking prisoners down under specious administrative charges, delaying or denying transfers, denying parole to those who were eligible, and the like, in direct retaliation against jailhouse lawyers for their lawsuits. Some retaliatory state actions took a decidedly more dangerous turn when a jailhouse lawyer was labeled a "snitch" by prison officials, a label that in some prisons can get a person killed.[17]

The law, as we have seen, is an elusive thing. Yet how can we say what the law is without looking at the people who wear the title "judge"? Whether one wins or loses in the wheel of fortune that is the law, a definitive factor is often the judge on the case.

In the view of the American wit H. L. Mencken, "a judge is a law student who marks his own examination papers." Radical historian Howard Zinn has opined that "the judge is [a] monarch" and his courtroom "essentially a tyr-anny."[18] One enters thinking it is a "bastion of democracy" or a "hall of justice," only to be sorely disappointed. The judge, Zinn explains, "is in control of the evidence, the wit-nesses, the questions, and the interpretation of law."[19]

When called as an expert witness in a trial in the mid-1980s, the historian expected to tell the jury about the history of civil disobedience in America. There was little objectionable about such testimony, for the accused were charged with doing some small, mostly symbolic damage to a nuclear submarine to protest the growing nuclear arms race. As Zinn recounts, the judge performed the additional functions of prosecutor and censor:

> The judge would not let me speak. From the very first question—Can you tell us about the history of civil disobedience in the United States?—as I began to answer, the judge stopped me. Objection sustained, he said loudly. I had not heard any objection from the prosecuting attorney.
>
> Indeed, at this point the prosecuting attorney, a young man, spoke up, Your Honor, I did not object.
>
> Well, said the judge, why didn't you?
>
> Because, the prosecutor said, I thought the ques-tion was relevant.
>
> I disagree, the judge said, with finality.[20]

Indeed, in a brief span of years following the American Revolution, the U.S. Supreme Court's chief justice (who had previously sat as a senator on the judiciary committee that determined the constitutional powers of federal judg-es), one Oliver Ellsworth, wrote in a 1799 opinion, "The common law of this country remains the same as it was before the Revolution." Judge Ellsworth's opinion reflects the inherent conservatism of courts, which look back to the hoary precedents of a long-dead past in order to answer questions of an ever-changing present and unseen future. The law is heavy with the weight of past precedents, which is the lens through which judges still look upon the world.

Perhaps the best insights into legal precedents came not from a jurist but from Jonathan Swift, who, in his satirical masterpiece *Gulliver's Travels*, observed:

> It is a maxim among lawyers, that whatever hath been done before may legally be done again; and therefore they take special care to record all the decisions formerly made against common justice and the general reason of mankind. These, under the name of precedents, they produce as authorities, to justify the most iniquitous opinions; and the judges never fail of directing accordingly.[21]

The law is a tool of class domination and, as we have seen, of racial domination as well. But it can sometimes be wielded against that domination by those who make themselves adept at its use. Although it favors the wealthy, it has occasionally been utilized by those who are without means, as shown by the wins notched by jailhouse lawyers who litigated for civil rights and constitutional protections.

But the law, in its elusiveness, can be readily and quickly changed.

This is precisely what happened in 1996, under the neoliberal reign of President William J. Clinton, in his infamous Prison Litigation Reform Act. Much like his welfare "reform" efforts, at the bottom line the law meant a diminution of the rights of the poor and powerless, and the strengthening of state power. Under the act, prisoners became limited in the number of suits they could file, dismissal of cases became easier to make, injunctions harder to obtain and limited in force and time, attorneys' fees sharply diminished; prison administrator defendants could waive answering claims (which defendants are required to answer as a matter of course in non-prison-related civil actions), and no suits could be brought against the state for mental or emotional injury.

What led to the emergence and the passage of the Prison Litigation Reform Act?

It was a convergence of several elements. Clinton's political opportunism, the efforts of the archconservative U.S. Senator Orrin Hatch (R-Utah), national actions on the part of the states' attorneys general, and the unquenchable maw of the nation's trash-flash media, which went berserk with a wave of stories about "crazy prisoner" lawsuits.

Every major American broadcast network (and their cable/satellite cousins) aired features about the jailbird who sued because he got creamy instead of chunky peanut butter in his commissary bag. Or the dude who filed a First Amendment challenge to the prison for not delivering his *Playboy* magazine on time.

Such reports were as common as popcorn in a movie theater. The problem with these reports is that they weren't true.

This revelation came to light not due to the stalwart investigative efforts of the *New York Post*, but in the thin, monochromatic pages of the *Prison Legal News*. The *Prison Legal News* featured a remarkable article penned not by a prisoner (as most are), but by a federal judge, who put the kibosh on the notion of the "flood of crazy prisoner junk suits." In the 1996 article, Chief Judge Jon O. Newman of the Second U.S. Circuit Court of Appeals (headquartered in New York) set forth his critical reply to a letter signed by the attorneys general of four states published in the *New York Times*.

The *New York Times* letter was an organized attempt by the National Association of Attorneys General to garner media and political support to change the law and restrict access to the courts by prisoners. In their joint letter describing the prisoner suits, the attorneys general used a series of lies, half-truths, and misrepresentations to buttress their arguments. Judge Newman would quote from their letter and contrast these assertions against the real cases filed. Newman's article is a telling revelation of how politics and media mesh to create deeply flawed law:

> "Typical of such suits is the case where an inmate sued, claiming cruel and unusual punishment because he received one jar of chunky and one jar of creamy peanut butter after ordering two jars of chunky from the prison canteen. Or the inmate who sued because there were no salad bars or brunches on weekends or holidays. Or the case where a prisoner is suing New York because his prison towels are white instead of his preferred beige."
>
> I wondered about the characterization of these suits, because, though I have seen many prisoner suits that lacked merit, it has not been my experience in 23 years as a Federal Judge that what the attorneys general described was at all "typical" of prisoner litigation.

New York Attorney General Dennis Vacco was kind enough to respond to my request for copies of the complaints in these three cases. Here is what I learned.

In the peanut butter case, the prisoner did order two jars of peanut butter from the canteen and one was the wrong kind. But he did not sue because he received the wrong product. He sued because, after the correctional officer quite willingly took back the wrong product and assured him that the item he had ordered would be sent the next day, the authorities transferred the prisoner that night to another prison, and his account remained charged $2.50 for the item that he ordered but never received. Maybe $2.50 doesn't seem like much money, but out of a prisoner's commissary account, it is not a trivial loss, and it was for loss of those funds that the prisoner sued.

As for the case of the beige and white towels, the suit was not brought just because of the color preference. The core of the prisoner's claim was that the prison confiscated the towel and a jacket that the prisoner's family had sent him, and disciplined him with loss of privileges. In the case, the prisoner stated, the confiscation "cause[d] a burden on my family who work hard and had to make sacrifices to buy me the items mention[ed] in this claim."

Lastly, the salad-bar-claim allegation turns out to be a minor aspect of a 27-page complaint alleging major prison deficiencies including overcrowding, lack of proper ventilation, lack of sufficient food, confinement of prisoners with contagious diseases and food contamination by rodents. The inmate's reference to the food was to point out that basic nutritional needs are not being met. The claim mentioned that the salad bar was available to corrections officers and to prisoners in other state prisons. It is hardly a suit about lack of a salad bar.[22]

The nation's media, however, anxious to juice up their audiences with sensationalist reporting of "those loony prisoner suits," or to hit their economic advertising market with high scores in the "sweeps" (or ratings) period, decided to offer their services to this ignoble crusade instead of simply reporting the truth.

They chose fiction over fact.

Many of us may recall those oddly entertaining stories about prisoners suing over something as silly as peanut butter and claiming violations of the "cruel and unusual" clause of the Eighth Amendment to the Constitution.[23] Many of us may have laughed at the absurdity of it. "The *nerve* of that dude," we may have snorted in derision. I've heard more than one prisoner, several of whom were jailhouse lawyers themselves, grumble that "guys like them make it hard for us to get our suits into court."

But was this actually so?

What changed the law was something far more insidious than the occasionally silly suit. It was the convergence of several social forces: State power, the media, and political opportunism at the highest levels of government.

Media subservience to its political and class masters was transformed into law, enacted into statute with the signature of a former professor of constitutional law morphed into an imperial politician: William Jefferson Clinton.

And how this became law is worthy of note. Like a thief

in the night the Prison Litigation Reform Act was attached as a rider (a usually minor clause attached to a bill) to an omnibus appropriations bill and signed into law, without a committee mark-up (a report from the Senate Judiciary Committee explaining its provisions), drastically changing the law and legal procedure.[24] This was thus a stealth law that altered the rules impacting the lives and liberties of millions of people.

Yet Bill Clinton, a constitutional scholar, affixed his presidential signature and the Great Seal of the United States to the bill, one of his many signals of abject surrender: playing nice with his political enemies while betraying his political allies, constituencies, and even his bedrock political principles.

In economist Michael Meeropol's view, the Clinton presidency essentially surrendered to the forces of the right wing on social and class issues like welfare, the budget, and taxes. In his bills from 1995 to 1997, Meeropol noted, Clinton "signaled surrender: the Reagan revolution was going to achieve its major goals."[25] It was a bipartisan triumph of neoliberalism and a betrayal of the progress made by the New Deal.

Clinton's administration represented a *Neo*-Deal, which promoted the interests of the well-to-do folks on Wall Street and their political drones on Capitol Hill and in the White House. It was a trendy period called the "Me Decade," but for the many poor and dispossessed souls in America's dungeons it was a decade of exclusion. For the poor and the working class, and more so for those millions who dwelled in the nation's prisonhouses, it was a time to be hated and scapegoated. On that, if nothing else, there was bipartisan consensus.

But as with any law, one may not accurately predict how it flies in the real world. That's obviously because of the unwritten law of unintended consequences. For while state repression was a silent norm in U.S. penal practice, the media served to provide the state with a glowing reputation for fairness and evenhandedness, and wreathe it in the illusion of fair, humane treatment of the imprisoned.

That would soon change.

In the aftermath of 9/11, and the subsequent U.S. invasions and occupations of Afghanistan and Iraq, the events at Abu Ghraib and Guantánamo Bay have had dire consequences for America's image and reputation abroad.

While it is generally known that the lower-ranking torturers and abusers of Iraqi prisoners were U.S. Army reservists, it is perhaps lesser known that several were prison guards in their civilian lives. Indeed, the ringleader with the most reported abuses was a guard at SCI-Greene in Waynesburg, Pennsylvania, the very prison where these words were written.

Long before U.S. Army Reserve Corporal Charles Graner brought pain, humiliation, and torture to Iraqi people detained in Abu Ghraib prison outside Baghdad, he was giving the blues to prisoners in Pennsylvania, where he was known as a brutal, sadistic, racist prison guard.

The real irony is, however, that the events of Abu Ghraib, meaning the ones released to American audiences—the naked pyramids, the hoodings, the wirings, the panties-on-the-head, etc.—if committed in an American prison, would have been insufficient for a judge or jury to award damages, for the Prison Litigation Reform Act (PLRA) signed by President Bill Clinton does not allow recovery *for psychological or mental harm or injury.*

This law violates Article 1 of the Convention Against Torture (CAT), a treaty to which the U.S. is a signatory. In any event, torture, whether mental or physical, amounts to a violation of international law: "For the purposes of this Convention, the term "torture" means any act by which severe pain or suffering, whether *physical* or *mental*, is intentionally inflicted on a person."[26]

There are also, in fact, U.S. laws against torture. But the law is an elusive thing. Even in this era of conservative courts, some judges found this more than their readings of the U.S. Constitution could accept.

One court has announced (albeit in footnote) that the Prison Litigation Reform Act's passage wasn't exactly on the up and up. In the case *Ngo v. Woodford* (2005), the U.S. Ninth Circuit Court of Appeals observed, "The PLRA's sparse legislative history primarily consists of PLRA proponents parroting the frivolous cases compiled by the National Association of Attorneys General. . . . [S]adly, several of the most widely cited cases of frivolous lawsuits were mischaracterized by the proponents of the PLRA."[27]

The opinion cited Newman's article and noted that the description of the facts of prisoners' lawsuits contained in the attorneys general's lists of frivolous suits circulated to Congress and the media were "at best highly misleading and sometimes, simply false."[28]

While the *Ngo* panel critiqued the Prison Litigation Reform Act, it did not declare it unconstitutional despite its fraudulent carriage into law. For, as we've learned, fraudulent law is still law, and judges on conservative courts are usually loath to seem supportive of something like prisoners' rights.

At least one part of the Prison Litigation Reform Act

was declared unconstitutional in the 2006 case *Siggers-El v. Barlow*. There, the U.S. District Court found that the law's provision prohibiting damages for emotional or psychological injuries (at least as applied to First Amendment claims) violated the constitution.

At trial, a jury awarded a Michigan prisoner, Darrell Siggers-El, nearly $220,000 in economic, punitive, and emotional damages. The prison officials sought a remitter, or new trial, in the absence of more than minor physical injury. The court rejected the new trial argument, holding that "to bar mental or emotional damages would effectively immunize officials from liability for severe constitutional violations, so long as no physical injury is established."[29]

To support its reasoning the court set forth a daunting hypothetical instance that seemed inherently unjust. In the example, a sadistic guard holds an unloaded gun to a prisoner's head, threatens to kill him, and pulls the trigger in a mock execution. "The emotional harm would be catastrophic," the court noted, yet it would be "noncompensable."[30] If, however, a guard pushed a prisoner without justification, and the prisoner "broke his finger," the court would allow emotional damages caused by the injury.

Siggers-El thus turned on congressional intent, for "Congress did not intend to allow prison officials to violate inmate First Amendment rights with impunity, resolute with the knowledge that First Amendment violations will almost never result in physical injuries."[31]

But as the Prison Litigation Reform Act became law through a legislative sleight of hand, who knows what Congress intended?

We can glean some idea from the words of Senator Orrin Hatch (R-Utah), then chair of the Senate Judiciary

Committee, who said the following when he introduced the PLRA bill on the senate floor:

> This landmark legislation will help bring relief to a civil justice system over-burdened by frivolous prisoner lawsuits. Jailhouse lawyers with little else to do are tying our courts in knots with an endless flood of frivolous litigation.
>
> Our legislation will also help restore balance to prison conditions litigation and will ensure that Federal court orders are limited to remedying actual violations of prisoners' rights, not letting prisoners out of jail. It is past time to slam shut the revolving door on the prison gate and to put the key safely out of reach of overzealous Federal courts. . . .
>
> While prison conditions that actually violate the Constitution should not be allowed to persist, I believe that the courts have gone too far in micromanaging our Nation's prisons.[32]

With this burst of bile, Hatch and his fellow senators fought mightily to nail up the doors to the courts.

The problem, it seemed, wasn't that there was too much violating of the Constitution in the nation's prisons; there were too many suits complaining about it. The solution?

Simple.

Change the law.

Ten years later a small part of the bill designed to lessen court access and to limit access to a huge class of unrepresented people, was declared unconstitutional. (Perhaps by 2096, the whole thing will be thrown out.) Through pretexts, subterfuge, and lies, a bill meant to deny millions of

Americans access to the courts by slashing lawyers' fees to the bone (thus discouraging them from taking such cases), disallowing routine defenses and procedures that are the norm for other citizens, was passed into law as a rider.

Is it surprising that a nation that began its existence with Slave Codes, then continued for a century with an equally repressive set of Black Codes, would institute, by hook or by crook, Prisoner Codes?

Such is the stuff American law is made of today.

3

WHEN JAILHOUSE LAWYERS
"REPRESENT"

In the world of hip hop and rap, an artist is said to "represent" when s/he speaks powerful, representative truths that accurately reflect the lives, experiences, and worldview of the urban poor—those who live in "da 'hood."

This is seen as high praise, and while it is a badge of honor rarely bestowed upon an artist, it is conversely a slap at an earlier age, especially that of the rhythm and blues and disco periods when Black artists acted, dressed, or spoke in ways that were imitative of whites and dismissive of Black cultural and aesthetic expression.

They did not "represent."

There have been times when jailhouse lawyers, by their occupation of the fiercest ground imaginable, acted to "represent" their fellow prisoners in ways that other lawyers rarely represent their clients.

In part, that is because street lawyers, by their very nature, have a state-created space, a bar so to speak, that effectively distances them from their clients. Indeed, the term itself is but a latter-day expression of a Latin word that encapsulates this relationship: *cliens*, which *Black's Law Dictionary* defines as "dependant," or "[o]ne who depend[s] upon another as his patron or protector."[1]

Thus, the social distance of class is presumed, and this

is often exacerbated by distances of broken loyalties to one's supposed client facing the court. This may be seen when a lawyer opts to serve the court, to the detriment of his client. This may also be seen when an overburdened lawyer takes on a case without reading anything about it or even meeting the client.

In an instance such as this, who is being served?

On the other hand, as prisoners, jailhouse lawyers and those they help have little, if any, of such distance between them. They fight for the lives and liberty of their fellows virtually for free, while many free-world lawyers, in an effort to negatively distinguish themselves from their clients, sell them into the depths of hell. It matters little whether they do this through intent or inattention; the results are invariably the same.

The state of Texas is infamous for its acceptance of lawyers who were drunk or even sleeping at trials—indeed, in the midst of capital trials where their clients faced death!

The courts, a group of elected judicial officers stacked with career prosecutors, have looked at such cases with little interest; some courts have reasoned that counsel slept through "unimportant" parts of the trial process.

Some jailhouse lawyers have undoubtedly served their "clients" poorly (usually defrauding them for venal reasons), but as there is rarely if ever a case when a jailhouse lawyer has been judicially approved to sit at trial in defense of an accused, it can safely be said that one has never slept through another's trial.

On the other hand, as the appeals stage rarely requires the personal presence of either counsel or the accused, jailhouse lawyers have served as appellate counsel,[2] simply because most folks can't afford appellate counsel, and even if the state appoints someone, s/he is apt to be less than motivated given the meager fees.

Sometimes while in the depths of the dungeons of the empire, and contrary to the seemingly triumphant laws of capitalism, *free* can prove to be better than *paid-by-the-State*.

The Billa Case

Cat was a young dude who was facing the most serious sentence that the law metes out—death.

Cat didn't know the law, but he knew he didn't feel optimistic when he received his lawyer's brief in the mail. He tried to read it the best he could, but as the feeling persisted, he called his pal, another death row guy named Barry "Running Bear" Gibbs, a man about his age who seemed to enjoy few things more than playing air guitar and reading law books.

Bear *did* read books constantly, and the day rarely dawned when he didn't call down the hall to Steve to ask him about some legal puzzle that confounded him.

When Cat asked him to look over his appellate brief, he readily agreed, but because this was a death penalty case, he asked me to give him a hand. We split the case into two parts: Bear would take the trial and I would handle the sentencing hearing. In Pennsylvania, a death penalty case involves two trials; the first is the guilt phase and the second is a sentencing phase.

The first is like any other criminal trial (except for the jury selection process, where everyone who opposes the death sentence is excluded). But the sentencing phase, because it involves the death sentence, and is based upon a wealth of U.S. Supreme Court precedent, is unlike any other such procedure in the law.

If one doesn't know that precedent, then important errors can be made or overlooked that can lead to the death of an accused.

We read the brief filed by Cat's lawyer, and then Bear began reading the trial transcripts and I the sentencing texts.

At Cat's trial, the prosecutor introduced evidence of other crimes, and Cat's lawyer, while objecting, failed to seek what's called a limiting instruction—a judicial statement to the jury which explains that while it may consider such evidence, it can only do so for a limited purpose.

That error would prove crucial to Cat's fate.

In spring 1989, the Pennsylvania Supreme Court issued its ruling granting Cat a new trial! In the words of Justice Rolf Larsen:

> While trial counsel vigorously objected to the admission of the challenged evidence, at no time did he request the court to give the appropriate limiting instructions to the jury. Not surprisingly, appellate counsel, who was trial counsel below, did not raise the issue of the failure of the court to give limiting instructions, nor does he raise his own ineffectiveness in failing to request such instructions. Technically, therefore, *this issue has been waived* . . . while appellant's trial/appellate counsel did not raise this issue of the court's failure to render the appropriate instruction, his jailhouse lawyer did in his *Pro Se* Supplemental Brief. In this supplemental brief, appellant asserts,

inter alia, that counsel was unconstitutionally ineffective for failing to request a limiting instruction on the jury's consideration of the evidence of the prior sexual assault. Under the circumstances, we agree.[3]

Not only had Cat won a new trial, but in the last pages of the opinion, the court reasoned that even if a new trial were not granted, his sentencing hearing was in violation of the Pennsylvania Rules of Criminal Procedure as well as the U.S. Supreme Court's precedent established in the 1988 case *Mills v. Maryland*.[4] In their view, Cat's sentencing violated the state's relevant rules and the U.S. Constitution: "The instructions to the jury at the sentencing proceeding needlessly deviated from the language of section 9711 of our Sentencing Code, were needlessly confusing, and in at least one instance, were sufficiently prejudicial to have *required vacation of the sentence of death* and a remand for resentencing."[5]

When Cat received word of the new trial, he was happy as a cat on a hot tin roof. His two jailhouse lawyers, both high school dropouts, had secured him a new trial and a new sentencing hearing.

His jailhouse lawyers did it without expecting real payment other than an occasional candy bar, and a hug.

Fearful of the very real possibility of being retried, reconvicted, and resentenced to death, Cat took a life bit. He would never again have to live in permanent lockdown, always afraid of getting poisoned by the state. His two jailhouse lawyers, by merely reading the law books and his trial transcripts (and writing his briefs), literally saved his life.

Other Representations

While it is exceedingly rare for a jailhouse lawyer to sit as defense representative of an accused at trial, it is often the case that an accused in prison may utilize the assistance of a jailhouse lawyer to defend against charges prepared by prison guards. Many states offer such an opportunity for those charged with institutional misconduct, but do not allow the assistance of street (or professionally licensed) lawyers.

Isaac L. Herron was one such jailhouse lawyer, who acted to represent Abu Bakr Muhammad, a fellow Tennessee prisoner. When in 1983 prison staffers retaliated against Herron, he promptly prepared and filed a civil rights suit, charging that the administration had punished him for defending Muhammad at his misconduct hearing.[6]

In his federal trial before a magistrate judge, Herron lost on all counts. The magistrate ruled that Herron could not assert an access-to-court claim based on his representation of another prisoner, and also that because the retaliation against him neither "shocked the conscience" nor constituted an "egregious abuse" of prison authority, it didn't violate the U.S. Constitution.

Herron wrote a *pro se* (lit., "for himself") appeal to the U.S. appeals court in Ohio. While it may seem strange for a case originating in Tennessee to be heard by an appellate court in Ohio, in fact, such occurrences are far from rare. This is so because the U.S. appeals courts sit in regional circuits, some of which may be quite far geographically, yet remain in the circuit. These courts are divided into eleven numbered circuits, plus the federal circuit in Washington, D.C. (For example, Puerto Rico is part of the First Circuit, even though most of its cases come from New England. Similarly, the Third Circuit, headquartered in Philadelphia, hears cases from Pennsylvania, New Jersey, Delaware and the U.S. Virgin Islands.) Herron's appeal thus went to the U.S. Appeals Court in Ohio, from the district court of western Tennessee. He also argued that staffers in the Cold Creek, Tennessee, prison violated his First Amendment rights to freely practice his religion, based upon his founding of the Church of God at Cold Creek. Herron added that when they fired his Church of God volunteer, by so doing they further interfered with his ability to practice and observe the tenets of his faith.

The Sixth Circuit determined that the magistrate-judge who heard his district court case had used the wrong analysis to decide the claims, and granted him partial relief.

In *Herron v. Harrison*, the appeals court used another case to "clarify" the law on retaliation cases and ruled that Herron had a valid case:

> The primary thrust of Herron's complaint is that CCCF [Cold Creek Correctional Facility] official[s] impermissibly retaliate against him for exercising his First Amendment right to file grievances and petition the courts for redress. In March of 1999, eight months after Herron filed his appeal in this case, an en banc panel of this court decided *Thaddeus-X v. Blatter* . . . (6th Circuit 1999). *Thaddeus-X* clarified the law governing prisoner retaliation claims where the retaliation is alleged to have been directed at an inmate's efforts to litigate on behalf of himself or others. . . .[7]

As *Thaddeus-X* case was now the controlling case, Herron had to be analyzed under this new standard.[8] The court essentially established two kinds of retaliation: a) general retaliation and b) retaliation for exercise of a specific constitutional right. Under this latter rule, Herron was allowed to amend his claim and try again:

> As an alternative ground for its holding, the magistrate-judge also concluded that none of the disciplinary actions that Herron alleges in his first supplemental complaint rise to the level of impermissible retaliation. The magistrate-judge drew upon pre-*Thaddeus-X* precedents in so holding, and mistakenly applied the general retaliatory standard to claims that allege retaliation against Herron's exercise of First Amendment rights. Thus, regarding Herron's most serious allegation that he was sentenced to five days of administrative segregation in retaliation for assisting Muhammad, the magistrate-judge found that "a prison disciplinary conviction and confinement to segregation for creating a disturbance neither shocks the conscience nor egregiously abuses authority." Under the proper standard expressed in *Thaddeus-X*, however, this court has found that placing an inmate in administrative segregation "could deter a person of ordinary firmness from exercising his First Amendment rights."[9]

Who is a person of "ordinary firmness," one wonders? Was Herron? What if he had quietly acquiesced during the five days of hole time? As "The Myth of Humane Imprisonment" has taught us, the holes of prisons are filled with jailhouse lawyers. Are they people of "ordinary firmness"?

Sometimes judicial opinions speak volumes in a few words. Jailhouse lawyers, we are learning, are often people of extraordinary firmness, who fight for a law that rarely fights for them.

Isaac Herron went to the hole for helping another man defend himself from a write-up. In a society that seeks to isolate people on the spurious grounds of race, ethnicity, or regionalism, perhaps his real "misconduct" was his solidarity with another who was targeted.

In the prison context—as in the greater social one as well—unity is feared; isolation is favored.

Herron shows us another way of "representing."

Jailhouse Lawyers Who Didn't Go to Jail—or Should I Say *Prison?*

For jailhouse lawyers, what is the supreme achievement?

Some may suggest getting one's conviction overturned, or, failing that, getting the case of a friend, homie, or client tossed. These are doubtless good things, but for one who engages in courtroom battle there is something that is a cut above these noteworthy and noble achievements—to do their best work in the trial court, and by so doing, never to arrive at the House of Pain. Those who beat their cases in the courthouse may spend a brief span in a county lockup or jail, but prison is not their lot. Those whose efforts have netted either acquittal or dismissal are an exceedingly rare breed.

We have already mentioned the exploits of one such man, Warren Henderson—the brilliant legal student of jailhouse lawyer Steve Evans—who beat a vigorous murder prosecution with a wealth of jailhouse snitches (many of whom were undoubtedly trying to angle for their own deals). Now we will discuss the cases of a small number of jailhouse lawyers who represented *themselves* in courtrooms that seemed determined to ignore or undercut their unorthodox methods of liberation. They faced the derision of career lawyers, the contempt of prosecutors, and cool disdain from the judges.

Yet they persevered.

These jailhouse lawyers were members or supporters of the revolutionary MOVE organization of Philadelphia, whose membership to this day rejects the system and, as a matter of principle, opposes representation by lawyers, opting instead for self-representation.

Using trial transcripts, published accounts, and personal recollection, this chapter tells their stories. These stories have gone largely unrecorded until now, since case reporters and law books only cover decisions by state or federal appellate courts that have ruled on convictions. These are stories of success—stories of dismissals and acquittals.

One of these cases stems from the May 13, 1981, arrest of half a dozen MOVE members, among them John Africa, MOVE's founder. In the early 1970s, MOVE was distinctly multiracial, in a time when most folks kept their racial walls high. It would not be odd, from a MOVE perspective, to see Chinese MOVE mothers, Puerto Rican MOVE fathers, or white MOVE daughters. According to John Africa's worldview, MOVE wasn't nationalist but *naturalist*, open in principle to all human beings.

When the level of government repression heightened and the police, in their automatic weapons–bearing hundreds, laid siege to MOVE's homes, the white faces, the

Chinese faces, the brown faces quietly, often tearfully—yet fearfully—disappeared from the front lines.[10] As repression intensified, MOVE got blacker, and while it never became entirely Black, that is its predominant hue today.

The May 13, 1981, arrest resulted in John and Alphonso Africa being charged with the illegal procurement of weapons and bomb-making materials, which, if they were found guilty, would have sent both men to federal prisons for well over a decade. The two, along with seven other MOVE men and women, were arrested in Rochester, New York, and after preliminary hearings were extradited back to Philadelphia. However, only John and Alphonso faced the weapons and bomb-making charges, based for the most part on statements from former members, several of whom took plea deals to avoid or mitigate jail terms.

In late June 1981, jury selection began in the U.S. District Court in Philadelphia, with Federal Judge Clifford Scott Green presiding. Facing these serious charges, the two MOVE men chose to represent themselves, an option that angered and frustrated court-appointed backup counsel, Messrs. John Snite and Stephen Patrizio.

It would be misleading, however, to say that both represented themselves, since Alphonso "Mo" Africa, actually did the yeoman's work, cross-examining the government's witnesses as well as examining his own. John, by contrast, spoke rarely, except to whisper ideas for questions to Mo. He spent the lion's share of this federal trial appearing to sleep through the testimony. Yet, though he spoke rarely, he demonstrated his strength, confidence, and mastery over his taxing situation in an altogether different manner.

As both men were held in a federal facility in New York, they were driven for hours through the dark of night to appear in court in Philadelphia by morning. The two men responded with what they called a "hunger confrontation"—commonly referred to as a hunger strike—to force the government to hold them in the vicinity of the city. The government responded to their protest by holding a hearing before the judge, seeking a court order to force-feed the men, ostensibly to protect their dwindling health.

While the U.S. attorney was making his argument, John Africa calmly rose from his seat, walked around to the carpeted area behind his chair, and pumped out fifty brisk push-ups. Neither he nor Mo had eaten anything in three weeks.[11] The judge peered down from the bench over his bifocals and denied the government's motion, stating simply, "He looks pretty healthy to me." In ways such as this, John's silent presence dominated the courtroom, making those rare opportunities when he did speak have all the more impact.

Given the massive local and regional publicity about the MOVE organization, jury selection was quite a challenge. During the first day, when the judge asked if any of the panel of sixty men and women present had ever heard of MOVE from regional media sources, the courtroom seemed to rise as one. Indeed, only one person didn't stand—some suspected a serious hearing problem.

When the judge next inquired if any of the prospective jurors had formed a "fixed opinion" that would influence their ability to sit fairly in the case, over half the panel, some thirty-one people, raised their hands and were dismissed. Before the day was done, the panel shrank by another ten, due to claims of hardship or other disability to serve. Before the defense or the prosecution began to challenge the throng, only twenty potential jurors remained.

Before the twelve men and women, Black and white, were selected, almost 200 people had been called, questioned, and dismissed.

From the very beginning, this case would depart from the norms of American trial practice. The Africas, defending themselves, simply refused to cross-examine many of the state's witnesses, opting instead to recall some of them as defense witnesses. Moreover, the trial featured a dearth of objections, thus allowing the government to question their witnesses to their heart's content.

One courtroom observer, a retired trainer from the U.S. Treasury Department's Bureau of Alcohol, Tobacco, and Firearms, told a reporter with amazement, "No objections, either side. Why, I saw fifty objections myself! I guess they allow a lot more on the record today."[12]

Assigned to cover the case for local public radio, I sat close enough to hear a lawyer tell John repeatedly, in frustrated stage whispers: "You gotta object! You gotta object, man!" John would calmly wave this off, as the trial departed daily from the realm of routine.

When I asked a MOVE member why no objections were raised, I was informed that John considered them legal tricks: when something would be objected to, it didn't matter if a judge sustained or overruled it, for the jury heard it anyway. "To act like they can take it out they head, just because a judge said so, is stupid," he was quoted saying.

The witness stand became a site swollen with ex-MOVE members, disgruntled spouses, and even siblings of the accused. It mattered not, for no objections were lodged. But the fact that no objections were made doesn't mean that nothing objectionable was said.

The government lawyers led with what they perceived

to be their hardest punch. They presented the testimony of one Donald Glassey, a white man described by government officials as a cofounder of MOVE, who, arrested in July 1977 for using false ID to purchase arms, became a government informant.

Glassey would testify for two days, without objection, that he had been ordered to procure rifles, black powder, dynamite, and other such items, to prepare the arming of MOVE against an expected police assault. Glassey, white, pale, and dressed in a jacket and tie, could not look more different from the men who sat in front of him accusing them of planning an armed battle with the city. He looked like a bespectacled college professor on the stand. John and Mo wore dungarees and dark blue sweatshirts at the defense table.

While Mo occasionally scribbled notes during the apparently damning testimony, John appeared to not even listen to Glassey's testimony, for his head was back, seemingly blissfully dozing behind dark glasses as Glassey told the jury of three men and nine women of a plan to arm MOVE on the orders of John, through Mo. Glassey told of plots to bomb hotels and embassies all around the world to bring relief to the local MOVE chapter by forcing the city to leave them alone.

On Thursday, July 2, 1981, Glassey ended his testimony against his former fellow MOVE members. As he was dismissed from the stand, he rose, as did the target of his assertions, John Africa. John walked toward him, the air was thick with tension. He stuck out his hand, and Glassey extended his, somewhat tentatively. Africa slapped his palm, slapping him five, with a smile on his face. Glassey looked startled and confused, as John put his arms out, grabbed him in a bear hug, and said, "I'm not going to hurt you. You're only doing what you have to do."[13] According to a reporter covering the courtroom encounter, a shaken Glassey later told her, "He's insane. Can you imagine doing that to someone who may be responsible for sending you to jail? You've got to be crazy."

Glassey later admitted to wearing a body wire for the government in an attempt to set up other MOVE members. Several young men were indeed arrested and convicted based on his undercover operation.

Glassey's testimony was followed by that of Jeanne Champagne Africa, who reiterated much of Glassey's statements, but from a decidedly different perspective. Although a former MOVE member, she had acquired the name Africa through marriage to another MOVE member, Ishongo Africa. She too presented an appearance quite distinct from MOVE members, for she dressed fashionably and wore her hair styled instead of in a natural fashion. She spoke, again without objection, about war plans for the coming confrontation, finding weapons in the basement of an apartment in which she was living, and a plot to have her ex-husband killed (because of his abuse of her).

Throughout the three days of testimony and the half a dozen witnesses, the government kept a dolly sitting in front of the jury, with several rifle barrels sticking out and what appeared to be several gallon jugs full of a dark brown powder. The dolly was rolled out every morning after the jury was seated, and rolled back every evening after the jury filed out. According to a Bureau of Alcohol, Tobacco, and Firearms agent who testified for the government, the boxes contained twelve pipe bombs, four sulfur incendiary bombs, three glass-jar bombs, components for some seventeen other such explosive devices, and several firearms. These items served as silent, daily testimony that was quite difficult to ignore.

When the prosecution rested, a quite unexpected witness for the defense was called forth. Phil Africa, born William Phillips, came from a prison cell to testify on behalf of his brothers John and Mo.

Phil was one of nine MOVE men and women who were awaiting sentencing on the collective convictions of third-degree murder stemming from the August 8, 1978, police assault on MOVE's home.

Before Phil could be cleared to testify, he was threatened by the federal prosecutor that he might be indicted for the very same offenses faced by his brothers. Upon advice of the government, the judge warned Phil that his testimony might open him to charges and noted his right against self-incrimination. Phil angrily pushed aside the threats and insisted that he would give testimony in defense of his brethren.

He began by labeling the government's chief witness a "liar" and a "coward." Phil testified, "This man was terrorized of jail and always has been." Speaking of Glassey, he continued, "He would lie to keep from going to jail. He was afraid of spending the five to ten years for standing up for what's right."[14]

Phil, who identified himself as MOVE's minister of defense, said that Glassey had lied repeatedly when he said John Africa ordered him to get the arms sitting in the dolly.

Mo Africa conducted Phil's examination:

MO AFRICA: Would John Africa ever tell Donald Glassey to make bombs?

PHIL AFRICA: Definitely not.

MO AFRICA: Did John Africa ever tell Glassey to purchase black powder?

PHIL AFRICA: At no time was there anything like that. . . . You got to remember that Donald Glassey comes from a family that's pretty well-to-do. To him it was always he could run home to papa or brother in Jersey.[15]

In yet another departure from trial protocol, Mo Africa gave his opening statement to the jury, but only after he had already presented several witnesses. He spoke for nearly an hour, extolling John Africa's work in bringing health and purpose to scores of MOVE members, and continued to call for "total revolution" in spite of the betrayal of some former members.

Among his comments during his opening argument were these, "For a long time now, the federal government has been trying to stop MOVE, has been trying to stop John Africa. [But] the power of righteousness won't be stopped. Before this trial is over, you'll see how sick Don Glassey was to betray MOVE. He was real sick to just go and spill his guts all over the place about John Africa after all he did for him."[16] Mo explained to the jury that when Glassey joined the group, he suffered from severe allergies and drug addiction, both of which John helped cure.

The next day the jurors spent hours listing to tapes of telephone calls, some forty-seven in all. The jurors heard Bureau of Alcohol, Tobacco, and Firearms agents posing as illegal weapons dealers, calling several MOVE members trying to lure them into buys. The jurors listened to several conversations between Glassey and other members regarding financial dealings. According to at least one published report, jurors fidgeted and appeared openly bored at the hours of tapes.

But an alert juror would have noticed what the defense wanted them to notice—none of the tapes featured conversations with either John or Mo.

Most of the MOVE Nine took the stand to defend their brothers, speaking about why they joined MOVE, and what the experience meant to them. They uniformly spoke of Glassey as a traitor, and of John Africa's impact on their lives and health.

The defense would recall Glassey, with Mo asking questions from a yellow legal pad. His questions seemed rhetorical, meant more to give information than any answer would or could elicit, such as, "How does it feel to be a traitor?" With questions such as these, what does it matter what the answers are? But the time of questions passed.

Once more departing from tradition, the defense, in essence, offered three closing arguments: the first read by Mo Africa, the second read by attorney Snite, and the third done extemporaneously by John Africa.

Both Mo and Snite would read excerpts from *The Guidelines*, a largely unpublished compilation of John's views of life, technology, society, and revolution.[17] What Snite read was hardly the stuff of a traditional closing argument and something hardly ever heard in a courtroom. He explained to the judge that he would read portions from *The Guidelines*—an act that he had doubtless never been trained for in law school—and proceeded to tell the jury in part:

Today this system is in the worst trouble ever, tomorrow it'll be still worse, and the day after tomorrow will be even more worse. I know you would like to think there is a way out by working through the system after what you have just heard, but it ain't and the Government got a hellish nerve punishing people for expressing dissatisfaction about a system the Government know won't satisfy.

This is why MOVE members are MOVE members. People don't leave things they're satisfied with, it is impossible to leave a state of contentment because there's nothing in that state to suggest a change. But you will notice everybody is looking for a way out of the system because everybody openly express dissatisfaction at one time or another.

But unfortunately, when you're of the system, all you know is the system, and though folks think they be fighting against the system, because the only reference they know is the system, they're doing as the system. For you see, the system can never change from bad to good, it can only go from bad to worse, because the fuel being fed to this fire continues to increase, making it hotter and hotter.

And if this analysis ain't convincing enough for you, check your history, look how calm people was fifty years ago, how settled people was a hundred years ago, how work oriented-people was two hundred years ago, and look at people now.[18]

The trial transcript reveals that Snite read his client's words for roughly fifteen minutes. As the remarks suggest, John did not spend much time directly addressing the charges against them. But, at the very beginning of Snite's reading, the basic issues of bombs, guilt, and innocence were addressed, and in ways that have perhaps never been done before. John didn't so much dispute the charges as dismiss them:

> People ain't gonna condemn the MOVE organization as a bunch of kill crazed, bloodthirsty murders [*sic*] when it is the Government spilling blood, killing life out of greed. But the Government is attempting to indict me for spilling blood, burning flesh, killing life, by saying I was making bombs. I ain't gonna spend a lot of energy talking about this bomb-making frame-up. My innocence is proven with every innocence of energy you breathe, every drop of innocence you drink, every morsel of innocence you eat. The very message you are hearing is me. My righteousness is represented all through this information.[19]

Then, as Snite continued to read, John managed to get down to brass tacks, so to speak, but with an interesting twist.

> I don't need no bombs, *but if you want to call life a bomb I'm for the biggest bomb existing.* It's already made and the MOVE organization is constantly dropping it, bombarding the system with truth. As far as those scientific bombs the FBI is charging me with making, I ain't gonna make no bomb. Bombs backfire on the people that create them and all those that believe in them, because bombs are explosive, destructive, corruptive. But wisdom is informing, and when you put

what is right to a person you ain't in danger of getting wrong back. That is the difference between what I use as my defense, my bomb, and what the government use as their so-called defense, their bombs.[20]

When Snite concluded his recitation, Mo stood, intending to read more from *The Guidelines*, but not without some hiccups between the judge and the self-represented accused.

THE COURT: Ladies and gentlemen, Mr. Snite has read to you certain guidelines on behalf of Mr. Leaphart [John Africa]. Mr. Robbins [the court is here referring to Mo Africa] at this time wished to read other guidelines. Is that correct, Mr. Robbins?

MR. ROBBINS: Yes. I'm going to read some guidelines. I just want to say this will be obvious that—it's obvious to everybody that not only do people that understand the MOVE organization have a lot of resentment for people like Don Glassey and Gina Champagne, but I know that the people who Don Glassey cooperated with, the Government—I know they don't even like Don Glassey because nobody likes a traitor.

THE COURT: Now, wait a minute. You're testifying again. If you're going to take the witness stand and testify, do so. If you intend to read a guideline that has something to do with you during the time in question, read it.[21]

Mo Africa then began to read from different sections of

The Guidelines on love, motherhood, and children. He read for about ten minutes, taking up eight pages of the trial transcript. He ended in a matter-of-fact way, "The *Guidelines* of MOVE are simple. It simply states that MOVE is opposed to anything that harms life no matter what that life is. I mean we will not go against our belief. We are dedicated to our belief."

With Mo's reading the defense formally rested. The U.S. attorney rose to present a rebuttal argument and spoke for over half an hour, warning the jury "not to be fooled by their philosophy that says a weapon is not a weapon unless it is used against a weapon maker."[22]

After the defense rested its case, John Africa was granted the opportunity to give a closing statement to the jury.

He did not stand.

He did not face the dock.

He sat calmly and spoke slowly at first, with a deep baritone voice amplified by the microphone jutting upwards from the Formica table. The sound system deepened and enriched his voice so that it seemed to echo off the walls and the tall-ceilinged chamber:

> Now, we have to understand what this case is about. This case is about evidence. Now, it's evident that we've got some bottles and pipes and we've got some so-called bombs over there that are supposed to belong to myself and my brother. But as you can see, evidently the bombs are on that side of the room. We've been charged with terrorizing the city and making threats on civilians and the like. And they want to find us guilty for this, but they don't want to find us innocent, and that's tragic because, you see, if I were run-

ning the system and I wanted to clear up the system, I wouldn't go around looking for guilty people. I would go around looking for innocent people and if I found some guilty people I would convert them into being innocent and not guilty.

Because when you're guilty, you're a criminal, according to the way this man [he points to the prosecutor] thinks. And when you're innocent, you're not.

I'm not a guilty man. I'm an innocent man. I didn't come here to make trouble or to bring trouble. But to bring the truth. And goddamn it, that's what I'm going to do. . . .

Now, ain't it obvious? Ain't it obvious? Don't you see bombs there before you? Do you see bombs on his table or do you see bombs on the perpetrator's table?

We're not here as it's said to cause trouble. We don't want trouble. Don't you find it troublesome to understand, to know that we had our babies killed? Don't you find it troublesome to know that we have had our pregnant women kicked in the stomach and have had their babies kicked out of their stomach? Don't you find it troublesome to lie to people?[23]

Here, he began to repeat himself about how the charges are set forth in writing. Moments later, tears would well from his eyes, as he discussed the losses that MOVE had suffered. His voice rose in a crescendo of pain and anger:

What is it that you want from MOVE that you haven't already got from MOVE? You've got our babies, you've got our pregnant women, you've got our

nine people in jail now. You've got lives on the table
to try to put us in jail. You've got Don Glassey, you've
took Sam, you've took Gina. What else do you want?
Who else do you want? Why are you trying to convict
me and my brother? You're the prosecutor today trying to convict me and my brother. Tomorrow you'll
be a lawyer in defense of somebody else. You don't
take the job serious. Neither one of you guys take that
job serious.

When you got my people in jail for murder,
you've got me in jail for murder. [Africa begins to
weep softly] Don't let these tears [the court transcript
reads "peers," but this is clearly in error] confuse you
with weakness. You might not know it, but there's
such a thing as sensitivity. I feel things that man
would be telling you a lot of words and then those
words would be descriptions of so-called evidence
that are supposed to apply to my brother and myself
concerning those things on the table.[24]

Although Africa began his closing argument calmly,
there were periods when emotions clearly got the better
of him, especially when he spoke of MOVE. However, his
mood then lightened and he seemed less a defendant sitting in the dock of a federal court than a teacher speaking
to students hanging on his every utterance.

It seemed incongruous, given its site and context, in
the midst of a serious trial, where the two accused faced
at least fifteen years' hard time, but what seemed to excite
him was this unique opportunity to share his views:

The MOVE organization lives by the principle of

life, the origin, the source. My mama, or the person
you heard referred to as mother nature—that's my
mama. That is your mama, too. Because I'm fighting
for air that you've got to breathe. Yeah, you do. And
if it gets too polluted, you're not going to breathe
that air. And I'm fighting for water that you've got
[to] clean, and if it gets any worse, you're not going
to be drinking that water. I'm fighting for food that
you've got to eat. And you know, you've got to eat it
and if it gets any worse, you're not going to be eating
that food.

We are not fighting people. We are not out there
fighting cops for the sake of fighting cops. Those cops
are fighting us and they are fighting us because they
want to uphold this industry.

You see, when you start threatening industry,
you've got a fight on your hands, and we are threatening industry and they know that. They know it and
the man knows it.

Don't you see? If you took this thing all the way,
you could have clean air, clean water, clean soil and be
quenched of industry. But, you see, they don't want
that. They can't have that. Everything you do, everything you know, everything you see in this courtroom
is designed by the system for the economics of the
system. There ain't a thing that you can look at in this
courtroom that you haven't been made to be dependent
on, including these lawyers. I can't defend myself in this
system. I've got to depend on these lawyers. They have
got to be sitting here. But, you see, you've got such a
thing as a lawyer lobby. You see, that is an industry and
they ain't about to give up that industry, you see.

But you must know that anybody that knows the principle of self has the means to protect self. That lawyer can't protect me. That lawyer wasn't speaking for me right now. I have to speak for myself, you see, because when he speaks I don't rest. When I speak, he don't rest.

And just like he can't speak for me, he can't talk for me. He don't know what I feel. He don't know what the man does to me when he tells me I'm guilty. He don't feel that. He can't feel that. Only I can feel that.

But they will tell you that you must have a lawyer because that lawyer is part of this industry.[25]

By this time John Africa had spoken for nearly forty minutes, and was returning to his earlier themes about crime, its causes, and the polluting impacts of modern industrial civilization.

Despite several judicial interruptions to complain about the length of his oration, Africa or his backup counsel, would respond politely, and he would launch on. He seemed to be trying to make this middle-class jury vibe with him, an African-American revolutionary, and to see the world from his perspective. "If you got crime in this system," said Africa, "then it is because you are teaching crime. If you are teaching crime, then you should not be the one to lock up the criminal, when you are as criminal as the person you are locking up."

Once again, the court interrupted, noting that he had "greatly exceeded" the time allocated for his closing and, indeed, the extension. Asked by the court if he had one last thing to say, Africa added, "I just want to say that I don't have anything against anybody in this courtroom and it is not the people that I'm against, but the idea that control the people."[26]

John Africa's closing statement lasted some fifty-three minutes. Rarely had an American jury heard such an argument. But these were not the last words they would hear. The federal prosecutor would have his rebuttal, and he strove mightily to ensure that this jury came back with the strongest condemnation that the law allowed for the offenses charged.

The judge gave a relatively brief exposition of the applicable law, and the jury had the case in its hands.

If the prosecutor, his thumbs curled in his suspenders like a carnival barker, seemed overconfident, this could be forgiven, for he seemed to have every reason to be. The main accused spent much of the trial napping. He strictly forbade his court-appointed backup lawyers to make objections. His long close was more a statement of his beliefs than an attack on the case.

The jury sat for almost two weeks with boxes of rifles, plastic milk bottles labeled TNT, and other exotic explosives under their noses. This was, after all, a trial of MOVE, which the corporate media strove mightily to liken to a coven from hell. The verdict seemed an all but foregone conclusion. The jury was out five days, deliberating over thirty hours on what seemed an open-and-shut case.

When they trudged back into the courtroom, none looked in the direction of the accused, usually a bad sign. The jury foreman, Dorothy Kelly, rose to speak on the jury's behalf and announced "not guilty" eight times for the four charges each man was facing.

The Africas turned to each other and gave palm slaps.

The judge thanked the jurors for their duty and ordered the two men released.

The courtroom resounded with shouts of "Long live John Africa!" as MOVE members and supporters surrounded the men.

The prosecutors looked stunned, as if in disbelief.

Moments later, the assistant U.S. attorney, L. Marc Durant, told a reporter, "It would be nice if I could say I thought we did this wrong or that wrong. Then, at least, I would have some rational reason."[27]

His co-prosecutor, William Carr, added, "You hear prosecutors griping about this ruling or that ruling, but in this case there were no rulings."

Mo Africa then read a statement given to him several weeks before the trial began by John Africa, explaining, "The reason it took a long time, the trial didn't go the way it usually goes. We represented ourselves, we wouldn't take advice of co-counsel, and when the evidence was brought back . . . there really wasn't no evidence and it wasn't clear."[28]

For MOVE members, the trial was known as "John Africa vs. The System."

When John Africa exited the federal court building, holding a cardboard box filled with cantaloupe, eggs, potatoes, and a pineapple, he declared to a group of supporters, "I whipped 'em."

John Africa had won by representing himself.

The Trials of Abdul Jon

Abdul Jon has been a MOVE supporter for decades, campaigning for the liberation of the MOVE Nine, who have been imprisoned unjustly since the August 8, 1978, police assault on the MOVE house in Philadelphia. As such, he has had his share of conflicts with the local gendarmes, and has had occasion to rumble for his freedom in local courts.

In most cases, he has represented himself, even when it was apparent that the judge had no interest in hearing from him. It's almost as if all the lawyers in the courtroom—judge, district attorney, and backup defense lawyer—wanted him to simply shut up, sit down, and let them do their jobs to decide his fate.

What made this difficult was Abdul's habit of writing his own motions and arguing on the record on his own behalf whenever he managed to set foot in a courtroom.

On November 16, 1981, Abdul was arrested when he came to the defense of another MOVE sister, Jeanette Africa. He came upon her while she was having a scuffle with a sheriff and he tried to intervene. Both he and Jeanette were beaten by sheriffs and local cops, so brutally that Jeanette's leg was broken by the cops' assault.

When they came to court some months later, Abdul, Jeanette, and another MOVE sister, Theresa, chose to represent themselves.

Abdul submitted his own motions in the municipal court, where the three were charged with aggravated and simple assault, and obstruction of justice, among several related charges.

The March 15, 1982, trial was contentious, funny, and insightful. The transcript that follows refers to Abdul as Jones, his court-appointed lawyer as Adam Renfroe, the assistant district attorney as Mr. Bell, and Ricardo Jackson as the municipal court judge.

THE DEFENDANT: (JONES) Right now I'd like to read into the record my motion for dismissal.

THE COURT: And, your motion for dismissal, that goes to the question of whether you've been brought to trial within the mandatory one hundred and twenty days?

THE DEFENDANT: (JONES) After completely reading my motion everything will be answered.

THE COURT: Is that the thrust of your motion?

THE DEFENDANT: (JONES) Excuse me?

THE COURT: You have been brought to trial?

THE DEFENDANT: (JONES) No. It takes up several issues.

THE COURT: Deal with the issues one by one.

THE DEFENDANT: (JONES) That's what I do here.

THE COURT: The first issue is what?

THE DEFENDANT: (JONES) The Commonwealth of Pennsylvania Criminal Trial Division 81-11-2206.2207.2208. Commonwealth versus Michael Jones, all right. Case: That I have been in continuous confinement since my arrest on the 16th of November 1981 more than one hundred days without ever once being brought to Court. Summary of arguments: On November 18th, 1981, while a patient in Guiffre

Medical Center, as the result of a brutal beating I received at the hands of my accusers, I was preliminarily arraigned by Judge Conroy and charged with Aggravated Assault, Simple Assault, Recklessly Endangering Another, Resisting Arrest—

THE COURT: Mr. Jones, not cutting you off but all that's right there. I know all that.

THE DEFENDANT: (JONES) That says a preliminary hearing if not waived that it should be held within not less than three days and not more than ten days. And the preliminary arraignment is for the purpose of establishing probable cause. I've been confined 10 times 10 days and have not heard even the first word of accusation thus far or been present in the courtroom to know if cause was shown. The Fifth Amendment says one shouldn't be deprived of life, liberty without due process and the establishment of probable cause is long overdue in this case.

THE COURT: With regard to 140-D [in the rules of criminal procedure], what is your argument there? That you have not had your preliminary hearing within 10 days?

THE DEFENDANT: (JONES) Right, exactly. It's been 10 times 10 days.

THE COURT: All right, do you have any response, Mr. Bell?

MR. BELL: Your Honor, the first date given for the preliminary hearing was 11/25, 146 of which is well within 10 days of the arrest.

THE DEFENDANT: (THERESA AFRICA) Abdul wasn't there.

THE COURT: The preliminary arraignment?

MR. BELL: November 16th.

THE COURT: 11/16 or 11/8. Which is it?

MR. BELL: 11/16.

THE COURT: All right now, at that time it was scheduled to be a preliminary hearing?

MR. BELL: That's correct.

THE COURT: And the first date given 11/25?

MR. BELL: Correct.

THE COURT: And that was the first preliminary hearing? And at that time there is no attorney of record.

MR. BELL: Correct.

THE COURT: And at that time the defendant failed to appear?

THE DEFENDANT: (JONES) Wait a minute. I was locked up. I didn't fail to appear. I was in lockup. I've been in the Detention Center throughout this time.

THE COURT: On January 7th?

THE DEFENDANT: (JONES) I was in the Detention Center. I've been in continuous confinement.

THE COURT: I'm not talking to you. Let me hear you.

THE DEFENDANT: (THERESA AFRICA) I told you this before. I told you he's locked up since this happened.

THE COURT: Let me hear from him, please. Then you can talk.

THE DEFENDANT: (THERESA AFRICA) It's the same. It's one case.

THE COURT: You're in custody on 1/7?

THE DEFENDANT: (JONES) Since the 16th of November.

THE COURT: Why was there not a bring down on January 7th?

MR. BELL: He did not answer the call because we checked up there to see if he was in custody.

THE DEFENDANT: (JONES) What are you talking about I didn't answer the call? What is he talking about?

THE DEFENDANT: (THERESA AFRICA) He's lying again.

THE COURT: At this point the argument that he has not had a preliminary argument hearing is well taken. And he hasn't had a preliminary hearing within 10 days.

MR. BELL: Preliminary hearings always get continued. They don't always go off within 10 days. He has to have a listing for a preliminary hearing within 10 days.

THE COURT: I understand that.

MR. BELL: But they always get continued. He got continued the first listing because he wasn't represented.

THE COURT: The matter went from 11/16 to 11/26.

MR. BELL: That's within 10 days.

THE COURT: Right.

THE DEFENDANT: (JONES) I never saw any courtroom on the 25th. All I saw was the 7th floor of the City Hall. I ain't had—I was not in the courtroom, you know, I wasn't there. I don't know what you all had. You know, I don't know what you all did. *I* wasn't there. I've been in lockup. I ain't—since coming to City Hall in this case I ain't never been no further than the 7th floor. Can you say otherwise?

MR. RENFROE: May I speak on behalf—

THE COURT: Let me count the number of days first. That's fifty-two days as of January 7th.

THE DEFENDANT: (JONES) Excuse me. You say I wasn't brought down? You say I didn't answer? Is that what you're saying?

MR. BELL: I'm saying you were not here. We checked to see if you were in custody and we were told you were not in custody.

THE DEFENDANT: (JONES) Who told you that? Let me see the writing on any of your documents to substantiate that I wasn't here.

THE COURT: Mr. Bell, from 11/16 to January 7th is fifty-two days. And at that time we're still in the preliminary hearing stage because at that time the charges were not reduced to M-1.[29]

MR. BELL: That is correct.

THE COURT: Now, it's obvious at that time we're beyond the 10 days. Now, what are the remedies for not having a preliminary hearing within 10 days?

THE DEFENDANT: (JONES) Dismissal.

MR. BELL: Well, Your Honor—we didn't have a preliminary but we had a listing. That's the gist of the argument. If the defendant shows up unrepresented how can the Commonwealth proceed? You can't have a preliminary hearing if the defendant doesn't show up.

THE DEFENDANT: (JONES) Wait a minute, if I didn't show up? You're saying—

MR. BELL: And they informed the Court Officer on that day that he was not in custody. You were sitting on the bench that day too as a matter of fact.

THE COURT: It was my case. I don't recall a notation that the defendant failed to appear. No service, District Attorney to serve or prepare a writ. I don't recall anyone informing me that he did not answer the call at the prison to bring him down.

MR. BELL: Well, I remember they called up and said he was not in custody.

MR. RENFROE: The burden remains on the District Attorney. If the Court files do not reflect that he didn't answer the call of the list then I would submit to the Court that the burden remains on the District Attorney to show that he didn't call or answer the call.

MR. BELL: It still doesn't matter, we take that as a Commonwealth request. We have every right in the world to have Commonwealth request at the second list of the case.

THE DEFENDANT: (JONES) What do you mean it don't matter?

MR. BELL: We're still within all the run dates in this case and it's not even an issue.

MR. RENFROE: It's still very much an issue, Your Honor.

THE COURT: I'm trying to determine wherein lies the responsibility for not doing something within the 10-day period provided by the rule.[30]

As the two sides wrangled, Abdul swam upstream. The lawyers, instead of listening to him, seemed to barely tolerate his presence, as if he were little more than an irritant.

He was that most dreaded of defendants: one who chose to represent himself, and infinitely worse, one untrained in the intricacies of the law. As such, he was not, nor could he ever be, a member of "the club." If Abdul sensed this, he did not let it quiet him, for he surged forward, making his arguments, often repeatedly, which were remarkable for their simplicity and clarity.

That, among other things, his support of MOVE, for example, may have provided more reason for their displeasure.

Abdul repeated over and over again that he was held in continuous custody for over one hundred days, "10 times 10," but he seemed to be speaking a language that few others in the business of the court understood. While the judge appeared to misunderstand his argument, the assistant D.A. downplayed its relevance, suggesting that it's simply how things are done. Then Abdul took a different tack; he directly questioned the DA (something not allowed under court procedure):

THE DEFENDANT: (JONES) Look, how many times have I been in this courtroom?

MR. BELL: This is the first time.

THE DEFENDANT: (JONES) Why?

MR. BELL: Because you were upstairs—

THE DEFENDANT: (JONES) Why was I upstairs?

MR. RENFROE: Your Honor, my motion is as to the preliminary hearing. At this point, I make a motion for the matter to be discharged because it was not properly heard within the three- to 10-day period specified according to 140-D of the rules of criminal procedure, sir.

MR. BELL: It doesn't apply at all in this case. He was given a listing within—

THE COURT: Mr. Bell, you do agree that something has to be done. You can't keep a person in custody without any type of hearing for 112 days.

MR. BELL: That's right. And the proper motion is to Room 714, in terms of reduction of bail. The Court took all that into consideration at the time it was re-manded. Further motion for reduction of bail should have been made and then the defendant, justifiably, might have been released or sign his own bail or whatever. But he didn't do it. It's his fault.

THE DEFENDANT: (JONES) Wait a minute. Right here I've got here: Application for Reduction of Bail that I submitted on January the 20th, 1982. That was never moved upon, it was said to be moved upon, on the 19th of February. Now you said I didn't do it. I have a habeas corpus right here that I filed around the same time as that. It was scheduled for the 19th and then it was never moved upon. So what are you talking about I didn't file any application for bail?

MR. RENFROE: If Your Honor pleases—

MR. BELL: I'm talking about February 19th.

MR. RENFROE: The proper time to file the motion is at the time that the defendant appears in Court. This is the first time the defendant had an opportunity to be heard in the Court of law. This being the first time, although a substantial period of time from the preliminary hearing until the matter was discharged as a felony and remanded. The proper time is the first time he's had an opportunity to be heard. This is the first time and we're making a request to discharge pursuant to that particular rule of law.

MR. BELL: Your Honor, he's beyond that. We're not even talking about a preliminary hearing anymore.

THE COURT: Well, it appears to me that there's been gross inequities to the defendant not having been moved within 112 days.

MR. BELL: Not having moved?

THE COURT: Not having moved to see that the matter was tried as a preliminary hearing or see that the matter was tried as a municipal matter.

MR. BELL: The Commonwealth was ready at each and every listing of the case.

THE COURT: You weren't ready on the 7th when you didn't have him down.

MR. BELL: That's not the Commonwealth's fault.

THE COURT: Okay. In the matter of Michael Jones, 81-11-22-6, 2207, 2208, this matter is discharged.

MR. RENFROE: Thank you very much, Your Honor.

THE DEFENDANT: (THERESA AFRICA) Oh, the case is done?

MR. BELL: Judge, you really gotta be kidding.

THE COURT: No. . . .[31]

Theresa Africa's innocent query was ultimately answered in the negative.

For within weeks it would be appealed by the district attorney's office and all three activists would be on trial for the same charges before a local but higher court.

Philadelphia and some other jurisdictions have a two-tiered local judiciary allowing for appeals to be made, just as in the federal judicial system and many U.S. state judiciaries.

After a series of false starts (several judges, sensing something rotten in Denmark, simply refused to take the case, passing it on to others), a trial ensued, and most of the more serious charges, such as aggravated assault, were dropped.

The municipal court hearing, however, gives us some flavor of MOVE proceedings, and some illustration of how strenuously the system opposed the allegedly constitutionally guaranteed right of self-representation.

Some students of the law look to the Supreme Court's landmark 1975 ruling *Faretta v. California* as its root. In that case the Court decided that a person may dispense with a lawyer, and represent oneself in a criminal court proceeding.[32]

This right to self-representation, however, despite the deep-seated resistance of the "legal industry" (in John Africa's words), went back much further than the 1975 Supreme Court decision.

Its roots lay in the American Revolution, when mostly English colonists announced their antipathy to lawyers.

In 1776, over a decade before the adoption of the U.S. Constitution, the state of Pennsylvania's "freemen" adopted a Declaration of Rights (and Constitution), the Ninth article of which provided that "in all prosecutions for criminal offences a man hath a right to be heard by himself and his council."[33]

Other states, like Massachusetts, have similar provisions. In Pennsylvania's constitution this clause has been included since then, and in all subsequent amendments, the latest being the 1968 document.

What does it mean that one "hath a right to he heard," when no one hears him?

American history is replete with sweet words written into documents by legal and economic elites, with another reality faced in the warring arenas of the courtroom. Abdul's case shows us how one had to reiterate his words repeatedly, incessantly, in order to be heard, finally. He was discharged, albeit temporarily, for a retrial was ordered, which he found out about only by chance, for a summons was mailed, not his house, but to another MOVE person's home, who called to inquire about court mail he received addressed to Master Michael Africa.

The Aftermath

It is one of those ironic twists of history that in the first of the cases we've examined, two revolutionaries were charged with federal crimes of possession of explosives and unregistered rifles and acquitted by a jury. It is ironic because one of these men, John Africa, was later murdered by state and federal cops using illegally obtained explosives.

Philadelphia police were illegally equipped with weapons provided by the U.S. Treasury Department's Bureau of Alcohol, Tobacco, and Firearms. Those weapons and explosives, including C-4, were used by the Philadelphia Police Department to kill eleven men, women, and children in a police massacre on May 13, 1985, when police bombed the MOVE house. (Among those killed was the same sweet-voiced Theresa Africa who was a codefendant standing with Abdul Jon in the dock.)

John and Mo Africa faced over a decade in federal prisons for the alleged possession of illegal weapons until their self-representation resulted in a stunning acquittal.

For the Philadelphia cops (and the federal cops and military who conspired with them) who used such weapons, and slaughtered almost a dozen people, there were no charges. To this date, only one person has been tried, convicted, sentenced, and imprisoned for their participation in the extraordinary events of May 1985. That person was Ramona Africa, a MOVE Minister whose only crime was survival—she was convicted of "incitement to riot"! She dared survive the firestorm of the bombing of her home and the slaughter of her sisters and brothers.

She spent seven years in prison. She too was a jailhouse lawyer who represented herself at trial. If this were not the case, she may have faced considerably more time than she eventually did, given the plethora of charges brought against her.

The jury acquitted her of most charges and most courtroom observers agree her conviction was a compromise verdict. It is an axiom of the "lawyer industry" that "one who acts as his own lawyer has a fool for a client." Of the millions who dwell in U.S. prisons, what tiny percentage of that vast number represented themselves? It would be difficult to arrive at any amount above one percent. These rebels, representing themselves against great odds, emerged from those dire situations with significant victories. Their challenges lay in the larger prison, the outer prison of society.

4

WHAT ABOUT STREET LAWYERS?

For most people, jailhouse lawyers are the exception and street lawyers are the rule. The United States is awash with street lawyers.

According to the the Bureau of Labor Statistics there were 1,637,000 attorneys, legal workers and judges in the United States in 2006.[1] That number has undoubtedly only mushroomed in recent years, most notably among women, who presently constitute the majority of law students training to become lawyers in America today.

Most folks encounter lawyers whenever trouble appears on the horizon: car accidents, divorces, important financial transactions, and the like. We are all conditioned to look for lawyers when our lives hit the inevitable snags of daily existence.

We are all inculcated with the myth of social equity—reinforced by TV, radio, and the corporate media—that law is essentially equitable, and that lawyers are necessary social agents who serve the interests of all. But these ideas exist side by side with other ideas that counter such perceptions, for deep within American memory is a profound distrust of lawyers, as reflected in the state constitutions of American colonies, where, in the opening hours of the American Revolution, articles were adopted that allowed for self-representation. This was especially the case in the nation's Northeast, the site of the original thirteen colonies.

Thus, while the social idea behind the necessity for lawyers is strong, there is also a counter-idea, one formed by centuries of social and communal knowledge. Though discussion of class is often absent in public life, many people who come from poor or working-class families bear deep scars from their lack of representation, stemming from the time when lawyers only worked for rich people. There is still a significant degree of truth to that judgment made over a century ago by a man who is still famed as a paragon of the profession, Clarence Darrow.

Darrow, who was invited to speak to prisoners at the local Chicago lockup, did so with amazing bluntness and clarity. His 1902 "Address to the Prisoners in the Cook County Jail," caused a sensation. His colleagues agreed that what he said was true, but it shouldn't be said to "those people," i.e., prisoners. Darrow's words were so striking that one prisoner leaving the speech termed it "too radical."

On crime, Darrow explained, "Some so-called criminals—and I use this word because it is handy, it means nothing to me—I speak of the criminals who get caught as distinguished from the criminals who catch them—some of these so-called criminals are in jail for their first offenses, but the nine-tenths of you are in jail because you did not have a good lawyer, and, of course, you did not have a good lawyer because you did not have enough money to pay a good lawyer. There is no very great danger of a rich man going to jail."[2]

Darrow began his lucrative legal career as a lawyer defending business and corporate interests. His 1894 meeting with socialist organizer Eugene Victor Debs, during the notorious Pullman Strike, helped push him toward his radical awakening. As a matter of conscience, Darrow resigned his corporate post and took on Debs as a client, a choice that would mean a substantial financial sacrifice for him and his family.

Debs was later imprisoned in 1918 for opposing World War I. For expressing his antiwar stance to a group of socialists and their supporters, Debs was charged under the Espionage Act, convicted, and sentenced to ten years in prison.

"They tell us that we live in a great free republic; that our institutions are democratic; that we are a free and self-governing people. That is too much, even for a joke. . . . Wars fought throughout history have been waged for conquest and plunder. . . . And that is war in a nutshell. The master class has always declared the wars; the subject class has always fought the battles."[3]

In Debs' day, millions of people identified themselves as socialists, including Clarence Darrow. But we know of Darrow because he was the exception, not the rule. Most lawyers today resemble the early Darrow, when he was a well-paid advocate of corporations, not the later Darrow, who took up the cases of social and political underdogs.

Few lawyers call themselves or think of themselves as socialists today, and that is hardly surprising. Most have never handled a criminal case (despite the heavy media coverage of such trials and movies depicting such events). The reason is simple. There's little money in it.

When lawyers leave law school, many with staggering debts incurred by years of undergraduate and law school study, why would they turn to criminal cases, in which a poor clientele is overwhelmingly represented?

Of all the lawyers in the United States, perhaps 6 percent work in criminal law. Darrow explained this issue in these words in his 1902 address:

> See what the law is: when these men [the rich] get control of things, they make the laws. They do not make the laws to protect anybody; courts are not instruments of justice. When your case gets into court it will make little difference whether you are guilty or innocent, but it's better if you have a smart lawyer. And you cannot have a smart lawyer unless you have money. First and last it's a question of money. Those people who own the earth make the laws to protect what they have. They fix up a sort of fence or pen around what they have, and they fix the law so the fellow on the outside cannot get in. The laws are really organized for the protection of the men who rule the world. They were never organized or enforced to do justice. We have no system for doing justice, not the slightest in the world.
>
> Let me illustrate: Take the poorest person in this room. If the community had provided a system of doing justice, the poorest person in this room would have as good a lawyer as the richest, would he not? When you went into court you would have just as long a trial and just as fair a trial as the richest person in Chicago. Your case would not be tried in fifteen or twenty minutes, whereas it would take fifteen days to get through with a rich man's case.
>
> Then if you were rich and were beaten, your case would be taken to Appellate Court. A poor man cannot take his case to the Appellate Court; he has not the price. And then to the Supreme Court. And if he

were beaten there he might perhaps go to the United States Supreme Court. And he might die of old age before he got into jail. If you are poor, it's a quick job. You are almost known to be guilty, else you would not be there. Why should anyone be in the criminal court if he were not guilty?

If the courts were organized to promote justice the people would elect somebody to defend all these criminals, somebody as smart as the prosecutor—and give him as many detectives and as many assistants to help, and pay as much money to defend you as to prosecute you.[4]

Though Darrow's words were uttered over one hundred years ago, they resonate to this day, for they reflect powerful social and political truths.

For his views Darrow was lionized by the poor and the working class; however, today the poor and working class view the profession with stark antipathy. Yet those feelings did not begin yesterday.

Before the United States came into being, "America" described a continent with scattered European colonies. In the regions where English was the predominant tongue, lawyers were seen as instruments of British rule and the British Crown, and thus hated, feared, and distrusted.

A U.S. Supreme Court case of the 1970s illustrates that period, and the nature of the colonial legal establishment, which sparked revolutionary ideas among the common folks:

The colonists brought with them an appreciation of self-reliance and a traditional distrust of lawyers.

When the Colonies were first settled, "the lawyer was synonymous with the cringing Attorneys-General and Solicitors-General of the Crown and the arbitrary Justices of the King's Court, and all bent on the conviction of those who opposed the King's prerogatives, and twisting the law to secure convictions." This prejudice gained strength in the Colonies, where "distrust of lawyers became an institution." Several Colonies prohibited pleading for hire in the seventeenth century. The prejudice persisted into the eighteenth century as "the lower classes came to identify lawyers with the upper class." The years of revolution and Confederation saw an upsurge of anti-lawyer sentiment, a "sudden revival, after the War of the Revolution, of the old dislike and distrust of lawyers as a class." In the heat of these sentiments the Constitution was forged.[5]

This was the majority opinion written by the late Justice Potter Stewart in the case known as Faretta v. California. In that case the Court decided that a person may dispense with a lawyer, and represent oneself in a criminal court proceeding. As we have seen, however, in practice lawyers and judges are hostile to such a concept.

In colonial Massachusetts, the 1641 Massachusetts Body of Liberties declared in Article 26, "Every man that findeth himselfe unfit to plead his owne cause in any Court shall have Libertie to imploy any man against whom the Court doth not except, to helpe him, provided he give him noe fee or reward for his paines."[6]

In the seventeenth century, Connecticut, Virginia, and the Carolinas also had prohibitions against pleading for hire. This is a kind of grassroots antipathy to lawyers, shown by colonial, prerevolutionary constitutions. And yet a century later, a telling statistic emerges.

Of the fifty-six men who signed the Declaration of Independence (no women signed) in 1776, twenty-nine of them, or roughly 52 percent, were lawyers or judges. They would erect a legal structure that would protect property yet deprecate freedom—at least the freedom of enslaved African people. The lawyers brought with them a sensibility that is at the heart of the profession, an inbred conservatism.

Even a millennium ago, when Rome was fresh, public schools were established to train lawyers, as servants of the empire, to administer the realm for their masters. Historian J. B. Bury, who has written several tomes on the latter days of the Roman Empire, observed, "Lawyers are always conservative and suspicious of change."[7]

Throughout that span of time, the essential nature of lawyers remains in place. One may well ask, "How can that be, when this is a democracy born in a revolution?"

Another great historian and political scientist, Alexis de Tocqueville, examined this very question when he came to postrevolutionary America in the early nineteenth century. He went to prisons, courthouses, alehouses, libraries, and government buildings of the new republic.

This Frenchman, born to an aristocratic family and to the period of monarchic restoration amidst the democratic innovations in the wake of the French Revolution, found something quite unexpected in America—an aristocracy of lawyers. In *Democracy in America*, which appeared in two volumes in 1835 and 1840, he writes, "A portion of the tastes and habits of the aristocracy may consequently be discovered in the characters of men in the profession of the law. They participate in the same distinctive love of order and formalities; and *they entertain the same repugnance of the actions of the multitude and the same secret contempt of the government of the people.*"[8]

De Toqueville was not, nor could he be, your average lawyer-hater. For he was, after all, a lawyer, who prior to his trek to the United States worked as a judicial officer in France. He was also an odd offspring of two divergent French institutions of aristocracy and revolution.

His grandfather lost his aristocratic head to the guillotine. His parents would be freed from prison and have their rank restored during the Bourbon Restoration. He therefore knew a thing or two about aristocracy. And when he looked at American and English lawyers, he recognized class kin.

He was a lawyer, of course, but he was a *French* lawyer. He saw the French Napoleonic Code or *Code Civil* as far more rational than the English or American law codes. This was due, de Tocqueville believed, to the Anglo-American penchant for precedence, which ties today's legal reasoning irrevocably to the past:

> This aristocratic character, which I hold to be common to the legal profession, is much more distinctly marked in the United States and in England than in any other country. . . . The English and Americans have retained the law of precedents; that is to say, they continue to found their legal opinions and the decisions of their courts upon the decisions of their forefathers. In the mind of an English or American lawyer a taste and a reverence for what is old is almost always united to a love of regular and lawful proceedings.[9]

Yet what could such a thing mean in the context of a state that claims to be a democracy? What does it mean in a state that marks its political legitimacy not in the grants of a crown, but in an anti-regal revolution? It means that at the very heart of the emergent democracy lay a profoundly antidemocratic principle—aristocracy. What should surprise us is our very surprise, for a moment's contemplation will reveal what is hidden in the stories of glory that accompany the mere mention of the people we know as our "Founding Fathers."

Jerry Fresia, in his remarkable work, *Toward an American Revolution*, gives a revealing portrait of these early Americans who stood at the forefront of the revolution against the British:

> The first was a very wealthy man. In 1787, many considered him the richest man in the thirteen states. His will of 1789 revealed that he owned 35,000 acres of Virginia and 1,119 acres in Maryland. He owned property in Washington valued (in 1799 dollars) at $19,132, in Alexandria at $4,000, in Winchester at $400, and in Bath at $800. He also held $6,246 worth of US securities, $10,666 worth of shares in the James River Company, $6,800 worth of stock in the Bank of Columbia, and $1,000 worth of stock in the Bank of Alexandria. His livestock was valued at $15,653. As early as 1773, he had enslaved 216 human beings who were not emancipated until after he and his wife had both died.
>
> The second man was a lawyer. He often expressed his admiration of monarchy, and, correspondingly, his disdain and contempt for common

people. His political attitudes were made clear following an incident which occurred in Boston on
March 5, 1770. On that day, a number of ropemakers
got into an argument with British soldiers whose occupation of Boston had threatened the ropemakers'
jobs. The British soldiers responded by firing into the
crowd, killing several. The event has since become
known as the Boston massacre. The soldiers involved
in the shooting were later acquitted thanks, in part,
to the skills of the lawyer we have been describing,
who was selected as the defense attorney for the British. He described the crowd as a "motley rabble of
saucy boys, negroes and molattoes, Irish teagues and
outlandish jack tarrs."

The life of the third man was more complex,
more filled with contradiction than the other two.
He was wealthy. He owned over 10,000 acres and by
1809 he had enslaved 185 human beings. States one
biographer, "He lived with the grace and elegance of
many British lords; his house slaves alone numbered
twenty-five." Yet slavery caused him great anxiety;
he seems to have sincerely desired the abolition of
slavery but was utterly incapable of acting in a way
which was consistent with his abolitionist sympathies.
He gave his daughter twenty-five slaves as a wed-
ding present, for example. And when confronted with
his indebtedness of $107,000 at the end of his life
in 1826, he noted that at least his slaves constituted
liquid capital. He had several children by one of his
slaves and thus found himself in the position of having to face public ridicule or keep up the elaborate
pretense that his slave children did not exist. He

chose the latter course and arranged, discreetly, to have them run away.[10]

Fresia reveals the identity of these grand Founding Fathers—George Washington, John Adams, and Thomas Jefferson, the first three presidents of the United States. They were aristocrats in everything but title, and they helped erect a legal structure that would protect the wealth and privileges of their class with democratic language, but a profoundly counterrevolutionary and antidemocratic application of laws and rules.

Alexander Hamilton, a contemporary of these men, spoke for many of his fellow "Founding Fathers" when he said, "The people, sir, are a great beast."[11] They worked to erect a structure that was meant not to serve democratic interests, but to obstruct them. When the royal court was banished by the fires of revolution, other courts emerged, courts which preserved, in a sense, the royal prerogative not of princes, but of property, wealth, and means.

That said, quite a few "Founding Fathers" and other men who met at the 1787 Constitutional Convention in Philadelphia frankly preferred royal blood to rule the unruly America.

James Dickinson of Delaware, a signer of the Constitution, wanted a monarchy. He refused to sign the Declaration of Independence. Nathaniel Gorham, representing Massachusetts, wanted a monarchy so much that he secretly corresponded with European royalty in an attempt to convince someone with royal blood to rule the United States. Hamilton, representing New York, greatly admired monarchy. William Samuel Johnson, representing Connecticut, was described by one historian as "the nearest thing to an aristocrat in mind and manner." That lawyer refused to assist in the War of Independence because he couldn't "conscientiously" wage war against England. Delaware's George Read, a wealthy lawyer who "lived in the style of the colonial gentry," wished to do away with states altogether and wanted a president who held his office for life with absolute veto power.[12]

Despite the way the paintbrush of nationalist history has colored them, they were men who were intensely anti-democratic and had a class affinity with the aristocracy. The American Revolution wasn't sparked by such men so much as it was muted, channeled, and co-opted to their ends.

In the states of this disunited Union, people were up in arms not just against their haughty British occupiers, but also against their well-to-do American allies, many of whom would later call themselves revolutionaries. The response of a key coauthor of the Constitution, Gouverneur Morris of Pennsylvania, reflects the anxiety of his wealthy cohorts toward their fellow colonists when he noted, "The mob begins to think and to reason. . . . I see and see with fear and trembling, that if the disputes with Britain continue, we shall be under the domination of a riotous mob. It is to the interest of all men therefore, to seek reunion with the parent state."[13]

The British Crown may have been forced out of its reign, but a new aristocracy, legitimized by wealth, continued to rule under the guise of democracy. In the courts of the land, for example, in the Quaker State of Pennsylvania, the royal court was succeeded by a legal court. Consider the statutory powers of the Pennsylvania Supreme Court:

The Supreme Court shall have and exercise the powers vested in it by the Constitution of Pennsylvania,
including the power generally to minister justice to
all persons and to exercise the powers of the court,
as fully and amply, to all intents and purposes, as the
justices of the Court of King's Bench, Common Pleas
and Exchequer, at Westminster, or any of them, could
or might do on May 22, 1722.[14]

This statute shows how a *state* court, which has jurisdiction over a relatively limited territory, claimed the powers of an empire, and indeed dated its powers to precede
the American Revolution! Did you notice the reference to
May 22, 1722? Westminster is the seat of English superior
courts of the British Kingdom. Why would a state court
claim such power? It is because, in the eyes of the law, the
law of England continued to have the force and applicability
it did before the Revolution.

Another such statute, written into code in 1972, gives
further insight into the conservative nature of the law. In
Pennsylvania's Title 1, or General Provisions, it is written:

(a) English law.—The common law and such of the
statutes of England as were in force in the Province of
Pennsylvania on May 14, 1776 and which were properly adapted to the circumstances of the inhabitants of
this Commonwealth shall be deemed to have been in
force in this Commonwealth from and after February
10, 1777.

(b) Provincial statutes.—The statutes enacted on or

before May 14, 1776 under the authority of the Late
Proprietaries of the Province of Pennsylvania have
the same validity and effect as statutes enacted under
the authority of the Commonwealth.[15]

In a way, this makes sense—for it promoted continuity
in the law, and therefore protected property relations that
existed before the revolution. And yet, isn't a revolution
supposed to disrupt existing property relations? Aren't revolutions waged to shatter unjust social relations, to make
room for new, more egalitarian ways of life?

Abraham Lincoln certainly thought so, and said so in
1848 on the floor of Congress. "It is a quality of revolutions, not to go by old lines and old laws, but to break up
both, and make new ones," said Lincoln.[16] But what Lincoln thought and what the Supreme Court thought were
two different things, for there are revolutions, and then
there are counterrevolutions. In the midst of the American
Revolution, the law, an inherently conservative and aristocratic institution, protected people with property interests and, by doing so, sustained unjust social relations that
seemed to have been settled by the terrible determinant
of war. Nor did the law lend its power or prestige to the
protection of personal rights.

As Howard Zinn has succinctly noted, "Very soon after the Fourteenth Amendment became law, the Supreme
Court began to demolish it as a protection for blacks, and
began to develop it as a protection for corporations."[17]

In what became known as *The Slaughter House Cases*
and *The Civil Rights Cases* (1883), the Supreme Court declared the Civil Rights Act of 1875 unconstitutional, and
then, to add insult to injury, the majority opinion adopted

the tone of a slave master, reprimanding Blacks for turning to the courts for relief from a wave of white terror. In the words of Supreme Court Justice Joseph Bradley:

> When a man has emerged from slavery, and by the aid of beneficent legislation has shaken off the inseparable concomitants of that state, there must be some stage in the progress of his elevation when he takes the rank of a mere citizen, and ceases to be the special favorite of the laws, and when his rights as a citizen or a man, are to be protected in the ordinary modes by which other men's rights are protected. There were thousands of free colored people in this country before the abolition of slavery, enjoying all the essential rights of life, liberty and property the same as white citizens; yet no one, at that time, thought that it was any invasion of their personal *status* as freemen because they were not admitted to all the privileges enjoyed by white citizens, or because they were subjected to discriminations in the enjoyment of accommodations in inns, public conveyances and places of amusement.[18]

Bradley spoke for a nearly unanimous court—only one justice dissented. This was the Kentucky-born John Harlan, who asked rhetorically what the meaning might be of national citizenship, or its rights, privileges, and immunities, if it couldn't protect people from the indignities, assaults, and pains of racial discrimination in the states where they lived? What were the recently passed constitutional amendments, but "splendid baubles, thrown out to delude those who deserved fair and generous treatment at the hands of the Nation"? Harlan called Bradley's opinion that Blacks were the special favorite of the laws "scarcely just."

Yet it would be the opinion of Bradley, the jurist from New Jersey, that would voice for Northerners and Southerners alike the core principle of white supremacy in American law, a historical echo of the dreaded *Dred Scott* decision written generations before by a profoundly different court.

In his dissenting opinion, Harlan referred to the *Dred Scott* case, particularly to the court's definition of citizen as categorically white:

> In determining that question, the court instituted an inquiry as to who were citizens of the several States at the adoption of the Constitution, and who, at that time, were recognized as the people whose rights and liberties had been violated by the British Government. The result was a declaration by Chief Justice Taney, that the legislation and histories of the times and the language used in the Declaration of Independence, showed "[t]hat neither the class of persons who had been imported as slaves, nor their descendants, whether they had become free or not, were then acknowledged as a part of the people, nor intended to be included in the general words used in that instrument;" that "they had for more than a century before been regarded as beings of an inferior race, and altogether unfit to associate with the white race, either in social or political relations, and so far inferior that they had no rights which the white man was bound to respect, and that the negro might justly and lawfully be reduced to slavery *for his benefit.*"[19]

That was the law before the adoption of the Thirteenth and Fourteenth Amendments, Harlan would argue to no avail. And while he didn't ascribe the malady to aristocracy directly, his words reflected a chilling similarity to such a system.

> The difficulty has been to compel a recognition of the legal right of the black race to take the rank of citizens, and to secure the enjoyment of privileges belonging, under the law, to them as a component part of the people for whose welfare and happiness government is ordained. At every step, in this direction, the Nation has been confronted with class tyranny, which a contemporary English historian says is, of all tyrannies, the most intolerable, "For it is ubiquitous in its operation, and weighs, perhaps, most heavily on those whose obscurity or distance would withdraw them from the notice of a single despot."[20]

Conservatism. Aristocracy. "Class tyranny." Even after the conflagration of war, civil rights remained the preserve of the wealthy, the well-connected, and the corporations, not for Black people, Native Americans, or struggling people. This was clearly shown in the *Santa Clara* case discussed in Chapter 1, which was decided two years before the *Civil Rights Cases*.

Such decisions as these drew editorial exclamations of approval from papers of the day, such as that great exemplar of liberalism, the *New York Times*, which opined, "The Court has been serving a useful purpose in thus undoing the work of Congress."[21]

These rulings, written within years of the Civil War

and within a decade after the passage of the Reconstruction Amendments to the U.S. Constitution, show us the ability of the law to adroitly ignore the terms of a statute, to give it the meaning that it wishes. In the Fourteenth Amendment, the civil rights of U.S. citizens are set forth with clarity:

> Section 1. All persons born or naturalized in the United States, and subject to the jurisdiction thereof, are citizens of the United States and of the State wherein they reside. No State shall make or enforce any law which shall abridge the privileges or immunities of citizens of the United States; nor shall any States deprive any person of life, liberty, or property, without due process of law; nor deny any person within its jurisdiction the equal protection of the laws.

But as far as the Supreme Court was concerned, the Amendment might as well have read, "All persons (*except niggers*)," for its rulings ensured this precise, narrowed effect.

As Howard Zinn has observed, "after the Civil War, the Fourteenth Amendment's phrase 'life, liberty or property,' which turned out to be useless to protect the liberty of black people, was used in the courts to protect the property of corporations. Between 1890 and 1910, of the cases involving the Fourteenth Amendment that came before the Supreme Court, 19 were concerned with the lives and liberties of blacks and 28 dealt with the property rights of corporations."[22]

This gives us some sense of the law as a social instrument, devoid of the merest morality. It is, without a doubt, a tool of what Justice John Harlan called "class tyranny."

However, if that is the law, what of its practitioners—lawyers?

From Law to Lawyers

We have seen the roots of U.S. law, domination, aristocracy, and empire. Yet these are generalities. What does it mean in the real world of flesh and bone, of death and life?

For some, like North Carolina's Russell Tucker, the idea behind the words "my lawyer" probably didn't sound strange until, years afterward, he learned that that very man was thinking and acting just like his prosecutor. Mr. Tucker, like millions of others, was a poor person, and as such couldn't afford to hire a lawyer, so the court appointed one for his trial, appeal, and post-conviction process. It was during the post-conviction stage that the court appointed David B. Smith, Esq. to act as his appellate lawyer. Smith, a longtime prosecutor, obviously came to the defense business with some "baggage" from his days as an assistant district attorney.[23]

Smith would note shortly after meeting Tucker for the first time, "At the end of the visit, I decided that I did not like Mr. Tucker." Smith would later state in a sworn court document, "My own beliefs against capital punishment were severely challenged as I read the trial transcripts in preparation for post-conviction relief." His research led him to a single, inescapable conclusion: "Mr. Tucker should be executed."[24]

Surely, given class and ethnic differences that often emerge in the legal system, it would hardly be surprising if many lawyers disliked some of their clients. In many cases, lawyer and client are imperfect strangers, people tossed together by a fate as blind as a lottery. In many cases, they come from different worlds. Yet Smith, a lawyer sworn to protect and defend the interests and constitutional rights of the accused, a death row prisoner named Tucker, went one fatal step further.

In his sworn affidavit, Smith relates, "I decided that Mr. Tucker deserved to die, and I would not do anything to prevent his execution." The lawyer then deliberately missed a court filing deadline, thereby putting his client on the fast track to death. Smith, in his own sworn words, became "an agent of the state." With "defense lawyers" like these, who needs prosecutors?

It is a measure of the madness that now reigns as U.S. law that Smith's next move stands out as remarkable. He filed a formal court document stating precisely how he sabotaged his client, and by doing so, helped procure a stay of execution for a death row captive. But what of the lawyer who does precisely the same thing and never files anything?

Prison cells and graves abound with people who were "represented" by just such lawyers serving the interests of the state without a hitch. By this method, they will doubtless be deemed competent under the governing standard known as the *Strickland v. Washington* rule.[25]

In this case, the U.S. Supreme Court determined that an attorney's court performance must be gauged from the perspective of a "presumption" of effectiveness. It has led to some pretty remarkable results in actual practice. What would you think if when you were on trial for your life or freedom, your lawyer was curled up asleep, snoring? Surely this would be a classic case of counsel's ineffectiveness, right?

In the 1991 case *People v. Tippins* an American appellate court ruled, "Although counsel slept through portions of the trial, counsel provided defendant with meaningful representation."[26]

What if a lawyer were awake, but high on drugs during your trial? An American appellate court decided in the 1990 case of *People v. Badia*, in which the lawyer admitted to using both heroin *and* cocaine during the trial,[27] "Proof of a defense counsel's use of narcotics during a trial does not amount to a *per se* violation of constitutional right to effective counsel."[28]

Perhaps a sleeping trial lawyer or a drug-crazed defense lawyer is not so bad. But that has to be the limit—it couldn't get much worse than that, could it?

A guy is on trial, and it is discovered that he is wearing what appears to be the same clothes that the alleged assailant wore during the day of the crime! Would a competent defense lawyer be remiss if he didn't do sufficient research of the trial evidence to prevent his "client" from essentially radiating the perception of guilt by his garb?

In 1983 a state court of appeals ruled in *People v. Murphy*, "Counsel's . . . seeming indifference to defendant's attire . . . [though] defendant was wearing the same sweatshirt and footwear he wore on day of crime did not constitute ineffective assistance."[29]

Despite the constitutional provisions in both U.S. federal and state constitutions for an "effective counsel for one's defense" against the charges of the State, in real life, these provisions do not ask more than for a lawyer to be alive and present—effectiveness is presumed. But perhaps I've been a bit hasty.

In the case *Vines v. U.S.*, a lawyer excused himself during trial and left. He had the court's permission and a one-word waiver from the defendant, and so he took half the day off.

Miguel Vines, a Spanish-speaking man, tried to get a new trial by filing a §2255, a federal habeas corpus, for surely, if a lawyer is not present for half a day of a two-day trial, he cannot be deemed effective. At the Eleventh U.S. Court of Appeals, two of three judges saw it differently. In the *Vines* opinion, the court majority ruled:

> Vines proffers no authority that would compel us to conclude that the temporary absence of counsel is necessarily a structural defect. The Supreme Court has held that the *total* deprivation of counsel amounts to a structural defect. . . . That holding is predicated upon the recognition that "[t]he entire conduct of the trial from beginning to end is obviously affected by the absence of counsel for a criminal defendant." . . . We conclude that the *temporary absence* of a defendant's trial counsel during a *portion* of the actual trial does not necessarily affect the conduct of the entire trial. . . . Though we do not countenance the abandonment of a defendant by his counsel even during the presentation of non-inculpatory testimony, we cannot say that such an absence compromises the entire trial of that defendant such that harmless-error analysis would be inapplicable. Because we find that Vines's counsel's alleged errors are capable of quantitative assessment and

that no inculpatory evidence was presented during the temporary absence of his counsel, we conclude that the absence of Vines' counsel constitutes a trial error subject to harmless-error analysis.[30]

Although it had been demonstrated that the lawyer was not physically present, the majority determined that although this constituted error, the error was harmless.

The lone dissenting judge wrote an opinion longer than that of the other two judges. In his view, the majority opinion was both inconsistent and a misreading of the precedent that they relied upon. The third circuit judge noted, "Unlike the majority, I am reluctant to find defense counsel's temporary absence during the taking of any evidence *during trial* excusable or harmless and to be the first federal court to do so. This truly is an unprecedented decision."[31]

The dissenting opinion, in a legal sense, is like the human appendix in a medical sense; it does not really matter whether it is included or not. It certainly made no difference in Miguel Vines' attempt to receive a new trial.

There should be no comparable cases that demonstrate how empty this notion of defense counsel has become in American law. Yet there are more.

A lawyer represented a client while he was in the throes of a raging mental illness. When the client learned of this after his conviction he filed an appeal in his death row case. In *Johnson v. Norris*, the Eighth U.S. Court of Appeals determined that the afflictions of the petitioner's lawyer didn't amount to a *Strickland* violation. In the words of the *Johnson* court:

At his trial and on direct appeal, the petitioner was

represented by Robert Smith. The petitioner's issues before this Court all relate to Mr. Smith's representation. In 1993, Mr. Smith surrendered his law license. Between 1994 and 1996, he was convicted of various felony counts of property theft. He is currently serving a fifteen-year sentence in the Arkansas Department of Correction. During his testimony before the District Court, Mr. Smith, for the first time, revealed that he had been diagnosed with bipolar disorder.[32]

The court suggests that the man's lawyer may have been sane during the trial, but for the sake of argument assumes that he was not. Indeed, when Johnson petitioned for Smith's medical records to prove his mental instability during trial, the court denied the motion.

When the court looked at the lawyer's performance under the *Strickland* standard, an insane lawyer wasn't necessarily an ineffective one!

The unprofessional and perhaps bizarre behavior that the petitioner now claims was a result of Mr. Smith's bipolar disorder includes lying to the petitioner about his experience in capital cases, submitting a false application for malpractice insurance, and a general lack of trial preparedness. . . . Whether a result of bipolar disorder, character flaws, or just bad lawyering, these examples did not rise to the level of constitutionally deficient performance, because they cannot be shown to have affected the outcome of the case.[33]

With all due respect to the mentally disabled, it is important to give some thought to the nature of the disorder that was glibly dismissed by the *Johnson* court. Bipolar disorder is a fairly recent term for another disorder that may be more familiar. Its manifestations are especially critical for one who uses his mind, his intuition, and his powers of observation, analysis, and concentration to defend the rights, freedoms, and property of another.

In *The Concise Columbia Encyclopedia*, the disorders are defined thusly, "Manic-depression or bipolar disorder[:] severe mental disorder, involving manic episodes (characterized by an abnormally elevated or irritable mood, grandiosity, sleeplessness, extravagance, and a tendency towards irrational judgment) that are usually accompanied by episodes of depression (possibly including lethargy, a sense of worthlessness, lack of concentration and guilt)."[34]

A lawyer may be drunk, inattentive, stoned on coke or scag, absent from the trial, or crazy as a loon—but s/he ain't legally "ineffective." Such are the bitter fruits of *Strickland's* "presumption of effectiveness."

While cases such as these surely mock the very notion of "assistance of counsel," do they not also communicate an abominable level of respect for those who practice as lawyers? What is the court really saying about the quality of American lawyers? If this is acceptable, what can possibly be unacceptable?

A lawyer who, when representing another in a death penalty case, has a disorder that may lead to irrational judgment or affect his powers of concentration, who is gripped by a deep sense of lethargy, is a lawyer in name only. Not only is he no good to his "client," he is of little use to himself.

Other Examples from the Demimonde

One day I was called to the cell window by a man I didn't know, who wished for me to read his brief.

"Yo, Brotha Mu!"

"Yo! What's up, brotha?"

"Listen—I know you busy, man, but I just wanna ask you a question."

"I *am* busy, bro'—but what's up?"

"Can a lawyer write a brief where there ain't *no* cases cited in the whole damn brief?"

"Whoa—what you mean, man?"

"There ain't no cases in this brief."

"This is a real brief to a real court, right?"

"Yeah—of course!"

"What court?"

"Superior Court."

"Of Pennsylvania?"

"Of course, brotha."

"You gotta mean there ain't no 'Table of Cases' which lists cases, in the first few pages of the brief, right?"

"Naw, man—there ain't *no* cases cited *nowhere* in this whole damned brief!"

"None?"

"None."

"I ain't never seen nothin' like that, man—send it up."

I read the man's brief, some thirty pages or so of half-hearted arguments in insipid prose that was clearly penned quickly.

He was correct. There wasn't a single case cited in the entire brief, from the first page of argument to the last.

The man was facing over a decade in state dungeons for an escape attempt and related arson charges. Apparently his lawyer thought so little of his case that he didn't bother to cite any legal authority for the position he presented in court. Not one case!

I was stunned by this state of affairs and recommended that he petition the court for another, presumably effective counsel. This was clearly a case where the lawyer was simply going through the motions. Instead of filing a brief, he was essentially writing the court a letter!

In the *Rickman v. Bell* death penalty trial of a man in Tennessee, a reading of the trial transcripts makes it difficult to determine who was the defense lawyer and who was the district attorney. The words of the defense lawyer during his sentencing argument to the jury leaves little work left for the prosecutor:

> I know this young woman was put in the trunk of that car. That's no secret. I know that. And I'm not happy about it. No, sir. I'm not happy. I'm ashamed. I'm ashamed that this crime has been committed in our community. And I want the family of Debra Glose-close to know that. That I'm ashamed. I'm ashamed that this young woman died in that oven. [Mr. D.A.], I'm ashamed. I'm ashamed, [Mr. D.A.]. I don't condone murder. I know criminal defense lawyers suffer from what is called guilt by association. When I go to church Sunday, they are going to waylay me out at the Bellevue Baptist Church.[35]

The *Rickman* opinion doesn't report the district attorney's reply, but I've often wondered if s/he didn't simply rise, turn to the jury, and say, "The State rests, Your Honor."

On review, the Sixth U.S. Court of Appeals reasoned, "The effect of all this was to provide Rickman not with a defense counsel, but with a second prosecutor."[36] What can it mean when defense lawyers are virtually indistinguishable from prosecutors?

In every law school throughout the nation, lawyers are trained and formed by their participation in moot court, where students perform as defense attorneys one day, only to play prosecutors the next. While enabling students to see legal practice from both perspectives undoubtedly can be enormously useful, it also trains the students in performing either function, taking either side when needed.

When they graduate from these schools they have established themselves as brethren of the bar association, distinguished from their fellow citizens. They are not officers of the community but officers of the court, to whom they have sworn a loyalty as deep as vassals once swore to serve feudal lords and princes. Thus the client is fully expendable, for a lawyer's loyalty is not to the accused but to the court, the bench, and the civil throne. Yet sometimes their loyalty is to neither.

The extraordinary William Kunstler, a radical icon of the American bar, told a group of criminal defense lawyers in 1994, "We are allied, as 'officers of the court,' with the judges and the prosecutors, when we should be exclusively, 'officers of the client.'"[37]

When I was a young reporter, I covered a major murder trial where nine accused were "represented" by nine attorneys.

One day, in the midst of the trial, as we returned from a lunch break, I espied two distinguished, three-piece-suited lawyers coming into court to "represent" two of the defendants. That day I was sitting in the public rows, instead of the press box (since the nine decided on a trial by judge, without a jury, members of the press occupied the jury box). The two lawyers, both well-known in the Black community, had their mustaches fringed with something white.

The woman sitting to my right nudged my elbow, and whispered, "Do you see that stuff?"

"What stuff?" I replied.

She answered, "Them two dudes been snortin' that stuff!" I wondered, did she say "snuff"? I looked again, and sure enough, the white "stuff" on their black mustaches glistened in the summer's heat.

I looked at the woman again, and looked back at the two lawyers. Surely these two lawyers—Black lawyers—representing Black people facing decades in jail, would not—*could not*—be snorting drugs while in the midst of their trial! I told myself that they probably had eaten sugar-powdered doughnuts for lunch, and looked at the woman on my right with skepticism.

Years later, one of those lawyers would be convicted on drug charges, and he would tell his sentencing judge that he had been high on cocaine *since the day he left law school.*

Those nine men and women were convicted and sentenced to thirty to a hundred years each in prison for third-degree murder. They were members of the revolutionary MOVE organization of Philadelphia. Mike Africa is the guy whose lawyer went to jail and told of his coke addiction. The other lawyer with the white dust on his moustache "represented" Janine Africa. Now these men and women are entering their thirtieth year in Pennsylvania dungeons. They continue to fight for their freedom.[38]

This isn't, nor could it be, a condemnation of people who make their living as dedicated advocates. But it gives us some insight into the nature of the business, and why some people have come to rely on and trust jailhouse lawyers, who have never been trained to function as district attorneys.

Much of the criticism of the distinctions between jailhouse and street lawyers focuses on their significantly different levels of education. Street lawyers usually have formal training for three or four years in a graduate school. Jailhouse lawyers, if trained at all, learn either by studying cases or by correspondence courses. Some learn by a variety of apprenticeships, working with others who are more knowledgeable or experienced.

Yet there are distinctions often jumbled together under the rubric of class that may more properly be posed as differences of perspective.

In this brave, new post-9/11 world where governments have accrued more power from a fearful citizenry, little-known events occurred that highlighted the differences between street lawyers and jailhouse lawyers.

Several states, Pennsylvania among them, quietly enacted new rules governing the treatment of legal mail received at their prisons. This rule change affected correspondence from courts as well.

In Pennsylvania's new regulation, a secret code would be assigned to lawyers who wished to correspond with their clients; this numbered, lettered code, upon reception at the institution, would be obliterated by pen or marker, and then the mail would be individually delivered to the prisoner, where it was inspected in his/her presence and logged.

Those lawyers who failed to acquire this new code would have two choices: they could come to a regional Department of Corrections (DOC) office and hand-deliver the mail, or their legal mail sent in without the code would be treated as regular mail. This meant it would be opened by the institution's mail room, inspected, resealed, and delivered to the prisoner with other regular mail.

Those lawyers who sought and received this new code number would have to swear (or avow) that their correspondence with such-and-such inmate would not include any materials prohibited by their rules governing contraband.

What would one assume that an average lawyer would do?

One might assume that those deeply trained in the intricacies of the law and grounded in the U.S. Constitution would vociferously protest such a regulation, right?

For isn't there sufficient precedence to protect lawyer-client correspondence and confidentiality?

When the rule went into effect, this writer waited and waited and waited for a legal protest to erupt.

It never did.

Indeed, it took three jailhouse lawyers, who fought long and hard for several years, to mount a protest.

And while they had occasional assistance from court-appointed counsel to assist in civil discovery, the bulk of the work was done by themselves.

Incidentally, one fact learned during that discovery process was that the DOC negotiated with defense lawyers from groups including the American Civil Liberties Union (ACLU), the Pennsylvania Institutional Law Project (an

ACLU affiliate), and the Defenders Association of Philadelphia to draw up the new procedure.

In *Fontroy v. Beard*,[39] the court found that one important perspective was missing from the confab:

> The inmates were not represented in the negotiations nor had any inmate or group of inmates authorized those groups to speak for them. The input from these groups was not from the prisoners' perspective. It took into consideration the attorneys' concerns. As Secretary [Jeffrey A.] Beard put it, the accommodations were for the benefit of the attorneys to make their job easier.[40]

In essence, the lawyers represented themselves first. As for other lawyers who did not join their party, tough luck. Every man (or woman) for him/herself.

It took three jailhouse lawyers, scattered in three separate joints across the state, to challenge and defeat the new rule.

Their argument was simple: the regulation violated the First Amendment, as it allowed the state to open legal and court mail outside their presence.

Derrick Dale Fontroy, Theodore Savage, and Aaron C. Wheeler prevailed because they dared to fight.

While the rule was put in place in October 2002, DOC heads claimed that the impetus actually arose some three years earlier. It was August 1999 when a man escaped from the central Pennsylvania prison at Huntingdon. The escape garnered statewide news coverage and sparked several investigations.

The DOC speculated that the escape was made possible, in part, through contraband sent through legal correspondence. The DOC also proffered a distinctly post-9/11 reason for the policy: the event of biohazardous material, such as anthrax, sent via the mails.

In *Fontroy*, the court found both of these justifications unavailing, for it found "no evidence" establishing that escape materials were sent in that way, and that even state investigations "implicated other inmates and prison staff in the hand delivery of the tools to the inmate."[41]

In addressing the DOC's newer reasons, the *Fontroy* court explained:

> Another concern that Beard gave for changing the policy was the possibility of a contaminant, like anthrax, being introduced through legal or court mail. Yet, he could not identify a single incident of powder having been contained in any legal or court mail.
>
> The concerns articulated now by the DOC were not the reasons given for the policy change at the time. The only rationale for the revision then was the prevention of escape. Now, the DOC contends that the risk of mail containing contaminant powder and the risk to staff attendant to opening the mail in the inmate's presence are additional reasons for the policy. Yet, there has not been a single incident of suspicious powder or assaults of staff surrounding the opening of legal or court mail in front of an inmate. These post-policy change reasons are not supported by any evidence.[42]

The point is, lawyers, even those among the most conscientious (like the ACLU), follow their training to acquiesce to, rather than to challenge, the imposition of repressive rules.

The case record included over three hundred docket entries, evincing a hard-fought campaign, by jailhouse lawyers fighting a rule that quite a few lawyers found objectionable.

Both types of lawyer may read, analyze, and write legal pleadings, but they do so from starkly distinct perspectives.

Rarely are they willing or able to negotiate with the state, even though it is their constitutional rights at stake.

That may be because their relationship to the state is markedly different.

They are not "officers of the court."

They are not street lawyers.

As such, they have no one to whom they can sell out.

For street lawyers, it is a different story. They often enter a courtroom fresh out of law school, yet woefully unequipped for the awesome responsibilities thrust upon them. Jerome F. Kramer, a lawyer writing in the *National Law Journal*, offered a rare criticism of the low level of training of American lawyers:

> Is it any wonder that, in an inherently adversarial profession, the lawyer's image is subject to increasing criticism by the media and lay public alike? Questionable scholarship and lack of skills training inherently lead to at least a perception of incompetence of the Bar generally. . . .
>
> The United States may be the only country claiming to be governed by law that turns an unskilled graduate loose on some unsuspecting client whose life, liberty or property may be at risk.[43]

5

THE JAILHOUSE LAWYERING OF MAYBERRY

The name Mayberry has a specific resonance in modern American culture. For millions of people drawn to the flickering lights of the television set, it evokes the easy living in a vanishing rural town, where people are sweet, where they care for their fellow sweet neighbors, and occasionally bake wonderfully sweet blueberry or rhubarb pies. Here, however, I refer to another Mayberry altogether, one that challenges this escapist fantasy.

Richard Mayberry is a legendary Pennsylvania jailhouse lawyer, one who has had some spectacular wins as well as some heart-rending losses. Mayberry has had immense legal experience spanning nearly half a century, and his cases have changed the nature of prison for many men and women.

Nearly half a century is surely an impressive length of time, and much of that span Mayberry has spent in prison hellholes, yet even so, he has used all the tools at his disposal to try to win his freedom and the freedom of others.

The 1960s had not yet struck their midpoint when his trial for prison breach and related charges began its long, complicated trek through the bowels of the courts. His battles to represent himself at trial brought derision from judges, who took umbrage at one not formally trained in the intricacies of the law—a prisoner to boot—citing laws in a courtroom.

In a matter of days, his running conflicts with the court would reach a critical breaking point, when the judge responded to Mayberry's verbal lashes with a weapon given uniquely to judges to wield—sentencing. At trial's end, the judge socked it to the *pro se*[1] litigant.

Indeed, Mayberry was sentenced to more time for what he allegedly did within the courtroom than for what he was charged with doing outside it.

It was a cool day in October 1963 when Mayberry and other prisoners were arraigned for prison breach, perjury, and related offenses. Pretrial hearings would commence in May and June 1965 in the since-abolished old Court of Quarter Sessions,[2] after which the trial proceeded before Judge Leo Weinrott. Pretrial and trial sessions were quite spirited, to say the least. In a moment of rage, Mayberry, quite literally, threw the book at the judge. (In truth, it wasn't a law book but a *World Almanac*.)

At trial's end, Weinrott threw sentences at Mayberry, condemning him to eleven to twenty-two years for direct contempt.

Mayberry appealed, arguing to the Pennsylvania Supreme Court that in all cases such as this, the U.S. and Pennsylvania constitutions required a jury trial, especially given the sentences rendered.

In 1969, Pennsylvania's highest court unanimously upheld Judge Weinrott's decision, saying it did not violate the state constitution. The court determined that constitutional guarantees "did not apply" to Mayberry, citing his book-throwing incident and finding that his trial began long before the relevant Supreme Court decisions that required a jury trial.

Mayberry relentlessly continued his appeals all the way to the U.S. Supreme Court. In January 1971, the Supreme Court handed down its *Mayberry v. Pennsylvania* decision.[3] The court, with no dissenting opinions, vacated Mayberry's convictions and remanded his case for a new trial. It determined that people should be given public trials before a different judge than the one before whom the contempt occurred, under the due process clause of the U.S. Constitution. In other words, to make trial proceedings at least look fair. The court also quoted liberally from the transcripts of the state trial, giving some idea of its temper.

On the trial's very first day, Mayberry announced his position: "It seems like the court has had the intentions of railroading us . . . [and] I would like to have a fair trial of this case and like to be granted a fair trial under the Sixth Amendment."[4]

Things went downhill from there. The judge, seemingly stung by the impolitic reference to "railroading," is curt and dismissive in the tone of his responses to Mayberry's concerns expressed at sidebar:

THE COURT: You will get a fair trial.

MAYBERRY: It doesn't appear that I'm going to get one the way you are overruling all our motions and that, and being like a hatchet man for the State.

THE COURT: This sidebar is over.

MAYBERRY: Wait a minute, Your Honor.

THE COURT: It is over.

MAYBERRY: You dirty sonofabitch.[5]

What began in sidebar soon erupted in open court, as Mayberry tried to question his witness on the stand:

MAYBERRY: I ask you, Mr. Nardi, is that area, the handball court, is it open to any prisoner who wants to play handball, who cares to go to that area to play handball?

NARDI: Yes.

MAYBERRY: Did you understand the prior question when I asked you if it was freely open and an accessible area?

THE COURT: He answered your question. Let's go on.

MAYBERRY: I am asking him now if he understands . . .

THE COURT: He answered it. Now, let's go on.

MAYBERRY: I ask Your Honor to keep your mouth shut while I'm interviewing my own witness. Will you do that for me?

THE COURT: I wish you would do the same. Proceed with your questioning.[6]

We often think of trials as nice, neat, and polite proceedings where solemn gentlemen discuss issues of weight and importance with intricate fairness and equity. What we see as trials today are descendants of other, older Saxon rituals in England, such as trial by ordeal, known as Judicium Dei—"judgment of God"—which meant trial by fire, or trial by water. These ordeals were based upon a person's social rank, fire for people of higher rank and water for common folk.

Under the fire ordeal, the accused would take up in his hand a red-hot iron one to two pounds in weight, or walk barefoot over nine red-hot ploughshares.

There was a hot-water ordeal as well as cold-water ordeal—both were harrowing.

The hot-water ordeal required one to plunge a bare arm up to the elbow into boiling water, with emergence unharmed proof of innocence. In the cold-water trial, one was cast into a river or cold-water pond. If one floated (without swimming) this was evidence of guilt. If one sank, s/he was acquitted.

The Norman conquest of England in 1066 brought with it the Norman trial, such as "wager of battel," which, as the name suggests, meant a battle between the accuser and the accused.

To begin this ritual, both accuser and accused made the vow to the assembled judges: "[H]ear this, ye justices, that I have this day neither eat, drank, nor have upon me, neither bone, stone, nor grass, nor any enchantment, sorcery, or witchcraft."[7]

In his *Commentaries on the Laws of England*, Sir William Blackstone records that both sides would dress themselves in prescribed armor, mount their best steeds, and launch headlong into battle for life or death. This ritual would last from daybreak until the stars appeared at night, or until one of the contestants died.[8] He who prevailed was seen as one ordained by heaven, and thus in the right. Some seven hundred years after its introduction, during the reign of George III, this practice was abolished.

This history continues in today's trials, albeit through words (and sometimes with books) rather than physical ordeals. Yet hidden in these unusually calm words is the same stunning violence.

For angering a judge, and for calling the trial a "kangaroo court," Mayberry was given the equivalent of a life sentence in some states—eleven to twenty-two years. What is the judge's sentence but an act of violence? This was Weinrott's revenge. And what of his learned colleagues of the Pennsylvania Supreme Court? Did they not add insult to injury?

In the face of this judicial malevolence, the judge's determination to frustrate Mayberry's efforts to win his trial, should Mayberry have played nice? Should he have simply concluded, "Oh, well—the judge doesn't want to let me win. I guess I'll just sit down now"?

Not Mayberry. He spoke truths to a court that was more accustomed to sycophancy, in words that didn't bow or scrape as if before a feudal prince: "Now, I'm going to produce my defense in this case and not be railroaded into any life sentence by any dirty, tyrannical old dog like yourself."[9] Mayberry's anger is palpable, open, not subterranean, as was the judge's:

MAYBERRY: You started all this bullshit in the beginning.

THE COURT: You keep quiet.

MAYBERRY: Wait a minute.

THE COURT: You keep quiet.

MAYBERRY: I am my own counsel.

THE COURT: You keep quiet.

MAYBERRY: Are you going to gag me?[10]

The words, coming from the mouth of one without power, were fueled by anger. The relative silence of the judge was belied by the stentorian violence wrapped within a single sentence. For daring to insult this judicial prince, Mayberry was sentenced to a generation in penal perdition.

Mayberry filed the first of several state and federal appeals against his draconian sentence, but most judges who resented his bitter diatribes against their class brother found Judge Weinrott's judicial revenge quite acceptable. Indeed, before his state criminal trial began, Mayberry filed an extraordinary petition against the trial judge, saying a trial before such a jurist would be in violation of the Constitution's due process clause. In most civil proceedings, when a petition is filed, a judge serves it upon the affected party and establishes a time to appear and answer the complaint. If the party fails to show up, the case is almost automatically awarded to the filing side. In the 1966 case *Mayberry v. Weinrott*, federal Judge Luongo would dismiss his petition—without even serving it!—and deny Mayberry his requested injunction.

Mayberry's trials and tribulations in state and federal courts proved to be quite unlike most other civil or even criminal proceedings. Indeed, it is a fundamental rule in most civil actions, at least at the start, to view complaints "in the light most favorable" to the plaintiff, or the one filing the complaint. While Judge Luongo used that language, his antipathy for the plaintiff doesn't allow him to actually apply that principle. He takes Mayberry's one—admittedly rare—case and looks ahead to the many who might wish to emulate his bold, rare maneuver, and shuts it down stillborn. While admitting that his court has the jurisdiction and power to grant the injunction, Luongo goes on to announce that such power must be used "sparingly," to preserve the "delicate" balance between the state and federal governments. What is lost in this "balance of powers" argument, however, is the powerless individual, the accused, whom the constitution was allegedly written to protect. In Judge Alfred I. Luongo's words:

> Intervention by injunction against criminal proceedings should be resorted to only to prevent manifest injustice in extraordinary cases involving the violation of fundamental constitutional rights or the denial of the basic requirements of due process of law.
>
> We have been admonished, in civil actions, to permit process to issue and to require the named defendant to appear and answer or otherwise move with respect to the complaint, rather than to dismiss on our own motion. . . . To follow that procedure in every suit under the Civil Rights Act against state judges at various stages of criminal trials would be unduly disruptive.

The issuance of process would thrust upon the state trial judge *the role of adversary to the complaining state court defendant, a role so inimical to the judicial function that it should [be] avoided whenever possible.*[11]

In other words, to avoid the "disruptive" appearance of equating a state court judge with an adversary, Mayberry's complaint, and request for an injunction are summarily dismissed, without even requiring the defendant to answer the claim!

Judge Luongo's attempt to protect the superior status of the judge and to protect the "delicate" balance between the state and federal powers, had to undo the reality that at trial the judge was in fact an adversary of the accused, and a dangerous one at that.

On Mayberry's direct appeal, Pennsylvania Supreme Court Justice Henry X. O'Brien would even obliquely say as much when commenting on the extraordinary sentence Weinrott laid down against Mayberry.

In a lone dissenting opinion—and at that only in reaction to the sentence—O'Brien wrote:

[I] believe that the sentence imposed here exceeded all bounds of reasonableness. . . . My research discloses no case in which the punishment meted out even approaches that here.... Although there is no doubt that the dignity of our courts must be upheld, by the contempt process, if necessary, in a Commonwealth where assault and battery is punishable by a maximum of two years' imprisonment, larceny by a maximum of five, voluntary manslaughter by a maximum of 15, and second-degree murder by a maximum of 20, *a*

> *maximum sentence of 22 years for interference with the*
> *courtroom process and insults to the judge is cruel and*
> *unusual.*[12]

The other six Pennsylvania Supreme Court justices did not agree.

As we've seen, Mayberry appealed all the way to the United States Supreme Court and won. But did he really?

At first blush it would seem so. When Mayberry and his codefendants returned to the state system, they were given new trials before a different judge.

Mayberry and his co-accused were again convicted of ten counts of contempt, and sentenced to nine terms of six months, and one term of three months, meaning that what was once a sentence of eleven to twenty-two years became one of fifty-seven months—or four years, nine months.

Not bad.

But that was not the end.

Mayberry argued that anyone facing such charges had a constitutional right to a jury trial, given the potential sentences faced.

Again the Pennsylvania Supreme Court disagreed, and his codefendants appealed to the U.S. Supreme Court, which Mayberry, for some reason, didn't do.

Mayberry instead launched a federal habeas petition and, based on his codefendants' cases, won a writ of habeas corpus.

In *Mayberry v. Frame*, a U.S. judge granted the writ, simply stating the obvious:

> Rarely would a court's path be guided more clearly
> than here, where the precedent is established by the

United States Supreme Court in ruling on co-defendants' appeals. Were this court to deny the relief requested, however, we would simply be performing an exercise in delay, causing petitioner a needless runaround. Mayberry's right to a jury trial is clear, and we will require that he be given one.[13]

Because Mayberry was acutely litigious, this was but one of his many suits, both civil and criminal, that would grace the pages of the law books.

For over a generation, the case *I.C.U. v. Shapp* formed the basis and foundation for the prison regulations governing the entire state. The abbreviation I.C.U. stood for Imprisoned Citizens' Union, which had launched a class action suit against various state prisons and the conditions of confinement in them.[14]

The suit addressed issues of health, overcrowding, and other problems like the glass cages then in operation at SCI Huntingdon in central Pennsylvania. These were, as the name suggests, large, glass-covered cages where men were confined as a punishment.

The I.C.U. case ended in a settlement, which required an agreement by all parties. Mayberry served as class representative and signed on behalf of thousands of state prisoners, and a court-agreed settlement went into force, creating new rules that covered the entire state system. The I.C.U. provisions became the foundation for every subsequent regulation that governed the entire state, and they lasted for decades, until the passage of the Prison Litigation Reform Act. A central theme of the Prison Litigation Reform Act was the newly granted power of states to shatter consent decrees[15] (like I.C.U.). The Pennsylvania prison system wasted no time getting a judge to grant the order to vacate and dissolve the consent decree. Once again, the law changed based upon the political forces arrayed to lobby for the change.

As with many jailhouse lawyers, Mayberry spent extended periods of time in the hole. While in one prison, having been thrown into the behavioral adjustment unit, also known as a BAU, he understandably sued. Given the length of time it takes to litigate, by the time he got to the court of appeals, he was no longer in the original institution. The state argued that his suit should be dismissed, because, given his transfer, it was moot.

The appeals court, however, disagreed. In *Mayberry v. Maroney*, Judges Markey, Weis, and Gibbons held for Mayberry:

> Mayberry, at the time of his original suit, was subjected to the confinement in the BAU although he is no longer an inmate of the institution housing the BAU, he remains an inmate of the penal system encompassing that institution and might in the future, therefore, be subject to confinement in the BAU. Consistent with *Conover* [*v. Montamuro* (3CA 1976)], we hold that Mayberry retains standing as an adequate representative of the entire class and reverse the second order of the district court.[16]

Judge Gibbons wrote a second concurring opinion, which agreed with the majority but added a criticism of the lower district court for refusing to resolve the issue. His words bear repeating if only because they throw light on the nature of the nation's judiciary: "If judges do not settle legal relationships, at least so long as they have not been modified by court action, there is little need for the priesthood of the judiciary, witch doctors would do as well."[17]

Mayberry had won another one, and would win many more, as well as lose a few. He continued to wage legal skirmishes on the littered battlefields of civil and criminal law.

Mayberry the Man

Mayberry is a relatively small, thin man whose decades in prison have made him wary of those around him. As with life anywhere else, he has earned his share of enemies and allies.

In appearance, he is the quintessential lawyer, and his deliberate Northeast Philadelphia accent could be heard in courtrooms around the region. Indeed, imagining him a lawyer is not much of a stretch, for in brief glimpses of him in the visiting room as he launches into a legal theory or principle, he seems to be lecturing young lawyers.

Given his milieu—an older white guy in a predominantly Black institution—he tends to form friendships among other whites, with whom he feels comfortable. Over a decade ago, a Black neighbor of his in the hole in the state prison at Huntingdon began to lay into him. Hasan, a permanent resident of the hole, seemed to bubble with rage as he called his name.

"Don't think I don't know who you are, Mayberry!"

"What are you talkin' about, Hasan?"

"Don't play stupid with me, man! I remember, when you was up Dallas—in the hole—and alla them nigger jokes you useta be laughin' about!"

"I don't wanna rap about—"

"Oh! Now that you are here—around alla brothas, you ain't got no rap, huh?"

"No—it's just that—"

"Just what? Youza racist! You useta be all cool with them guards up there—when they was rollin' on brothas up there!"

"If I was workin' with 'em, how come I stayed in the hole, Hasan?"

"Do you deny that youza racist?"

"I'm sayin'—"

"I'm askin' you! Do you deny that youza racist?"

"I'm sayin', right—"

"You ain't 'sayin' nothin'! I asked you a question, white boy!"

A moment of silence passes, and every ear on that side of the block is perked in anticipation and tension.

"OK—OK, I'm a racist!"

Hasan laughs in triumph. "You think I didn't know that? Didn't I tell y'all? Didn't I tell y'all?"

"And you know what else, Hasan?"

"What, you white devil?"

"I may be a racist, but I love a nigger like you!"

"What did you say, white boy?"

"I said, I love a nigger like you!"

"What the hell you talkin' about?"

"Well, you came in here for killin' 'bout four niggers, didn't you?"

Hasan seethes in silence.

"Yeah—so you killed four (or was it five?) niggers; you came to death row, that's another nigger. You pulled your brother into this stuff, and he doin' life—that's another nigger. And you broke your Momma's heart—that's seven niggers!"

"Yeah—I'm a racist! But I love niggers like you!"

The block, like Hasan, seethed in silence.

Mayberry on Jailhouse Lawyering

Mayberry, although quite highly regarded for his legal acumen, is actually quite self-effacing and quiet, and would be the last person to consider himself a jailhouse lawyer. He's not the only one who shuns the title.

Mayberry's objection is actually quite logical. "No, I do not consider myself a jailhouse lawyer," says Mayberry. "I do not define myself in such limiting terms. I know something about law, and I've been practicing law for many years. But that is not what I am. I know a little about a lot of things, for example medicine, politics, history, chemistry, etc., but does that make me a 'jailhouse doctor,' 'jailhouse politician,' 'jailhouse historian,' 'jailhouse chemist,' or 'jailhouse anything'? I'm a man who has learned and put into practice those subjects and areas of expertise necessary to accomplish whatever I needed or wanted."[18]

Mayberry actually echoes many men and women who shun the establishment-sounding title of jailhouse lawyer, as much for the reasons he convincingly explains, as perhaps a reflection of the cultural distaste in which lawyers are held, especially among prisoners and other poor folks.

Like many jailhouse lawyers, Mayberry didn't study formally. As he explained in an interview in 2005, "I learned by reading books, and self-study. I was my own teacher.

Mainly while spending long years in solitary confinement in state prison."[19]

How did he begin his lone trek to the field of jailhouse law? It began when he was, predictably, in the hole. His first case actually predated the famous Supreme Court *Johnson* case by half a decade. As he recalls it, "First case I ever filed in Federal Court, and won, was *U.S. ex rel. Mayberry v. Myers and Prasse*, 225 F.Supp. 752 (E.D. Pa. 12/4/63). I filed a complaint from the hole at the State Penitentiary at Graterford, and won the right to send out and buy law books. In 1963 there were no law libraries in Pennsylvania prisons, and being caught with a law book was an automatic trip to the hole for possession of contraband."[20]

He remains, many years later, a brilliant and imaginative litigator, his continued reluctance to don the title of jailhouse lawyer notwithstanding. For the many men he assisted and the others he taught—if only through his indefatigable example—he remains a jailhouse lawyer.

He is a member of no bar association, he claims no cachet from any school, and yet his work stands as a testament to one man's power to resist, with intelligence.

6

A WOMAN'S WORK IN STATE HELL

When, or perhaps if, we think of women in prison, our minds might conjure up a cheap B movie featuring various oversexed vixens clad in remarkably stylish and revealing clothing. But reality is far from a B movie. Prison is a hell for all who inhabit it. It is meant to be. Prison is a form of state terrorism, designed to instill terror in the poor and the powerless.

Black, radical, feminist scholar-activist Angela Y. Davis has opined that the generality of crime has come to take the place of communism as the enemy of capitalist society. "Communism is no longer the quintessential enemy against which the nation imagines its identity," writes Davis. "This space is now inhabited by ideological constructions of crime, drugs, immigration, and welfare. Of course, the enemy within is far more dangerous than the enemy without, *and a black enemy within is the most dangerous of all.*"[1]

As the social order continues it devises other ideals of social danger, among them women.

In the United States today, there are more than ninety thousand women in prisons. Of that number, over 80 percent are mothers, who have left more than 167,000 children behind living in a tenuous freedom.

According to some thinkers, the surge in Black imprisonment could be traced to the emergence of the Black liberation movement of the 1960s and 1970s. Similarly, the heightened imprisonment seems to bear some relationship to the emergence of the women's liberation movement and the struggle for the Equal Rights Amendment during the latter period of that movement. This suggests that prison serves a profoundly political function, to discipline, subvert, and disempower social movements by disabling potential members. Conviction brings with it a concomitant loss of the tools of civil activity, specifically the vote, and social mobility such as the ability to acquire licenses or professional clearances. Women, upon leaving prison, are less able to secure the economic wherewithal to support and protect their families and children.

For those still in prison, there are women who have taken it upon themselves to do the hard work of jailhouse lawyering, working to protect and defend the legal rights of other imprisoned women.

One such woman is Jane Dorotik, who, although she does not consider herself a jailhouse lawyer, has done much to redress the grievances and injustices facing her sisters at the Central California Women's Facility (C.C.W.F.) in Chowchilla. The facility, along with the adjacent Valley State Prison for Women (V.S.P.W.) is the largest prison complex for women on earth—and it is overcrowded. The two units house over 60 percent of all female prisoners in the state.

Dorotik, in a recent interview, opined, "There is such a great need for jailhouse lawyers—these women have so little else, so few avenues to find help. Most of them have exhausted any financial resources they have had long before they arrive here, and pro bono[2] help from the law community is negligible."[3]

Like Mayberry, Dorotik neither uses the title jailhouse lawyer nor has studied formally. "My study has been all informal," she says, "in search of my own justice and freedom, and also in the recognition that someone has to help all these women. My own efforts have been more towards helping these women help themselves."[4]

She sees her essential role as providing hope to many who are without hope:

> I believe the greatest accomplishments I have had would be in giving women hope, if they work hard enough and persistently enough they will be able to achieve their freedom . . . but it takes commitment and relentless effort.
>
> I have had an awful lot of success in writing 602s (internal appeals)[5] against many practices that go on behind these walls. One practice that is so very prevalent—and yet in many ways so easily overcome—is the practice of Case Records [a department of the prison administration] miscalculating an inmate's sentence. Typically what will happen is a woman will come in to the law library with a tearful story of "I know the judge gave me four years with half time, but my counselor said no, I really have to do six years because of my controlling case."
>
> This, or some version of this, [is] so very common, and the "error" is never in the inmate's favor, always more time is added on with some convoluted explanation of "controlling cases." We got the abstract of judgment and minute order[6] (including credits) from

the court, not from the prison's case records. We 602 case records, pointing out the discrepancy between what the judge decreed and what the prison case records are now saying, and we get it corrected. Rarely, we have to write to the judge himself, indicating that C.D.C. [California Department of Correction] is attempting to override the sentence the judge ordered, but usually a simple 602 corrects it. This I would say is the most appreciated effort, because the inmate is finally able to get out of here when the judge says, not [in] the C.D.C.'s time frame.[7]

Dorotik's work in the law library is centered on the most pressing concerns of the women in Central California Women's Facility and all prisoners—freedom.

Her activity mirrors the reality of the virtual explosion of the women's prison population in the latter years of the twentieth century and the emergence of the twenty-first. As manufacturing jobs leave the United States and as the drug economy further permeates urban—and increasingly rural—America, the prison apparatus is brought more and more to bear on women. And, as Dorotik's jailhouse lawyering experience shows, there is official reluctance to let them go.

As Black feminist scholar Joy James has detailed, given the simultaneous explosion of male incarceration, the rise in female imprisonment has been widely overlooked.

Discussions around human rights abuses within penal systems tend to ignore the conditions of women. Traditionally women made up a small percentage of the prison population, yet their incarceration rates have recently increased over 300 percent, as compared with a 214 percent increase for men. Between 1930 and 1950 two or three prisons were built or established nationwide per decade for women; in the 1960s seven more were built; in the 1970s seventeen were created; in the 1980s thirty-four were opened to house women. In 1994 black women represented 82 percent of women sentenced for crack cocaine offenses; for drug offenses overall, they made up 50 percent. Female offenders are mostly women who ran away from home; a quarter have attempted suicide; more than half have been abused sexually.[8]

It is hard to look at such statistics without coming to the conclusion that there is a de facto war against women in this society. Indeed, the so-called drug war has had a profound impact on the lives of women and on the nation as a whole. Like many other rhetorical wars announced by politicians and enacted by political institutions such as legislatures, courts, and prisons, they mask deeper social and racial agendas.

Independent scholar Richard L. Miller has argued that the underlying premise of the so-called drug war shares parallels with, if not borrows from, the Nazi regime of legalism. While some may question such an assertion, who can deny that the programs of both the Nazis and the Nationalists of South African apartheid have points in common with historical precedents of the Black segregation codes and Indian reservations in the United States?

Only two modern nation-states had racial restrictions on naturalization—Nazi Germany and the United States.[9]

As for the Black Codes (or legal codes that were put

into force after the termination of the U.S. Civil War), the U.S. Supreme Court, in *U.S. v. Cruikshank*, explained them as legal strictures that "imposed upon the colored race onerous disabilities and burdens, and curtailed their rights in the pursuit of life, liberty, and property to such an extent that their freedom was of little value."[10]

In the U.S. Supreme Court case *Fletcher v. Peck* we glean some idea of how U.S. law viewed the rights and privileges of the Native American people. John Quincy Adams gave his view of Indian title by arguing this before the Court in 1802.

> Their cultivated fields; their constructed habitations;
> a space . . . for their subsistence . . . was undoubtedly
> by the law of nature theirs. But what is the right of the
> huntsman to the forest of a thousand miles over which
> he has accidentally ranged in quest of prey? Shall the
> liberal bounties of Providence be claimed by a few
> hundreds? Shall the lordly savage not only disdain
> the virtues and enjoyments of civilization himself, but
> shall he control the civilization of the world?[11]

In delivering his coup de grâce, Adams argued in terms that marked his contempt for Indian life, liberty, and property for generations: "What is the Indian title? It is mere occupancy for the purpose of hunting. It is not like our tenures; they have no idea of a title to the soil itself. It is overrun by them, rather than inhabited. It is not a true and legal possession."[12]

With such terms, white law despoiled Indians, putting them beyond the realm of law, on reservations.

Miller argues that the point of agreement is in the

ability to promote the power of the state over the body, as shown by the margins of the so-called drug war, which found expression through various segments of society:

> If research challenging the drug war is permitted, getting the research findings published in mainstream scientific journals is difficult. Some scientific journals, like the popular media, seem to have an editorial policy promoting the drug war. Analysts examined "cocaine baby" research reports in files of the Society of Pediatric Research. In eighty-one percent of reports claiming that cocaine harmed fetal development, medical personnel failed to determine if the pregnant women used cocaine. In seventy-five percent of reports claiming that cocaine caused no harm to fetal development, the scientists confirmed cocaine use by the pregnant women. Despite additional factors making reports of cocaine's benign effect on fetal development more reliable than "cocaine baby" reports, the analysts found that medical journals generally refused to publish reports that pregnant women could safely use cocaine. The analysts concluded that journals preferred politically correct reports that would help scientists get research grants from government agencies.[13]

Why this attention on the drug war, and how has it had an impact on society? At the forefront has been its impact on imprisoned women. The fact of the matter is that the majority of women are imprisoned for nonviolent economic and/or drug-related crimes, such as check forgery or fraudulent credit card use.

Despite this rise in female imprisonment for drug-related crimes, drug addiction treatment has not increased proportionately.[14]

Dorotik labors in a system that holds more women than any other prison system in the United States, and is the largest in the world. As of 2005, some 8,000 women were imprisoned at Central California Women's Facility and Valley State Prison for Women. She looks out from her perch in the law library and sees a vista of injustice:

> Anywhere between 10 to 25 percent of those incarcerated are actually innocent of the crime they were convicted of. [There is] a 60 percent reversible error rate on . . . death penalty cases. . . . This is horrifying. How can a society tolerate such an error rate? What would IBM, or Microsoft do if their error rate was so high—and this would only be in business machines or processors, not people's lives (and freedom).[15]

Although prison remains largely a male enclave, with the expansion of the prison-industrial-complex it is becoming increasingly a women's issue. As prison number and size expand to feed upon those who do not fit in the present economic system, an increasing number of women are finding themselves incarcerated.

At Chowchilla, women like Jane Dorotik continue to seek to help others by filing those 602s.

Midge DeLuca Goes to Prison

If Midge DeLuca had been asked about prison before she had the misfortune of going there, she might have blinked at the question, and swatted it away as a minor annoyance. It was as far from her presumed destiny as the moon. She had no clue.

Her road to the House of Pain began in the doctor's office, where she learned that a lump in her breast meant cancer. The Big C. It terrified her, and she responded to that very real fear by the very human answer of avoidance of the unpleasant.

She tried to chase away the demons with alcohol, only to awake in her car after a nightmarish car accident that left one person dead and another seriously injured.

This was January 1999, and still, with her middle-class upbringing, her education, and her profession, it never dawned on her that this unfortunate and tragic accident of drunk driving would translate into prison for her. When the judge sentenced her to seven years with an 85 percent time-served demand, she was quite literally stunned.

In a sense, it was two sentences—one to prison, and the other, because of her stage-three breast cancer, very possibly one of death.

She would later write, "I NEVER thought this could happen to me!"[16]

She was put in a place where fear was the only common denominator, and this fear of dying in prison propelled her toward the law:

> So when I got to E.M.C.F.W. [Edna Mahan Correctional Facility for Women in Clinton, New Jersey], I was sent to the MAX Security because my crime is [a] violent one—so in the MAX—I started to learn the law; because [I] was not getting the medical treatment I needed [and] didn't want to die in prison. You see I

learned how to get the medical care that I needed. I learned the law [and] started to write [and] became very vocal. Audre Lorde, my favorite poet, wrote "only our silences will hurt us"—so after I read that—I decided I was going to help other women, who were truly sick [and] needed medical care—I was going to help them [and] become their voice. I began to write for the prison paper [and] expressions of my concern were being read all around the prison. While I was in the MAX security (or for that matter *all* the time), the medical department hated to see me coming! I helped many women in the MAX—get the needed medication, dialysis treatments, help w[ith] their Hep[atitis] C or HIV, whatever their concerns, I began to help. There continues to [be] such a need in the MAX—to get the help that is needed. I became friends with the women (inmates) who worked in our law library. I learned what my rights were in regards to my medical care [and] the care of others—I've never been in prison before—BUT, I was not afraid—these are our rights [and] just because we were incarcerated *did not* mean we weren't entitled to medical care. So I spoke. . . . Women see me coming [and] speak—[and] I help![17]

She was sentenced to seven years, and did five years, eleven months and twelve days in the Edna Mahan Correctional Facility for Women. She remembers her time with a shudder:

I had to do two and a half years in maximum security because I am considered a violent criminal. And there you did practically nothing. Movement is real restricted, there [are] very few jobs unless you want to get into sewing or food service so really in maximum security I did barely . . . anything but write and read.[18]

When asked to recount the most difficult part of her prison experience, she didn't hesitate:

> Oh my God, just being there. In maximum security I absolutely can say I hated it. There was not one day when I woke up that I didn't want to kick myself for what I had done. I was also at the time battling breast cancer so getting medical help was a real chore. I had a real difficult time in maximum security. It wasn't that I was afraid or anything else. It's not a life. It's purely an existence in maximum security. I was so happy when they sent me out to minimum because there I was editor of the prison paper and I worked as a paid professional in education so there's a lot more opportunity for the women who can get out to minimum. But not everybody can go to minimum. Not only because of space but also because of your crime.[19]

To fight prison is one thing, but to fight cancer too? She describes her battle:

> I was diagnosed in January '99. I had waited much too long and the lump was protruding from my skin. I had a mastectomy in January 2000 and then I was sentenced in April 2000. I really believed that my judge wouldn't sentence me and send me right away. But he did.
> Medical care in the prison is just deplorable. I had to travel to St. Francis Hospital in Trenton

to get my chemo. You're in a van and you're going twelve to fourteen hours a day [of chemo]. It was just deplorable and it was only an act of God that it's in remission today because [of] the care and the diet and everything else, I battled on a daily basis. And I still battle and I still help women who have serious health issues. They can't get the help, they can't make the phone call.[20]

What saved her when she went to prison was writing to everybody she could—both in and out of the system:

[W]hen I arrived at Clinton in April, I had medical orders—because I was right in the middle of chemo— to continue my chemo on that regular cycle, which I didn't. And it was just letter after letter after letter, just writing to people, having family here write and call people. I became involved with some really good women's prison activists, Bonnie Kerness and Gail Muhammad, and we just wrote and wrote and wrote. That's where I learned the [law] and that's when I learned really what rights prisoners have.[21]

Her advocacy and constant badgering led to predictable responses from the staffers. Her cell was constantly shaken down. But it didn't deter her. What sticks in her mind is the degradation and humiliation of prison. She firmly believes that the state saw the women as a mere commodity:

I believe in the state of New Jersey that we are just a dollar sign to them.

It's all about money, it's not about rehabilitation. I believe that very strongly. The GED classes have waiting lists up the arm. And then we have supposedly a graduation at Clinton and only two women out of 1300 get a GED, come on. You know? I believe that we're a business for them and they don't want to see us improve. They would much rather see us fail.[22]

Midge counts among her friends many of the inmates at the Edna Mahan Correctional Facility for Women and also incredible people like jailhouse lawyers "Adrian," also of E.M.C.F.W., and Antoine Graham of Trenton State Prison. Although the memories of prison were grim, these jailhouse lawyers were the flickers of brightness. "What impresses me most about any jailhouse lawyer is the hope that they give you—knowledge is there of course—but the *hope* lets you believe you can do this—I tried to exude hope to anyone who asks me for help."[23]

On April 27, 2006, she emerged from the darkened façade of prison into the light of freedom.

She told a reporter for the *Trenton Times* that prison gave her a new perspective. "Prison changed my whole outlook on life. . . . I grew up in lily-white Millburn. I didn't known what a black person was until I went to college. Prison opened my eyes to much injustice and racism."[24]

She went through her most daunting fears—breast cancer, alcoholism, and prison—to count herself as a survivor.

Theresa Torricellas—Paralegal

In Corona, California, another jailhouse lawyer is hard at

work helping people who for the most part are unable to do their own work. Unlike some others, Theresa Torricellas does consider herself a jailhouse lawyer, if only somewhat ambivalently:

> Do I consider myself a JHL [jailhouse lawyer]?
> Kinda-sorta, though I'm loath to take on others' legal battles for them at this point since it can interfere with my major goals (such as pursuing relief from my own conviction and sentences) and provide more of a workload than I can reasonably handle or follow through on. The biggest problem with JHLs, in my own view, is 1) there aren't enough of them, and 2) many of the ones there are don't really have skills adequate to their task (not to mention all the handicaps they operate under as incarcerated persons).[25]

Why does she consider herself a jailhouse lawyer?

> Because I have developed a level of knowledge and a certain level of expertise that renders me particularly useful for 1) analyzing prisoners' legal problems/issues, 2) providing advice in respect to what the prisoner might be able to do about it (if anything) or how to proceed. I think I'm a fairly good consultant when it comes to typical prisoner-related issues. Even if I don't have all the answers, I have at least some of them a good portion of the time, and frequently know where to find the answer if I don't know [what] the answer is.
>
> I'm familiar with available legal resources and how to use them for the most part. Prisoners rou-

tinely seek me out for answers to their legal questions or to consult with. Several call me "lawyer" and I had one call me the "D.A." (after I grilled one of the associate wardens here with some tough questions at a community [question-and-answer] session set up by the administration in regards to new property regulations being implemented).

I just had another prisoner (a tax attorney on the outside, but serving time on a conspiracy to commit murder charge) tell me yesterday that she had sent a letter to the principal of the Ed. Department here at C.I.W. [Corona Institution for Women] to "suggest" that he hire me as a law library clerk, because the clerks presently on the job 1) don't know anything, and 2) can't find anything (resource materials). I was a law library clerk, but they bounced me after nine months, because I 602'd a staff librarian. A 602 is an administrative grievance. The law library now is total hell, and I am pursuing numerous individual and several class action 602s in regards to numerous and various deficiencies in the law library and the (new) librarian's failure to accommodate request[s] for legal materials and resources which are supposed to be in the law library and readily accessible per the Gilmore [case].[26]

Much of Torricellas's work seems to revolve around what the California system terms 602s, which are designed to address individual and collective issues in that state's prisons. In explaining her 602-related work, she notes:

I intermittently take on the preparation and pursuit of

class action 602s concerning group issues, primarily because I think it ought to be done, and I'm afraid if I don't do it, it won't get done. Occasionally I become involved in personally handling or managing other prisoners' legal work, but because I don't have a lot of free time available for this (and I'm already fully engaged in my own crime case and parole hearing issue writ litigation), I'm kind of picky about others' legal work. If it is something relatively simple that won't require too much of my time, or if there are extenuating circumstances I might be willing to help (as in do the work for them). Other than that, I have an open door policy to any prisoner who is sincerely in need of advice or guidance in their legal matters, and try to give folks the benefit of my insights and experience.[27]

Like several other jailhouse paralegals, Torricellas studied formally to become a paralegal. In fact, she studied with several paralegal schools, although she did not complete her last course of instruction:

I did complete several paralegal courses with S.C.I. [Southern Career Institute] of Florida, but they were almost too easy and simple. I later enrolled in a paralegal academy (I think they were called American Academy of Paralegals) which was more or less run/operated by prisoners with the assistance of an outside person. Their curriculum was TOUGH, but I loved it for this reason . . . and because they focused on the type of legal matters [likely] to be of the greatest importance to incarcerated persons. That being criminal conviction rates, post-conviction remedies, appeal and prisoners' condition of confinement issues. I was not able to complete the curriculum because I ended up swamped in the capital lawsuits I had filed previously and unable to handle everything all at the same time. [M]ost of what I learned is through experience, through working as a clerk at the prison law library, even for the short period of time I spent there, [which] helped to expose me to new different types of legal issues and problems (that are subject to appear frequently with prisoners as a class) I otherwise would have been in the dark about had I not worked there.[28]

With the growing imprisonment of women comes the need for more jailhouse lawyers to assist them.

Many women, consigned to the bowels of the nation's prisons, have rejected that sexist notion of their invisibility or weakness. Using their minds and their hearts, they dare to confront many of the problems that arise in the House of Pain and struggle to find solutions. They work to open the prison gates for some and to address prison conditions for many others. In the place expected to contain powerlessness, we find women of power and will.

7

THE RUIZ EFFECT: HOW ONE JAILHOUSE
LAWYER MADE CHANGE IN TEXAS

David Ruiz was many things. Robber. Thief. Convict. Lifer. He was also a jailhouse lawyer, writer, and painter. He was something quite different to the family from which he spent so many years separated. History will remember him for but one of those things: jailhouse lawyer.

It was in 1971 that Ruiz penned a thirty-page civil rights complaint against prison conditions in Texas. He dutifully sent it to the assistant warden, so that the document could be notarized before being filed in court.

It was the last time he would see the complaint, for it was tossed into the trash and Ruiz was thrown into solitary. At the time, Ruiz, having been imprisoned for nearly a decade, should've known better. But he learned quickly. Ruiz redrafted his complaint, but this time handed it to a lawyer, who passed it on to a federal judge named William Wayne Justice.

By spring 1974, the *Ruiz v. Estelle* case would be merged with that of seven other prisoners' civil suits, and within several months the United States would take the rare step of intervening in the case on the side of the prisoner-plaintiffs.[1] The rest is history. Texas would no longer be the same.

Ruiz v. Estelle would uncover the naked violence, favoritism, and brutality that was rampant in the plantation-style prison system. When Ruiz and several other jailhouse lawyers filed their suits, the state prison system was an eighteenth-century anachronism.

Texas prisons featured not just double-celling but triple-celling, with conditions of misery ripe for disaster. Texas prisons featured dormitories that were clear and present dangers to prisoners.

As Judge Justice explained in his 1980 opinion:

The constant threat to the inmates' personal safety posed by over-crowded living conditions in both the multiply-inhabited cells and the packed dormitories presents the most obvious harm. Penologists who testified at trial were virtually unanimous in their condemnation of double and triple-celling. Director Estelle himself noted the exigent problems associated with double-celling, making reference to the increased opportunity for predatory activities and the enhanced difficulties respecting supervision and control. TDC [Texas Department of Corrections] inmates are routinely subjected to brutality, extortion, and rape at the hands of their cellmates. Some of the most heinous examples have occurred in triple-celling situations, where two-on-one confrontations practically guarantee the capitulation of the abused third cellmate. However, the problems of violence also occur all too frequently in double-celling situations, where one inmate often dominates the other. The evidence made it clear that, even if inmates were doubled in cells large enough to accommodate two persons, the effects of violence and the climate of fear would remain.[2]

What really distinguished Texas (and other southern) prison systems was the "building tender" program, by which prisoners were armed by guards to assist them, and even perform their duties.

Texas prison officials argued that building tenders generally performed innocuous roles merely to assist guards. The judge, however, found otherwise:

> [C]onclusive evidence shows that, in reality, building tenders are allowed to do a great deal more than merely assist officers at routine tasks. For instance, building tenders are used by TDC officials to gather intelligence concerning the activities, expressions and attitudes of other inmates. More importantly, they quite often literally serve in the capacity of guards. In the words of one of the defendants' expert witnesses, these inmates do the guards' "dirty work," serving as enforcers of the ranking officers' will in the living areas, and harassing, threatening, and physically punishing inmates perceived as troublemakers.[3]

And guess who were deemed "troublemakers"? As Judge Justice explained:

> TDC officers routinely harass and punish those prisoners whom they perceive as litigious. These inmates, known as "writ writers," are ear-marked by TDC officials as troublemakers and are constantly hounded wherever they go within the prison system. Their persistence in legal activity can cause them to lose even minor comforts or privileges which TDC prisoners are otherwise capable of enjoying.

Practices designed to retaliate against writ writers have ranged from the overt to the subtle, from the imposition of inconveniences to the perpetration of violence. . . . Some writ writers have been moved from the general population to administrative segregation. There, they have spent months, and even years, for no discernible security reasons.[4]

Judge Justice documents a plantation-style prison system that borrowed liberally from the actual slave plantations, e.g., building tenders, in the role of overseers, being armed with weapons supplied by guards.

They were deadly instruments in a virtual reign of terror—one nicely ignored and denied by the state.

To make matters even worse, the prison system's use of building tenders in this manner was a clear violation of Texas law. Texas blindly violated its own state laws for several simple reasons: It was cheap. It worked. Judge Justice wrote:

A Texas statute expressly prohibits the use of inmates in a supervisory or administrative capacity over other inmates and forbids any inmate to administer disciplinary action to another prisoner. Disregarding the statutory provision, TDC has compensated for the chronic shortages of civilian security personnel by using inmates to perform security functions. TDC officials agreed that a large number of inmates hold jobs in which they assist officers; notwithstanding, they deny that these inmates exercise supervisory authority over other inmates . . .

Building tenders have unofficially been given such specific powers as issuing orders to other inmates, assisting in taking daily counts of the population, keeping track of inmate movements, escorting inmates to different destinations within the prison, and distributing correspondence and commissary scrip. Some are authorized to be in possession of keys outside the presence of civilian personnel, and others operate the automated opening devices which control access to cell blocks, day rooms, and other parts of the institution.[5]

Given this power dynamic, and the racial/ethnic composition of prisons as largely of people of African and Mexican descent, with a predominantly white rural staff, this was a recipe for abuse, corruption and officially sanctioned injustice.

This was the system that Ruiz and seven other jailhouse lawyers exposed to the bright light of day.

Ruiz and his cohorts were threatened with death by other prisoners—building tenders—for daring to sue the prison.

Judge Justice found:

> TDC officials have [. . .] caused violent attacks to be perpetrated on writ-writers, in retaliation for their legal activity. Various inmates testified that they have repeatedly suffered brutality at the hands of TDC employees because of their writ-writing. One notoriously violent inmate was instructed by higher-ups to prey upon one of the plaintiffs in the instant action and "scare him off the Ruiz case." He accordingly proceeded to—non-fatally—slit the writ writer's throat.[6]

Such death threats caused Ruiz to be transferred into the federal prison system until he petitioned to be returned.

In a 2002 interview with reporters from the *Houston*

Chronicle, Ruiz described a state-supported system of fear and intimidation, enforced by building tenders. As Ruiz explained, "They had permission to carry knives, hammers, black-jacks [and] sticks." He described the joint as a "jungle" where only "the strong survived."[7]

Neither the death threats nor the other threats of violence deterred Ruiz from his intentions.

The *Ruiz* case spelled the abolition of the building tender system in Texas and opened the door to the courts for other civil actions. It also opened the door to recreational facilities, better health care, improved sanitation, and fire safety requirements.

It also opened an antiquated, backward system to the twentieth century. The *Ruiz* class action, which initially earned him a spell in the hole, would eventually force Texas to spend billions of dollars to bring the system into some semblance of modernity.

The Ruiz case has come to stand as law over the Texas system for thirty years.

In 2001 (now Senior) Judge Justice would describe the case as "a history unto itself."

In November 2005, David Resendez Ruiz, a man who spent all but four years of his adult life in prison, would die, reportedly of liver cancer, at the age of 62.

Houstonian (Texas) artist and former Black Panther Bob Lee called his death "a severe loss."[8]

Lee (known as "da mayor of the Fifth Ward") called Ruiz "one brave man," with few to fill his shoes. Ruiz, joined with seven other jailhouse lawyers, brought change to a system that was determined to resist change. They demonstrate the positive impact that jailhouse lawyers, against tremendous odds, can have.

8

FROM "SOCIAL PRISONER" TO JAILHOUSE LAWYER TO REVOLUTIONARY: ED MEAD'S JOURNEY

Ed Mead is perhaps best known as a cofounder of the prison legal monthly *Prison Legal News*, the journal edited, written, and published by prisoners since 1990.

Mead, along with *Prison Legal News* editor Paul Wright, began the project when both men were entombed in Washington's state prison and engaged in the struggles of jailhouse lawyers to research, catalogue, and interpret the cases emerging from the nation's growing prison population.

Today, Mead heads the board of directors of *California Prison Focus*, a publication that seeks to meet the needs and address the problems of California's vast prison population.

In an interview with Prison Radio, Mead recounts his prison experiences, from his days as a young man who was unjustly jailed, to his growth and development into a revolutionary activist who sought a true transformation in the political, social, and economic scene.

MEAD: Long ago and in a galaxy far away I went to prison as a social prisoner; I had been convicted of a crime that I didn't commit. It was the only time, you know—I've been doing time since I was 13 years old, I'm 63 now and I've always been guilty. But this one time I was convicted of a crime that I didn't do and

191

they sent me to prison. So the first thing I did I hired the best jailhouse lawyer in the place. Every week on commissary day I'd be carrying sacks of commissary in to this guy. And there were a whole lot of other people in the institution who he was doing work for. But he keeps stringing me along, maybe write a letter for somebody, do some little thing and that was okay for most of his clients but unlike them I was in the law library all the time studying the books. I didn't know much, I'd find some sentence that seemed to fit my situation, I'd run to him "Well, what about this? What about that?" I'm sure I was a pain in the neck to him.

PRISON RADIO: What conviction did you get? That you were working on. What year?

MEAD: It was 1968. I had been suspected of breaking into a National Guard armory and stealing five M-60 machine guns, a truckload of M-14s, ammunition, C-rations, smoke grenades, grenade launcher, and stuff like that. They could not prosecute me on that. But they did lock me up in jail. But there is no way I could be convicted of it. While I was in jail some kid decided that he was going to try and escape. He got hold of a pickax and was beating on one of the outside walls, on a wall that led to the outside; it wasn't a wall that surrounded the prison but it was a dormitory that had a wall that looked out. There was a Native American youngster about 20 from a remote village, didn't speak much English, didn't say much. He said it was me who was beating on the wall with a pick. I was there on this federal offense knowing that I was going to get out. It was just an outrage that I was even in jail, they were just so mad that they had to do something; but my release date was coming up pretty quick. And the guy who was beating on the wall looked a bit like me, about my height and had blonde hair. It was a mistake that somebody could make who hadn't been around many Caucasians. Well, he got up on the stand and testified that it was me; a whole bunch of other prisoners got up on the stand and testified that it was not me. Well the guy who was beating on the wall got up and testified that it was him beating up on the wall. I had a judge instead of a jury. I thought that would have been better because of my prior record. The judge knew about the armory and just found me guilty and gave me the maximum sentence and sent me off to McNeil Island Prison in Washington state.

PRISON RADIO: What was your sentence for that?

MEAD: It was ten years for attempted escape. I was just outraged that this could happen. The fact that I had actually done the armory and that it all kind of evened out was a concept that was foreign to my notion of fair play. So I got to doing more and more of my own work and filing my own appeals.[1]

Mead had learned some important lessons about the nature of the criminal justice system. In many ways, his lessons of life were just beginning. His unrewarding experience as one of the joint's best jailhouse lawyers taught him at least one more important lesson.

MEAD: Well, I wanted more out of him than he was willing to give. And so I said, well, I'll just do my own legal work then. And so I did. I took a job on the back dock of the kitchen cleaning out garbage cans. It was a dirty filthy job and I always smelled like garbage. But I . . . didn't have to spend much time there, so I spent as much time as I could in the prison law library reading the books . . . and over a period of years that knowledge accumulated and I [started] using it on a daily basis.

I became a jailhouse lawyer [and] began doing legal work for other guys as well, won some cases. When you win then other people come and they want help. And pretty soon, after a few years . . . there were so many people who needed help and so little time that I had that I would sort out who I could help on the basis of how much they could pay me. One point I looked at myself and you know what? I had become what had disgusted me; I had become that guy that was originally doing my work.[2]

But that was just the beginning of Mead's growth and development. It was the early 1970s, and he soon came face to face with people and ideas that would transform his life and his thinking—revolutionary politics.

MEAD: Some people from the antiwar movement were starting to come into the prison. One of these people was Chuck Armsberry. A White Panther out of Portland. He was convicted of arms violation, firearms violation. So he came in and he filed something . . . he calls it 'the genocide complaint' [but] he doesn't just file it, it's actually a political event. He has a lawyer and about seventy-five people on the outside march to the federal courthouse carrying signs about the genocide complaint, about how 70 percent of the prisoners at McNeil Island are from California, how poor their families are and [how] isolating people out on this remote island is a form of genocide against this category of people.

I didn't understand it, but I said to myself, "Well, I'll show this guy how to file a prisoner rights suit." I had been watching the court and seeing how things were going in terms of the rights of prisoners in terms of access to law books. And so I filed a class action habeas corpus petition in the Federal District Court in Tacoma claiming that the institution had an affirmative obligation to provide us with legal research materials. . . . I would do legal work for people and they would buy books and I would put them in the law library. That's how we got our books.

The District Court threw out the case, saying that you can't file a class action habeas corpus. I appealed it to the Ninth Circuit Court of Appeals and I won on the issue and also on the class action habeas status. But by the time that victory came, it was a shallow victory, because what I produced was nothing.

The genocide petition produced . . . something called the Steilacoom Support House. Steilacoom was a little ex-military town across the water from McNeil Island Prison. That suit was the organizing impetus for raising enough money to buy a large house in Steilacoom that would house twenty family members. People at the Steilacoom Support House would drive, pick up people from the airport and train stations, bring them to the Support House, feed them, drive them to the dock which was about three blocks away. When the ferry came in after the visits, they'd pick them up, bring them back to the Steilacoom House, where they would feed them and they would have clean sheets and everything like that. The genocide suit that Chuck Armsberry filed, him and his partner Paul Bayou, created something in the physical world that was progressive and good. My little ego trip lawsuit. . . . I won it but it didn't accomplish a thing. There was no . . . substance to it. And so with the introduction to Chuck I got to thinking about things.[3]

McNeil Island Prison, the oldest prison facility in the nation's Northwest, began as the first federal prison in what was then known as the Territory of Washington. It was originally constructed in 1875 but was declared obsolete a century later, and the federal government began its dismantlement.

A few years thereafter the state government devised a plan to lease the facility from the federal government for state use. Today, the rebuilt state facility sprawls over eighty-nine acres of the seven-square-mile island. That's where Ed Mead began to glimpse life in a larger scope than the circumscribed area of criminal consciousness.

PRISON RADIO: How much of a life did the genocide lawsuit have in the courts?

MEAD: Not much of a life at all because it was totally frivolous. But he understood that going to the courts expecting justice is an exercise in futility; he was just using that as an organizing tool whereas I was under the delusional belief that the bourgeois courts were actually going to dispense justice to the underprivileged.

PRISON RADIO: In 1968?

MEAD: Or earlier even.

PRISON RADIO: But you were charged with liberating weapons from that armory, what was that for? What little revolution was that going to fund?

MEAD: Well, that wasn't going to fund a revolution. It was a criminal thing, not a political thing. Unfortunately. But the FBI feared that these weapons were going to fall into the hands of the Black Panthers who were the big boogeyman of the day. I didn't know who the Black Panthers were.[4]

Despite the fears of the FBI, Mead was profoundly apolitical. Against his better judgment, he was hustling other prisoners, trading his legal acumen for cigarettes. While the radical member of the White Panther Party[5] had caused Mead to ask some questions about his life and the work he was doing, he could hardly have defined himself as a radical. He was a convict. He was a jailhouse lawyer. But he was also learning things about the world beyond the razor wire. He began to read radical literature. He explains:

Starting to read some of this stuff, I noticed that the

people who advocated longer prison sentences and doing away with parole and supported the death penalty and in every other way were against prisoners were the ones who supported the [Vietnam] war. Then the men's advisory committee, our little resident "self government" at McNeil Island, called a work strike in 1971 and the administration did everything it could to try and undermine this thing coming off, but come off it did. And typically they overreacted, causing us prisoners to dig in our heels. It was a bitter fight, we were throwing stuff out of our cells down on the tier lighting them on fire, breaking windows. It was total war and I'd never been in anything like that, never experienced, you know, this kind of direct conflict before. And I was just starting to become political. So the strike went on day six or seven, something like that, there were 600 demonstrators on the dock over in Steilacoom in support of our strike and with them was Pete Seeger, the songwriter and singer, and Jane Fonda. If there was any doubt about which side I was on, that doubt was all removed. Whatever these lefties are about, I'm with them, I'm a radical, I don't know what kind of radical I am, all I know is their enemy is my enemy. And so I started reading in earnest then. I started reading the easiest stuff, the anarchist literature and whatnot.[6]

Mead's new political awakening gave heft and focus to his jailhouse lawyering. It also gave him a sense that he was part of something bigger than himself, bigger than prison itself. He began to join with others to do broader, deeper legal work.

MEAD: I started filing more prisoner rights litigation. The chief of classification of parole called me into his office and at this time there was a clique of us doing law work and we are like a well-oiled machine. We're cranking suits out and we're just really good, we're tight. And so, Tennyson was his name, he calls me into his office, and he says "OK, look here," actually this was on the law book lawsuit, he says, "Now you can go to the camp. This lawsuit thing is a pain in the ass. Dismiss that suit and you can go to the camp and be on your way out of here. Or give us a hard time and you're going to find yourself on a bus to Leavenworth." I wish I could say that I spit in his face and said, "Bring on your mother-fucking bus, pig!" but I didn't. I didn't say anything. But what I did do was go back to the law library and told them of the bribe on the one hand and the threat on the other. And having ran back there and told everybody, now I can't dismiss the lawsuit because I'm committed. So, sure enough in short order I was on a bus to Leavenworth where I tried to organize a prisoners union and continue litigation and stuff. So that's why I did so much time, because I was very active on the inside at a time when a lot of prisoners weren't active or actively trying to organize.

PRISON RADIO: But you had a ten-year sentence.

MEAD: Yeah, I had a ten-year sentence. Actually I did just under six/eight; six/eight [six years, eight months] would have been my three-quarter time. But I got out on a writ. I got out as a result of legal work probably after six/five or something. And I was on lockdown. I had a copy of The Little Red Book[7] at Leavenworth and they discovered that and used it as a pretext to lock me down for the duration of my stay there.

PRISON RADIO: And then how long were you out?

MEAD: Well, I got out, I fell in Fairbanks, Alaska. I stayed in Fairbanks for two weeks and moved to Seattle to join a revolution; I went to the Steilacoom Prisoner Support House. Spent three months there, then moved to Seattle, started the Washington State Prisoners Labor Union and worked on a newsletter with some other comrades called *Sunfighter Prisoner Newsletter*, worked with the National Lawyers Guild. Was a full-time prisoner activist from then on. I was on the streets for two to three years until I was arrested in the George Jackson Brigade action, bank robbery as it were.[8]

This time, Mead would draw several life bits and spend eighteen years in the joint. He was shipped to Washington's state pen in Walla Walla and sent to the feds after his organizing in Walla Walla got on their nerves. Also, his group, the George Jackson Brigade, was still active in the "propaganda of the deed"—bombing symbols of capitalism and class domination.

Sent to the federal prison in Marion, Illinois, he returned a few months later because of his hunger strikes, feces-tossing, pillow-ripping, and other organizing efforts.

He was active during the height of the prisoners' rights movement, but conservative and increasingly repressive courts spelled the end of that era. One example of that trend can be seen in the case *Jones v. North Carolina Prisoners' Labor Union*, which severely limited the right of prisoners to associate given the "operational realities" of prisons.[9]

Another element in that trend was the dearth of outside organizing, as former radicals succumbed to the "Big Chill" of the Reagan era.

Mead, as a revolutionary who was active in and out of prison, began to see the law as a class instrument. "We came to understand that the courts are a part of the State's apparatus of repression . . . and the State is the means by which one class suppresses the interests of another class. And since the police and the prisons are a part of that and the courts as well, none of these enforcement mechanisms are going to abolish themselves. Once you get beyond the point of litigating over 'we want more peanut butter on the main line,' if you're looking for substantial issues, then the courts aren't the place to go."[10]

On expanding on those limitations, Mead examines the prison system as a state function essentially designed to fail. It is, in his view "a factory" that doesn't work.

MEAD: And the way I look at it is that the prison is the factory that turns out a product. And that product is angry people who are released to the streets full of rage, which gets taken out on their family members, their neighbors, and the community. And to try and treat individual products that the factory spews out, it's spewing them out faster than you could possibly fix the problem. You need to focus on shutting the factory down. And the courts aren't going to be of any assistance in that. I mean, like I say, they may order that you have more peanut butter on the main line but they're not going to do anything significant or fundamental in terms of serving the public interest. And that is the limitation of jailhouse lawyering, you can get yourself out but there will be another one to replace you. You can get a friend out; there will be another one to replace him. You can file a prisoner rights suit but they'll just not enforce it. . . .

PRISON RADIO: The Special Master won't enforce it?

MEAD: Right. Or if it's enforced, after a while it just dissipates, like a puddle of water evaporating and nobody really notices that it's gone. Those are the limitations. The main thing is to put jailhouse lawyering in a context of class struggle. And when you put it in that context its limitations become abundantly clear.[11]

The law is inherently conservative. And, truth be told, it is becoming increasingly so. But beyond the courts, there is tremendous potential in prisoners' (and ex-prisoners') power. Those in power know this, which is precisely why so many people are routinely disenfranchised because of their time in prison.

For example, Mead explains, "If they could vote, if they could have voted in the 2000 elections, George Bush would not be president, 100,000 and more Iraqi women and children civilians would not be dead. It is a *big* deal." Here, Mead is actually talking about the potential impact if ex-felons voted in one U.S. state. In post-apartheid South Africa, for example, not only ex-felons, but imprisoned persons still have access to the national franchise.

But Mead's studies and life experiences have taught him to look beyond elections, to the social transformations of popular revolutions. That was in his heart when *Prison Legal News* was founded.

MEAD: When I started *Prison Legal News*, the idea was to make social prisoners rights conscious. Rights-conscious prisoners, class conscious.

PRISON RADIO: As a progression.

MEAD: Right. I'm not doing *Legal News* anymore because I think *Legal News* is passé. In the absence, militancy breeds resistance, in the absence of an out-side movement prisoners have to compensate for this. First of all let me just say what I see my role as in all of this. I see myself as a propaganda officer in a revolutionary movement that does not yet exist. Ho Chi Minh started the National Liberation Army with nine propaganda officers in Vietnam and won the country and threw out U.S. imperialism and French imperialism and Japanese imperialism. I see my role as I see prisoners in the classic Marxist sense—as likely to be bribed dupes of reaction as likely to be revolutionary. But they lack the discipline of the working class. And my role, as I see it, and I probably won't be success-ful, but in thinking about what I'm doing, I believe there will be a communist party, and there will be a mass struggle, and my little niche in this whole thing is to deliver those prisoners I can, class-conscious, disciplined, forged in struggle, to the feet of this com-munist party, as a contribution.

For this one man, jailhouse law was a doorway into other realms of social reality, where the courts, for all their pomp and ceremony, were largely irrelevant to the larger social struggles rippling through society.

What Mead learned was that jailhouse law was simply a means; it was not an end.

It had, in Mead's view, severe limitations.

9

JAILHOUSE LAWYERS ON JAILHOUSE LAWYERS

Jailhouse lawyers are, by and large, a rather funny bunch. Many seem to be self-effacing and quite low-key about their accomplishments. Indeed, many of those interviewed for this work take umbrage with the very term "jailhouse lawyer."

Perhaps this stems from a natural desire to distance oneself by flying below the treacherous radar of prison, which remains a deadly place where furious envies may arise.

Perhaps it stems from the sense of real anger directed at real-world lawyers, and this self-effacement serves as a subtle defense against the projections that almost inevitably occur.

And perhaps it is a genuine response to what may often seem to be an insurmountable challenge; while the highs may be high, the lows are hellish, and there are many people in prison whose cases cannot be helped by even the most conscientious of jailhouse lawyers.

In the American context at least, such a response to such a challenge may be readily forgiven, for the United States has approximately 2.3 million people in its prisons.

Jailhouse lawyers alone, often facing official opposition, cannot make an appreciable dent in such a wall of human woe. Yet one jailhouse lawyer whom I never had the opportunity to interview or correspond with, managed to have an incredible impact on the criminal justice system. His name is now well known—at least among street lawyers and jailhouse lawyers. But in April 1962, when his handwritten petition for writ of certiorari was filed in the U.S. Supreme Court from the state prison system in Florida, perhaps a dozen people in the state knew he existed.

He was a 51-year-old homeless man with only an eighth-grade education, and he was charged with breaking and entering a local pool hall. When he went to trial, the state refused to provide him an attorney, and he appealed after conviction.

His name was Clarence Earl Gideon.

A year later, the U.S. Supreme Court ruled in *Gideon v. Wainwright* that the Sixth Amendment promise of "assistance of counsel" applied to all criminal cases.[1] At the time of his filing, nearly half of the people convicted in courts could not afford a lawyer and thus, like Gideon, had to either try to defend themselves or sit silently while the state exacted its pound of flesh.

Gideon was awarded a new trial and, with counsel, was acquitted of the charge and released. See Appendix A for a facsimile of his document, from the early days of jailhouse lawyering.

In his response petition for writ of certiorari, Gideon wrote clearly and simply, "Petitioner can not make any pretense of being able to answer the learned Attorney General of the State of Florida because the petitioner is not an attorney or versed in law nor does not have the law books to copy down the decisions of this Court. But the Petitioner knows there is many of them. Nor would the petitioner be allowed to do so."[2]

One need only look at the continuing debacle in New Orleans, Louisiana, to see that today, over forty years since *Gideon* became the "law of the land," hundreds, if not thousands, of people are still being held in jails and prisons without meaningful access to counsel.

In many ways it remains a promise unfulfilled, as shown in an earlier chapter that reviews the lengths to which "ineffectiveness of counsel" has been stretched.

In such a context, we can see why many men and women turn to those imprisoned with themselves to try to find some hope in a den of hopelessness.

Former death row captive (and now lifer) Roger Buehl accepts the term "jailhouse lawyer" when he describes his work; he has earned a paralegal certificate and taken additional college courses in English and writing.

While he accepts the term, he qualifies its usage by comparison to the skills of street lawyers: "So, yes, I guess it's true that I'm a jailhouse lawyer; I have the knowledge and skills to do anything a licensed lawyer can do, and I work as an advocate for both paying and indigent clients."

When he speaks of other jailhouse lawyers, he doesn't concentrate on the "big" cases, but applauds the day-to-day services provided to the imprisoned, to support social change. Says Buehl:

> The most impressive accomplishments of jailhouse lawyers are not necessarily any particular wins in litigations or cases, but rather, their improvements in the system. During the 1960s and 1970s, jailhouse lawyers were primarily responsible for the recognition and enforcement of prisoners' civil rights. To a lesser degree, jailhouse lawyers also played an important

part in initiating positive advancements in our criminal justice jurisprudence. Legal work aside, jailhouse lawyers have been—and are—instrumental in empowering prisoners, simply by educating and informing us about our rights and showing what's possible, even beyond these iron gates, and by facilitating contacts and communications between the inside and the community outside. For example, even nowadays jailhouse lawyers often arrange for guest speakers to enter prisons to lecture and answer questions on subjects of interest to prisoners. Unfortunately, many of these laudable accomplishments have been seriously eroded by the get-tough-on-crime fervor of the 1980s, which resulted in the federal Prison Litigation Reform Act and the laws imposing term limits for filing state post convictions and federal habeas corpus petitions.[3]

Buehl is an able and creative litigator and an award-winning writer who has worked with the imprisoned all over the state. He is thorough, well-prepared, and determined when it comes to litigation. He has taken many men deeper and further into their criminal and civil cases than they ever could have gone themselves.

Richard O. J. Mayberry almost echoes Buehl when he considers the accomplishments of jailhouse lawyers that he finds most impressive—"their willingness to fight against overwhelming odds against the entire legal machinery of the state, to continue fighting despite the retaliation inflicted by the prison authorities and the sacrifice of rights, privileges, amenities. The fact that they are willing to stand up and not be intimidated by the prison guards, officials, and their accomplices."[4]

Ron Williams, unlike most on death row, had a college background, having earned a BA in communications. When he reached the state's death house, he used his education and organizational skills to teach folks how to rumble back in their cases, and also how to learn. That said, he would be the last to consider himself a jailhouse lawyer.

"The term carries too many negative connotations," says Williams. "With the average grade level (of education) being about the fifth to sixth grade, many people prey on the less fortunate for whatever they can get. I've seen too many people lose their appeal rights permanently and issues that should have been won, that were argued incorrectly."[5]

Williams was determined to dispel the negative connotation of jailhouse lawyer, and struck out to do so upon reaching Pennsylvania's death row. "Jailhouse lawyers usually charge people, [but] my policy was different," says Williams. "When I went to death row in 1985 I refused to buy a radio or a television, so all I had was books, legal materials, pens, and paper in my cell. Then I offered to help anyone who was trying to do legal work, because I planned to fight my case. They laughed at me, told me I wasn't a lawyer, but a few people took me up on it."

Williams' method was essentially—to borrow an old Black Panther adage—*Each one, teach one.* "When we started," says Williams, "I had about six people and the only debt they owed me was that I had the right at any time to designate them to train someone new who had less knowledge and ability than *they* did. First, I would not do anyone's work for them. I would help you to learn how to do it yourself, so that if the administration transferred or moved any member, they would be qualified to operate independently at least at the level they had achieved. By having those I taught teach others, it kept me from being forced to cover the same material and areas, plus it reinforced what they had learned while we advanced."[6]

Williams was so intensely law-centered in his speech and behavior that guys on the row began referring to him by a witty and sardonic moniker, "Chief Justice Fat Burger."

But what began as a jibe at his then-considerable girth and his penchant for spouting law cases every day, became in time a term of respect. For Burger wasn't all rap. He did what was exceedingly rare in the jailhouse lawyer's art: like the pugnacious Muhammad Ali, he predicted victory. And like Ali, he won!

In 1986, he predicted that he would get both himself and his younger brother off of death row. By 1989, they were both off the row and living in the prison's general population.

There were many men to whom he taught the basics and who took it from there to fight their own cases and sometimes secured new trials or reversals. While hardly household names, they are known to those on death row: Lonnie Baker, Carlos Santiago, Michael Travaglia, Barry Gibbs, and others. Of these men, Burger says, "While I have helped numerous people, nothing is like the struggles on death row, because if you make an error you kill your friends."

"Jailhouse lawyers are most effective in the research and development of issues and arguments," says Williams. "They concentrate, and are more creative than attorneys, who are caught up in numerous cases with a vast array of issues. The good ones take time and teach their clients so they can help themselves. A good jailhouse lawyer doesn't want a client tied to him after he learns to effectively research."

Chief Justice Fat Burger continues to learn, teach and litigate for the greatest goal of all: freedom.

✦ ✦ ✦

One of Williams' students, Barry "Running Bear" Gibbs, has become a talented jailhouse lawyer and doesn't eschew the title. That may be because he wrote the main brief in the *Billa* case (see chapter 3) and got his friend off death row. He therefore has good reason to embrace the title, because "the Pennsylvania Supreme Court called me that in one case," he says.

He doesn't dispute it because of the effort that he puts into his work. "There's a lot of crackpots who send crazy stuff into the courts," says Running Bear, and that "makes it tough for the rest of us."

When someone asks Bear about his education, he uses a joke to answer, "I tell people I've studied law at State Pen University." (In Pennsylvania, the home of Penn State, that usually brings a smile.)

Inspired by Burger, Running Bear continued his studies. "I had to study law—at 18 [in 1984] I found myself on death row, and it was sink or swim." Bear adds, "I had only an eighth-grade education and a GED. I refused to get a TV and spent my time studying law—mainly reading countless reports, wearing out a *Black's Law Dictionary*, and keeping up with new procedures in recent rules of court. That provided a good start."

Despite his extensive experience in jailhouse lawyering, Running Bear only needed to think a moment to recall his best jailhouse lawyer stories.

"Rich [Mayberry] went on tilt in the courtroom, called

the judge a 'tyrannical dog' and threw a book at the judge," recounts Running Bear. "He ended up with eleven to twenty-two years for eleven counts of contempt of court, but he eventually gave all the time back. Usually it's the judge who throws the book at someone! Then there was Damon Jones, who gave a long eloquent speech in the courtroom about his right to be heard. Eventually, the judge finally agreed with him and asked him what he wanted to say. Damon responded that he had a Fifth Amendment right to remain silent, and would speak no further."[7]

✛ ✛ ✛

David M. Reutter is a jailhouse lawyer in Florida who feels the title is appropriate, although he adds one qualifier—he is "in retirement." He has worked in both civil and criminal law, and he had some informal training. "A large part of my legal training included legal writing," says Reutter. "Early on, I realized my writing skills were deftly inadequate to battle with the Attorney General's Office brigade of lawyers. To cure this, I began reading every brief and pleading prepared by a lawyer. Explaining my objective and giving a promise not to discuss their case often resulted in other prisoners allowing me to read their documents. I learned much from that endeavor. A writing textbook, *The Practical Stylist*, is still in my personal library for reference. That was a well-spent fifty dollars. In essence, I am a self-taught jailhouse lawyer and writer."[8]

The field abounds with lawyers who are poor writers, whose work is obtuse and prolix. They may have learned legal principles and theories, but they didn't learn clear writing skills.

What was important for Reutter to learn is a skill for all lawyers, jailhouse or street.

✣ ✣ ✣

Antoine Graham doesn't consider himself a jailhouse lawyer, but others do. He has spent over nineteen years in New Jersey's prisons and decries the dismissive nature of younger prisoners.

Graham, who did not have formal paralegal training, explains, "The system is not anything like it used to be. In this day and age it is a whole new generation of prisoners, and 85 percent of the young kids have very little on the mind. They are not about helping themselves with regards to their cases, and mainly that is because many have just given up. Many that I knew in the system have their minds on [the] negative, and they are not trying to do anything positive for themselves. If they would devote just half the energy that they spend on the basketball court on [their] cases, the prisons would not be as filled as they are."[9]

✣ ✣ ✣

Charles "Dutchman" Van Dorsten of Muskegon, Michigan is a self-taught jailhouse lawyer who takes his work seriously. Dutchman takes great pride in his work and looks for the same quality in the work of others. When he compares his brand of briefing with those of street lawyers, he thinks his is much better and better designed to prevail for the client in the long run. "I have found that many of the reversals given in the federal system are subsequent to having a court-appointed lawyer prepare a client's brief," says

Dutchman, "often leaving me with the impression that it will not prevail in state court, but will be seriously reviewed and the errors considered in the federal court, which will most likely bring the client some relief. I believe that to be because of the personal bias of most lawyers that feel their clients are guilty and therefore will not raise every issue of meritorious error, which is the reason for most jailhouse lawyers' successes."

When asked to give his opinion of the best in the field, Dutchman turns his view toward others in Michigan. "Jailhouse lawyer Paul Dye dropped out of school in the ninth grade at age 14," says Dutchman. "At age 28 he came to prison, completed his GED, became a tutor in the academic school in Jackson, took the JCC [Jackson Community College] paralegal classes and got his conviction reversed twice—as I have—and is getting ready to get it reversed for the third time—as I am."

Another who has gained Dutchman's admiration as a jailhouse lawyer proficient in both criminal and civil law is Alfredo Robinson, his friend. "The Michigan Department of Corrections [MDOC] began using Pharmachem Sweat Patches on prisoners so they could tell if the prisoner used any drugs, attempting to save tens of thousands of dollars spent on urine tests," recounts Dutchmen. "Alfredo took it upon himself to challenge the practice. He challenged the use in federal court and forced the MDOC to stop using the patches because they were not approved by the FDA [U.S. Food and Drug Administration] and [violated] our bodily protection liberty interests. Also, he got down in the mud and slugged it out with the courts, winning a re-sentencing for his woman, Taurus Duncan, in 2003, [by] developing the issues and brief overturning her guilty plea life sentence and obtaining a twenty- to forty-year sentence which secured her almost immediate release after twenty-six years in prison."[10]

Hustlers in Hell: Some Lame Jailhouse Lawyers

There was once a man in central Pennsylvania's Huntingdon Prison who, cast in the hole for some infraction, took to his gate to loudly announce his legal prowess to all within earshot. He bellowed onto the block, "I [he stated his name] am the *prince* of paralegalism! I am the best paralegalist to *ever* do the law—not just in this jail, but in the state! I handle all kinds of cases! They scared of me when they see *my* name on a petition!"[11]

This guy was engaging in a none-too-subtle form of advertising, one that, in other forms, is done by lawyers in the free world every day.

He knew that here was the classic captive audience, and so he launched into a jailhouse/hole version of ambulance chasing.

As there are serious and conscientious jailhouse lawyers who are students of the ever-changing facets of the law, there are also others who have earned the enmity of others.

Jane Dorotik is critical of the "I-have-the-one-and-only-method-or-answer-to–your-questions" quality of many jailhouse lawyers. But in Roger Buehl's view, the worst are those who take advantage of others for personal or financial gain. "The most despicable, for me," says Buehl, "are those who profess knowledge in the law, and represent themselves to be jailhouse lawyers, but are not. There are many jailhouse wannabes; they know just enough to sound and appear knowledgeable in the law to a layman, and are able to get clients in that way—and because they charge less for 'services' rendered. Such wannabes, however, often do more harm than good, and it's usually impossible to correct their mistakes or oversights later on. The wannabes also do a lot of harm in their own litigations, in that they'll lose winnable cases and thereby set bad precedent."

Ron "Chief Justice" Williams sounds a similar note. "Many people who claim to know the law are egocentric and petty," says Chief. "They are users who often destroy what minimal chances a man has to get back in court and win."

Mayberry is a bit more philosophical in his outlook, for his view is formed by decades in prison and long stretches in the hole. In stating what least impresses him about jailhouse lawyers, he says, "In jail everybody, with a few exceptions, has an angle. Mostly everybody is trying to get out of jail, or make things as tolerable as possible while in jail. Everyone has value systems, things they put value on. Jailhouse lawyers often place value on their or others' rights. The inalienable rights all men have from God, or from the Constitution or laws."

In all things under the sun, there are positives and negatives. Why should it be any different in the hothouse environment of American prisons? There are good guys and bad guys. There are lizards and legends.

Yet, in a place designed to crush the souls of men and women, there are people who, with time, attention, study, an artful phrase, and the odd starburst of insight can and do work together to help, to uplift, and even to free others.

10

THE BEST OF THE BEST

Determining the best of the best can only be a subjective enterprise, one colored by the biases and insights of the writer. Yet the presence of certain almost measurable characteristics—selflessness, excellence, will, and perseverance—informs our view of those who stand head and shoulders above many others.

For many jailhouse lawyers, Paul Wright and his award-winning *Prison Legal News* are examples of distinction and worth. The journal has been, and continues to be, a teaching tool for jailhouse lawyers in every state of the union, providing the latest cases, analyses, and criticisms of the prison-industrial-complex.

If correctional staffers and politicians are to be believed, the holes and dungeons of their keeps are inhabited by those who are said to be "the worst of the worst." As we have seen in "The Myth of Humane Imprisonment"[1] report, holes are places to which jailhouse lawyers, more than all others, find themselves consigned.

A cynic might argue that administrators use their disciplinary regimes to try to break jailhouse lawyers from their dogged adherence to the U.S. Constitution. For they are seen as perennial troublemakers, even though they rarely engage in violence, and unless they want to challenge them in court, usually scrupulously avoid violating prison regulations. Their institutional "crimes" are rooted in the allowances allegedly preserved in the laws of the land.

If you ask some jailhouse lawyers to name the best among them, several names will emerge again and again. Richard Mayberry will appear on many lists, even though he would probably disavow such recognition. If one asks him, the name George Rahsaan Brooks (or Rahsaan Brooks-Bey) will be heard. Brooks-Bey has had a long and resistant career as jailhouse lawyer, organizer, and rebel. Not surprisingly, when Mayberry made his opinion known, Mr. Brooks-Bey was in the hole.

When Brooks-Bey is asked why he considers himself to be one, he explains, "I consider myself a jailhouse lawyer because it identifies and distinguishes me. System lawyers first put that handle on us as a derogat[ion]. We knew we were not inferior to them because we were correcting too many of their errors. Plus, we knew our range of law was broader because we fought all problems prisoners had: real estate, civil torts, and criminal law. Most criminal lawyers are lost when taken out of their limited field of 'criminal law.' I had to explain the Anti-Terrorist and Effective Death Penalty law to at least ten lawyers who viewed themselves as 'experts' in their fields."

Although Brooks-Bey did not formally study law, he *has* studied its intricacies on his own, and his study led to civil cases and legal precedents that have impacted the lives and rights of men and women held in dungeons throughout the state of Pennsylvania and, in the case of federal suits, across the country.

He considers his best win *Brooks v. Andolina*, decided in 1987, "because it stopped prison officials from punishing inmates for exercising their First Amendment freedom of expression and precluded prison officials from retaliating against inmates for exercising these rights."[2]

Brooks-Bey doesn't consider himself merely a jailhouse lawyer, for his life—although surely severely attenuated by his imprisonment—is full of other facets. "I am also a prisoners' rights advocate," he says. "I have participated in numerous workshops, seminars, work stoppages, strikes, etc. Also, I founded the NAACP[3] prison branch at SCI-Graterford and wrote [its] Constitution. I have also held lifers' [meetings] throughout the state. I was one of the prisoners at SCI-Greene that formed the crime impact and cultural enhancement groups and I am a founding member of the peers group here at SCI-Fayette."

Given his long tenure in state prisons, Brooks-Bey has a wealth of stories about cases and controversies against the prison system, both as jailhouse lawyer and as activist.

"I was the class representative in the case of *Stanton Story v. Robinson* [No. 75-29657]" says Brooks. "I drew up the class action lawsuit and fought the deputy attorney general. All the plaintiffs were confined in the hole at SCI-Pittsburgh.

> Stanton Story was convicted of killing a policeman; Robert Joyner was accused of being a Black Panther and killing a park police; Larry "Kareem" Howard was found guilty for breaking Russell "Maroon" Shoats out of Holmesburg City Prison; and I was found guilty of allegedly stalking a rapist, catching him, and beating him to death along with allegedly robbing him. Every time we were taken to federal court in downtown Pittsburgh we had two police

cars in front of us and two police cars and a car full of U.S. marshals behind us in a prison bus made to seat eighty prisoners. The police and marshals would turn on their sirens and bully all drivers to let them pass. It was summertime and we would holler political slogans out of the window at all the drivers: "Blessed are those who struggle for a cause!"; "Oppression is worse than the grave!"; "Jail the real criminals—the police and U.S marshals!"

Once we reached the courthouse and were being escorted down the corridors to the courtrooms, we would holler: "Workers of the world unite against oppression!" Of course, all the federal workers would run and hide in their offices. I told the Magistrate Judge Mitchell that none of the plaintiffs would stand unless he removed the picture of George Washington, who possessed slaves. He refused to remove the picture, and we refused to stand. I told him I would not refer to him as Your Honor unless he could prove to me that he had actually done honorable things and that I would refer to him as only "judge," because he was here to judge the issues. Judge Mitchell said he had no problem being referred to as judge. I told Judge Mitchell that he was not being just because he had a water pitcher, ice, and a cup and the plaintiffs had none of the same at our table. He ordered the U.S. marshals to put a pitcher with ice and cups at our table. I then told him I took offense to the U.S. marshals using tax dollars to transport us to court when the federal government did not violate our rights and state tax dollars should be used. To my surprise, the U.S. marshals joined in on our argument, and the case was transferred to Judge Webber to determine who should pay for our transportation to the federal courthouse. Judge Webber ruled that the state should transport us to the federal courthouse and the federal marshals should secure us and all the prison guards to transport us back to the prison.

Prison officials appealed to the U.S. Court of Appeals for the Third Circuit, who upheld the decision but modified the district court's opinion, stating: inmates should be transported to the nearest county jail by prison guards and picked up by the U.S. marshals and transported to the district court. Prison officials appealed to the U.S. Supreme Court, [which] upheld the district court and U.S. Court of Appeals' decision. This is a landmark decision. After the U.S. Supreme Court decision, our case resumed. When the case resumed, Commissioner Robinson, the lead defendant in our case, had been forced to retire due to drunk driving. He was now the Commissioner of [a] county jail. Robinson and county sheriffs with shotguns blocked the jail's entrance. Prison guards called the U.S. marshals who had to remove us from the prison van, place us in two separate cars, then transport us [to] the district court.[4] We prevailed on our case, the Restricted Housing Unit [RHU] at SCI-Pittsburgh was closed, and a new RHU was built. We were given two hours of outdoor exercise as opposed to the fifteen minutes we were given before prevailing on our lawsuit. We were given laundry service, and lids on our food trays, and RHU guards were precluded from strip-searching us four times when we received visits."[5]

When asked to name those he considers the best, Brooks-Bey reflects back, "When I did time in New York, I felt Jerry 'the Jew' Rosenberg and Martin Sostre were the best jailhouse lawyers."

Rosenberg was on New York state's death row before his sentence was abolished in the wake of the U.S. Supreme Court's 1972 *Furman v. Georgia* decision, which put strictures around the usage of the death penalty.[6]

Sostre fought a series of classic cases, both civil and criminal, back in the 1970s. His case drew support from both Black Muslims and Black Panthers, because he was targeted by the state for his activism during the 1960s.

Sostre opened the Afro-Asian Bookstore in the Black community of Buffalo, New York. His bookstore became an important local center for Black radical thought and internationalist education, as Sostre intended. "I taught continually—giving our pamphlets free to those who had no money," says Sostre. "I let them sit and read for hours in the store. Some would come back every day and read the same book until they finished it. This was the opportunity I had dreamed about—to be able to help my people by increasing the political awareness of the youth."

Sostre was busted on trumped-up charges of narcotics, riot, arson and assault, and convicted and sentenced to forty-one years and a month. Throughout his incarceration he filed many civil suits, winning several landmark cases, including *Sostre v. Rockefeller*, *Sostre v. Otis*, and *Sostre v. McGinnis*. In the latter case, the Second U.S. Court of Appeals ruled that Sostre possessed "freedom from discriminatory punishment inflicted solely because of his beliefs, whether religious or secular."[7]

Today, Sostre lives in Manhattan with his wife and children.

When Brooks thinks of the best jailhouse lawyers, he thinks of those who have had the broadest systemic, or prison-wide impact, explaining, "I judge a jailhouse lawyer by the wins he has and by the changes he brought about in law or prison conditions." When asked to name them, Brooks doesn't miss a beat, "Since no jailhouse lawyer has brought more changes in the law or brought about more wide-ranging prison reform than [Richard] Mayberry and myself, I feel we are the best jailhouse lawyers in Pennsylvania."

Far from Pennsylvania in the Lone Star State sits a 61-year-old legally blind man named Iron Thunderhorse (né Coppola), who still considers himself a jailhouse lawyer. Thunderhorse, like Brooks, is as much activist as litigator, and was the "jailhouse lawyer membership coordinator" for the National Lawyers Guild. He cofounded the Committee to Safeguard Prisoners' Rights (CSPR), a kind of lobby group, which began as a subcommittee of the National Lawyers Guild.

When Thunderhorse was asked to opine on the best, he wrote, "There's a guy in New York, Jewish I believe, killed a cop in the '50s. He's considered the granddaddy of us all. The other best were all CSPR—including Mary Glover (Ypsilanti, MI), who won the *Glover vs. Johnson* case; Mike Costello in Florida; Richard Lee Owen II (Indiana), who was the only other jailhouse lawyer besides myself allowed to represent other prisoners in federal court in Houston; Dan Manville, Jenny Potts, Johnny Draper, Alvaro Hernandez, G.W. Gambee, Calvin Sellers, and of course me."[8]

Many of the people Thunderhorse names are perhaps best known in the nation's Southwest, but several are known nationally. The "Jewish guy" seemingly refers to Jerry Rosenberg, who survived the Attica massacre and is still doing a life bit despite what some observers insist was a woefully unfair trial. Dan Manville is known as the coauthor of the widely used *Prisoners' Self-Help Litigation Manual*, the sourcebook for thousands of jailhouse lawyers across the United States. His manual explains the state and federal legal structure, outlines litigation strategies, and provides forms and formats. Manville is also one of the few men who successfully bridged the gap between jailhouse and street lawyer.

"It's a success story," Thunderhorse explains. "Dan Manville did time in Michigan, got out on parole, and was editor-in-chief of the *Prison Law Monitor*. I was briefing editor. Dan attended Antioch School of Law in Washington, D.C., graduated, did an internship under Al Bronstein at the ACLU Prison Project, returned to Michigan and passed the bar exam. He had his own practice and now he's an adjunct professor of law at Wayne State University. He teaches a workshop of law students to operate a law clinic. If a prisoner's civil suit survives summary judgment it gets referred to this clinic and Dan shows a team of students how to help the *pro se* litigant."

In Roger Buehl's consideration, only two names arise when he looks for the best in the business. "Some of the best jailhouse lawyers in Pennsylvania include Richard Mayberry and Charles Diggs," says Buehl. "Both know the law, are competent writ writers, and have litigated and won cases. There are others, of course, but those are the names that come to mind. As for myself, I have litigated and won cases too, including capital cases."

Like Brooks-Bey, Mr. Diggs has had a long and extensive career in civil, criminal, as well as state and federal areas of law and jurisprudence. Like Warren Henderson, Diggs has had his share of *pro se* acquittals as well.

Matthew Clarke of Texas tells a tale of an unexpected win by a man whom many had written off. "The most impressive jailhouse lawyer I ever saw was a mentally deficient prisoner at Michael Unit who got a stacked deuce for striking a guard," writes Clarke. "The state waited over two years to prosecute him and he insisted that the jail time had to count towards the sentence (effectively eliminating it), even though the sentences were cumulative. Since the underlying sentence expired shortly after the sentencing in the second case, this would result in his immediate release. Every jailhouse lawyer he talked to told him he was wrong. He asked me, but it was 1989 and I didn't know enough to answer him. He ignored all of them, filed his writ petition, and was released a couple of months later."[9]

Clarke doesn't include himself among the best, but he has done remarkable work and his efforts as a certified paralegal have had good effects on others with him in Denton County, Texas, where he has been imprisoned since 1994. He says:

I got so many guys out of jail using a "fill-in-the-blank" pretrial petition for a writ of habeas corpus that they put me in ad[ministrative] seg[regation] to keep me from talking to other prisoners. I then distributed copies around.

To accomplish this I wrote an article on how to get out of jail and had it published in *The Paralegal Bench*. I then distributed copies around the jail by leaving them in the law library when I visited it. This positive outcome isn't so much a result of my litigation skills as it is a result of the jail's illegal policy of holding prisoners for many months, even years, without ever taking them to court. This violated a statute—Article 17.151, Texas Code of Criminal Procedure—so it was easy to put together a simple, successful writ that required the prisoners' release from jail, but not dismissal of the charges.[10]

Clarke's article in *The Paralegal Bench* is three-quarters of a page long and explains the Texas statutory provision that mandates release (pending trial) for those who have had to wait over specified time periods. His article is a brief but clear work of statutory history, citations to relevant cases, and some analysis of present law.

His writ is similarly quite straightforward, and the document is an example of a jailhouse lawyer's clarity of style and purpose. (See Appendix B.)

In his article, Clarke explains:

A little-known provision in the Texas Code of Criminal Procedure (C.C.P.) can result in immediate release of many Texas jail pre-trial detainees. Art. 17.151 was first passed by the Texas Legislature in 1977 and has remained since then. It provides for the release of a defendant who is being held in violation of them. It provides for the release of a defendant who is being held in jail pending trial if the state is not ready for trial within the following time limits: a) 5 days if accused of Class C misdemeanor; b) 15 days if accused of a Class B misdemeanor; c) 30 days if accused of a Class A misdemeanor; or d) 90 days if accused of a felony.[11]

Although Clarke may quibble, it seems clear that he has done some remarkable work. Though not as complex as brief writing, it was undeniably effective. And it served—albeit briefly—a prisoner's ultimate dream: freedom.

Talented and Anonymous

Contrary to popular belief, there are thousands of prisoner-litigants who shy away from the limelight. They seek neither publicity nor added attention.

The following woman who shuns the appellation jailhouse lawyer also shuns unwanted and unneeded publicity. Out of respect for her, this writer will not use her name or identify her. I'll call her Adrian.

Adrian looks at the term "jailhouse lawyer" as synonymous with "troublemaker," and as such feels uncomfortable accepting it. "I do *not* consider myself a jailhouse lawyer," says Adrian. "In my perception, such individuals are those who challenge prison policies with civil lawsuits, seeking to change the status quo, often merely for the sake of change. I do not do this. I have provided assistance to other prisoners in court pleadings which challenge their convictions and/or sentences, something which they have a right to do in our criminal justice system. The phrase 'jailhouse lawyer' carries a connotation of a troublemaker, an agitator, a gadfly to prison administration. I hardly consider myself this kind of person. Moreover, because the prison law library has finally assigned an inmate who is capable of doing that job . . . I have actually decreased my assistance to other prisoners in the past year."[12]

One might think that Adrian shuns those jailhouse lawyers who tend to give the craft a bad name because of bad lawyering, but such is not the case. Although she is quite a good and clear writer, a plus for either jailhouse or street lawyers, she shuns the law itself, and its underlying structures. Though not formally trained in the law, she reveals a deep perception of its inherent shortcomings.

"I detest lawyers and the stilted, contrived formality of our legal system," says Adrian. "I have grave doubts about the wisdom of a system wherein the mediocrities who populate the legislatures throughout the country can enact criminal laws which are actually written by unelected legislative 'aides' and voted on by legislators who are often uneducated about the effects on real people of the laws they vote to enact. My legal education is entirely self-taught and was compelled by my own criminal cases circumstances. That education is ongoing. Simply put, I began to educate myself in this business because I needed to do so, not because of any burning desire to change the prison system."

She uses her skills reluctantly, admitting, "I take no pride in litigation, and would prefer not to do it." Despite her lack of pride in her litigation work, it has been successful. If asked about successful litigation efforts, she notes, "I suppose I must point to the New Jersey Superior Court

Appellate Division opinion in the case *Vasquez v. N.J. Dept. of Corrections* . . . wherein the court reversed a final administrative decision by the EMCF superintendent denying a friend of mine permission to marry based solely on the subjective recommendation by the prison marriage committee that my friend and her fiancé were 'not appropriate candidates for marriage.' This paternalistic blather had nothing to do with any prison security risk. And I so argued in the brief I wrote for my friend. The court agreed and, relying on *Turner v. Safley*, 482 U.S. 78, 107 S.Ct. 2254 (1987), they overturned the denial and ordered the DOC [Department of Corrections] to allow the marriage to proceed. I have had other successful litigation in the courts, and a loss or two as well, but this is the only published opinion."[13]

With all due respect, Adrian, it looks to me that you are indeed one of those damned jailhouse lawyers—and a pretty good one at that.

Running Bear

Running Bear rarely engages with prisoners' rights–type litigation, and usually sticks to straight criminal law. He was the main jailhouse lawyer leading the appellate defense in the *Billa* case, discussed in Chapter 3. That case was one of several that he won for his clients.

A student of Chief Justice Fat Burger, Bear explains his limited role as a jailhouse lawyer as "mostly to advise folks who don't understand the legal process. If they have counsel of record, I try to work with the attorney, point out case law or new ways to proceed. Where there are no attorneys, as is often the case in post-conviction proceedings, sometimes I have to draft motions, petitions, and briefs myself."[14]

His work is perhaps closest to Adrian's heart, as it is hard-core criminal law; in fact, it is capital case law—the hardest in the business. His most important achievements as a jailhouse lawyer? Helping three people to get their death sentences overturned, one of them being himself. He describes "hearing a kid yell up to me that the PA Supreme Court just overturned his capital case based on a brief I wrote" as one of his most treasured memories of his jailhouse lawyering career. "Saving someone's life via pen and paper is a rewarding and unforgettable experience."

Running Bear has reversed his own conviction thrice and continues his journey to freedom. Yet he remains immensely grateful to Chief Justice Fat Burger for his early teachings, when he was a young man entering death-row hell. "Being eternally grateful to my teacher, I asked, *How can I thank you?* His response—*Teach someone else.* I've tried to do just that and respond to [my clients'] questions to me *How can I thank you?* the same way—*Teach someone else.*"

This he does as he continues to work as a jailhouse lawyer. His goals? Simple ones—saving lives, finding freedom.

The Best? Or the Luck of the Draw?

Sam Rutherford, a prisoner-litigant in the state of Washington, rejects the term "jailhouse lawyer." He finds it "childish" and "degrading." From his perspective, most of the prisoners who consider themselves to be jailhouse lawyers "are barely literate idiots who usually do more harm than good."

Rutherford earned a paralegal studies certificate in 2004 from the Blackstone Career Institute, formally known as Blackstone School of Law. In characterizing himself, he sounds downright humble. "I would describe myself as a prisoner who knows *a little* about the law and has been lucky enough to have a few successes over the years. In fact, the more I learn about the law, the more I realize how little I know. I am certainly a far cry from being a lawyer." That may explain why one of his goals, once free, is to go to law school.

Nonetheless, in Rutherford's opinion, one's ability has little to do with how a case turns out. In a way reminiscent of Adrian, his views force us to rethink the notion of "best," for he questions the fundamental fairness of the playing field.

"[E]xperience has taught me that a non-lawyer's skill as a litigator has very little to do with success or failure," refects Rutherford. "Whether a prisoner wins or loses a case has more to do with the judge he or she draws and that particular judge's mood on any given day. For example, I have lost cases where I clearly out-litigated my opponent because the judge was pro–law and order and would have ruled against me no matter what authority I cited or arguments I made. On the other hand, I have seen prisoners win cases based on briefs that were barely legible simply because the judge wanted to rule in the prisoner's favor. In other words, *pro se* criminal appellate and prisoner rights litigation is a lot like playing the lottery—you'll win if you get lucky enough to draw the right judge."[15]

Rutherford's observations fly in the face of the faith that many people, even jailhouse lawyers, place on the law. The courts are chock-full of hanging judges, unfair judges, vengeful judges and incompetent judges. Seen in this light, Rutherford's insights lead us to admit again that the notion of "best" jailhouse lawyer is a subjective judgment.

Subjective or not, in this author's opinion, what makes the jailhouse lawyers described here excellent is their brilliance, their tenacity, their will, and sometimes their hearts that care for the least of these.

11

THE WORST OF THE WORST

In an entirely different sense than the way I use it, U.S. military authorities, politicians, and prison administrators seize on the usage of the phrase "the worst of the worst" to justify the barbarities practiced against prisoners. They use it to justify the isolation, abuse, and torture of prisoners in places like the federal lockup known as Marion Control Unit in Illinois, and in various such units in two-thirds of the states, and more recently—and infamously—at the U.S. military prisons in Guantánamo Bay, Cuba, Abu Ghraib, Iraq, and Bagram, Afghanistan.

Of course, characterizing their captives as the "worst of the worst" is usually a pretext deployed to deflect criticism of official treatment. But such pale excuses have somewhat limited utility in light of the testimonies, photos, and videos that have emerged from the U.S. torture centers around the globe.

In the infamous photos from Abu Ghraib prison in Iraq, one can see the almost manic glee reflected in the shiny, white faces of Americans—several of whom were American prison guards in their civilian lives—as they thrilled at the abuse, torture, and humiliation of stripped Iraqi men, at the prison that had been made infamous by the pains inflicted upon opponents of the fallen regime of Saddam

Hussein. Only the Americans, with their electronic toys capable of sending digital images abroad, could have outdone the Ba'ath Party in depravity and infamy.

What millions saw in the garish reflections of Iraq was but a foreign edition of the reality of American prisons: places of legalized torture, humiliation and abuse—practices exported from domestic U.S. hellholes to ones overseas.

As law professor David Cole has observed, the epithet "worst of the worst" (an expression used repeatedly by U.S. Vice President Dick Cheney on television) could hardly apply to many ensconced in the Guantánamo torture and interrogation camp, for only 8 percent of the detainees are alleged to be fighters for Al Qaeda.[1] Among those detained there are people from China known as Uighurs, a Muslim ethnic minority speaking a Turkic tongue, who are being refused re-entry to their homeland despite having been cleared of terrorism charges. Constitutional lawyer Michael Ratner, who has written widely about this and represented people encaged in Guantánamo before the U.S. Supreme Court, notes:

> The U.S. military dropped leaflets in Afghanistan offering large sums of money for information leading to the capture of terrorists. Many apparently took up the offer and turned in innocent civilians for their bounty. A military interrogator at Camp Delta estimates that as many as 20 percent of the men in captivity at Guantánamo are innocent. Dozens of prisoners—if not more—are described in U.S. intelligence reports as farmers, taxi drivers, laborers, and shoemakers. Ac-

cording to these reports, at least 59 individuals from Afghanistan and Pakistan were captured and shipped to Guantánamo despite not fitting the screening criteria for such a transfer. As one military official who served as an interrogator observed, "If they weren't terrorists before, they certainly could be now."[2]

Are these people—or their torturers—*the worst of the worst?*

Snitches

That said, among jailhouse lawyers there really is a "worst of the worst."

While we've written of jailhouse lawyers who are poorly trained, conniving, and even dangerous (because of ignorance, venality, or inattentiveness), there is a far worse breed—snitches.

There are two general classes of snitch: the jailhouse snitch and the accomplice snitch. The jailhouse snitch, as the name implies, is one who offers authorities an alleged prison cell confession to exact a deal from the prosecutor for another pending case. The accomplice snitch gives up tape against his codefendant, usually for a reduced sentence.

Despite their ubiquity in criminal cases, some courts have begun to awaken to their danger to the trial process. For example, the Mississippi Supreme Court has warned against "an unholy alliance between con-artist convicts who want to get out of their own cases, law enforcement who [are] running a training ground for snitches over at the county jail, and the prosecutors who are taking what appears to be the easy route, rather than really putting their cases together with solid evidence."[3]

Yet worse than these are the jailhouse-lawyer snitches, those who use their skills and access to elicit the trust of a prisoner, only to betray him or her on the stand.

Because many jailhouse lawyers handle criminal appeals, they are privy to both the formal and informal records and information upon which convictions are based. To the particularly unscrupulous jailhouse lawyer, proximity to troubled prisoners provides the perfect opportunity for betrayal.

Indeed, there have been several cases arising from such conduct, with some surprising and unexpected results.

In 1987, a man was stabbed to death in the Arizona State Prison in Tucson, Arizona. Ruben Melendez was indicted in the killing, based in large part on testimony by another prisoner whom Melendez had chosen to represent him at a separate prison misconduct hearing.

After he was convicted of the institutional charge, and was awaiting his subsequent state criminal trial, his prison-appointed "inmate representative" contacted the prosecutor and offered to testify at trial against several of the prisoners based on his representations of them.

Shortly before trial, Ruben Melendez filed a motion to suppress communications made to the prisoner who had served as his jailhouse lawyer to help him prepare for and defend himself at the institutional hearing.

The trial court agreed and granted the motion, and the district attorney appealed.

Arizona's court of appeals reversed the lower court, and Melendez appealed to that state's Supreme Court.

Calling the case one of "first impression," the state's highest court upheld the trial court's decision to bar the testimony of his jailhouse lawyer at trial.

Arizona's Supreme Court decided in *State v. Melendez* in his favor because he had "a reasonable expectation" that his inmate representative would be subject to the same confidentiality rules that would have been in effect had he opted for a street lawyer for his disciplinary hearing (which is allowed under Arizona prison rules).[4]

The Arizona Supreme Court, relying upon the Arizona constitution, found that to permit the state to introduce testimony garnered from communications between a defendant and his formal "inmate representative" would, under the circumstances, be fundamentally unfair and thus a deprivation of due process.[5]

The court reached this conclusion even though it was conceded that there was no attorney-client privilege between a prisoner and a jailhouse lawyer, explaining in its opinion:

> In the case before us, the state—through the [Department of Corrections]—allowed Defendant inmate assistance and representation, and permitted Defendant to meet and consult with his representative. The state now seeks the representative's testimony at a trial regarding the very conduct that served as a basis for the disciplinary proceeding in which he represented Defendant. The effect of such testimony is to take what the state offered Defendant as a "right" to representation and turn it into a trap, depriving Defendant of his due process right to fundamental fairness.[6]

A study of the cases and legal treatises informs us that Melendez's experience wasn't as rare as one might think, simply because the art of jailhouse lawyering affords the unscrupulous a unique opportunity to take advantage of their less informed brethren.

At least one legal scholar has argued that instances such as these necessitate the legislative or jurisprudential grant of what she calls a "jailhouse lawyer–inmate privilege."

Julie B. Nobel authored an article in the *Cardozo Law Review* in which she argues that, in other legal contexts and in other cases, courts have held that lay representatives and their clients have rights of privileged communications, based upon the function being performed by the representative, rather than the representative's status as a prisoner or even training as a lawyer.[7]

She also cites court decisions supporting the right of lay (or non-lawyer) representation, and concurrent rights of privileged communications. Among her favored cases is *Welfare Rights Organization v. Crisan*, where the California Supreme Court held that the attorney-client privilege protects confidential communications between welfare claimants and their lay representatives.[8]

In Nobel's view, functionalism should triumph over form:

> A functional analysis promotes the extension of communication privileges to relationships that are functionally similar to the traditional privileged relationships. In 1887, the court in *Benedict v. State* held that confidential communications between an accused and his lay representative were privileged although the representative had not been admitted to the bar.

Since then, functionalist arguments have continued to promote the application of the attorney-client privilege to certain relationships in which the adviser is not an attorney. The majority of case law expanding the attorney-client privilege in this way concerns patent agents. In more limited instances, this approach has been used to support a communication privilege between clients and the lay representatives who represent them in administrative proceedings.[9]

Nobel argues that this right should be extended to jailhouse lawyers.

As laudable as her goals are, Nobel's proposal will not address nor resolve the problem of jailhouse-lawyer snitches.

Attorney Evan R. Seamone has suggested another possible solution. In an article published in the *Yale Law & Policy Review*, Seamone proposed that jailhouse lawyers not only be certified but be administered a Jailhouse Lawyer Bar Examination, with a stringent code requiring competence, client loyalty, and confidentiality.[10] And while both ideas have obvious merit, they require the State to actually undermine its counter-interest in utilizing prison as a structure of repression and control.

While it is unlikely that conservative courts would ever grant such privileges, it is equally remote that U.S. legislators would ever attempt to pass legislation to this effect. Some states have created privileges for journalists, psychiatric social workers, priests, and others privy to secret communications. In Pennsylvania, for example, confidential communications are protected by specific statutes involving news reporters, clergy, psychiatrists/psychologists, school personnel, sexual abuse counselors, or those involved in crime-stopper or anti-crime programs. These provisions govern both civil and criminal proceedings.

Yet there are few effective legislative lobbyists for jailhouse lawyers, and it's perhaps a safe bet that few members of the legislature would rush to support such a provision.

If one were to rely purely on logic rather than politics, the arguments of both scholars would have some appeal. Yet as another legal scholar, David Kairys, has opined, "Law is politics by other means."[11]

This needn't mean that such a goal isn't attainable, it merely posits certain political realities. In other words, the solutions are political, rather than merely legal. In the meantime, the issue of jailhouse lawyers who have joined the macabre army of snitches remains an ongoing problem that has worsened over time. There are numerous cases where snitches have misused their jailhouse lawyer access to betray their clients. Some cases have made their way to the newspapers, where journalists have reported state and federal prosecutions assisted by jailhouse lawyers.

In 1993, New York's *Newsday* described how the FBI coerced jailhouse lawyers to snitch on an Arab suspect they wanted to prosecute. Florida's *St. Petersburg Times* reported that a jailhouse lawyer snitched not on one, but on "several" of his clients for a reduced term.[12]

Are these not the worst of the worst?

The answer, of course, depends on one's perspective, for the politicians and the corporate media assign one meaning to the phrase and prisoners, generally, have quite another view.

But it's not as though the courts have suggested that snitching is cool. Over a century ago, state and federal courts called the practice of snitching into question. Mississippi's high court, in the 1894 *Wilson* case, and in *Dedeaux v. State* in 1921, ruled that snitch testimony was to be received "with caution," and seen as a "polluted" source of evidence.[13]

In 1909, the U.S. Supreme Court determined that snitch testimony "ought not to be passed upon . . . under the same rules governing other and apparently credible witnesses."[14]

Yet the various wars on crime that followed the Nixon years created a new, politically driven fog of war, and the lessons and admonitions of years past have been lost in this fog.[15]

It is time that jailhouse lawyers were removed from the arsenal of state power and returned to the defense.

Jailhouse lawyers are men and women who work for the well-being and liberation of their fellow prisoners, not for consigning more of them to the hell of time in prison.

12

THE SOCIAL ROLE OF JAILHOUSE LAWYERS

There is an old African-American saying: "It doesn't matter what you call me; it matters what name I answer to." For many jailhouse lawyers, it matters not if they are called writ writers, jailhouse lawyers, or another name altogether, what matters is the social role these men and women answer to—the role they fulfill that bridges a void in the prison system.

Jailhouse lawyers serve best when they can help a fellow prisoner right a wrong or obtain redress for a particular grievance against the state. They fulfill their role when they are able to save a life or open the latch on the cage. They also help when they are able to redress broad, institution-wide, or sometimes statewide grievances. The role of jailhouse lawyers serves to ameliorate a problem that may have broad impact within the prison system, and thus pushes back a particularly repressive act or set of actions contemplated by prison administrators and their political bosses.

In *Brooks v. Andolina*, for example, the U.S. Court of Appeals held that under violation of the First Amendment to the Constitution, prisoners could not be punished for writing a letter that complained about the behavior of a guard.[1] Based on the 1974 Supreme Court case *Procunier v.*

Martinez, the case forbade the state from censoring outgoing correspondence because of complaints against prison staffers.[2]

What, one wonders, could be the downside of such a thing? Cases such as these reinforce the role of the law as an arbiter in social relations and further the image of a fair dealer between litigants on both sides.

Yet it is important to note that cases such as these are civil cases, and as such operate under a different set of rules from those that apply to the majority of criminal legal proceedings. What seems fairly straightforward in the civil context becomes something else entirely when it comes to the life, liberty, and protections of a litigant who seeks standing in the realm of criminal law.

There is an ancient Latin saying that has come to us through England, and before that from Rome: *Rex no potest peccare*—"The King can do no wrong." It is an odd concept in a nation that claims its origin in a statement proclaiming, quite boldly, that the King of England had wronged the people of the American colonies—I speak here, of course, of the Declaration of Independence. Yet the modern legal system is replete with principles that hearken back to that hoary period. Of course, there are no references to the King, but substitute "the state" for "the King" and it fits perfectly.

That doctrine survives in the idea of sovereign immunity, which protects states and officials of states, such as judges, district attorneys, and occasionally prison officials from some of the most atrocious acts imaginable. Additionally, the Prison Litigation Reform Act has worked to make it considerably harder to break through the legislative brick walls surrounding the courthouse.

If we were to translate *Rex no potest peccare* into modern terms, the phrase would say "The state can do no wrong."

Isn't such an idea absurd? Yet, such ancient ideas and principles still hold sway in U.S. courts. It is at this junction that jailhouse lawyers often unwittingly serve the interests of the state by propagating the illusion of "justice" and "equity" in a system devoted to neither.

The prison system is erected upon an unjust, imbalanced, and unfair structure. It maintains and indeed heightens such injustices by its daily existence. Jailhouse lawyers, at times, project to the larger public consciousness the essential fairness of the judicial structures of the state. Thus jailhouse lawyers support the propaganda interests of the state, that it is a fair and equitable arbiter of social and class conflict.

Jailhouse lawyers also serve to release pressure from the pressure cooker that is prison; they present the illusions of legal options as pathways to both individual and collective liberation. As former political prisoner and jailhouse lawyer Ed Mead explains, "courts have defined what's actionable in increasingly narrow terms, and the procedural hurdles . . . have increased so much that . . . it's difficult to make any progress. . . . But in terms of prisoners organizing, in terms of building a movement, in terms of moving things forward, litigation is not the answer. . . . The real need is for political organizing on the inside. It used to be against the law for workers to combine, to organize, to unionize, and workers just went ahead and did it. And that's how they won their rights. And that's the same with prisoners."[3]

If the so-called Rehnquist court and its successor have shown us anything, it has been its naked antagonism to the interests and legal options of prisoners, showing the limits of the law as a liberating vehicle for the millions of imprisoned within the United States—the Prisonhouse of Nations.[4] It is one thing to be an adversary of the State, a role that some jailhouse lawyers relish, but it is something quite different to be an unwitting and unwilling instrument of it.

It can be argued that by their very existence jailhouse lawyers serve the system, especially in the sense that the system denies the rights of the imprisoned to real, meaningful "legal access to the courts" and consents to accept, as a kind of substandard fall-back measure, the assistance of jailhouse lawyers, some of whom are as venal as proverbial ambulance chasers are among street lawyers. If folks have constitutional rights to "access to the courts," why is there no concomitant access to real lawyers to challenge their convictions or their conditions of confinement? In many states, post-conviction counsel is nonexistent. There is no "right to counsel" in a civil context. The burden, therefore, falls on jailhouse lawyers.

Thus, the paradox of being a jailhouse lawyer—to be at once both *subversive to* and a *subject of* the law. Many jailhouse lawyers may not recognize themselves in such a portrait, but, as in the hidden painting of Dorian Gray, a true likeness is reflected.

Nonetheless, as true as this may be, we cannot forget the simple fact that for every case that wins, perhaps a hundred are lost. That is partly due to the sheer vagaries and caprice of American law, to divergent abilities among a wide range of people, or to situations such as Sam Rutherford has eloquently opined, "I have seen prisoners win cases based on briefs that were barely legible simply because the judge wanted to rule in the prisoner's favor."

If Rutherford is right, then the legal system is simply

a "lottery." How can one speak reasonably about the "fairness" of such a system? In such a case, what is to be done? What is the socially conscious, politically aware jailhouse lawyer to do?

Perhaps an old African-American proverb, drawn from centuries of social, political, and cultural struggle can provide an answer: "Speak truth to power." That means, if it does not hurt one's clients, to speak truths about power, the law, and history in the context of one's briefs and legal pleadings.

There is, thankfully, yet another option. Jailhouse lawyers aren't simply, or even mainly, jailhouse lawyers. They are sons, daughters, uncles, nieces, parents, sometimes teachers, grandparents, and occasionally writers. In short, they are part of a wider, broader, deeper social fabric. There are literally thousands, if not tens of thousands of journals, community papers, newsletters, Web sites, and other media that may be explored as outlets to reach people and spread these truths for a wider social discussion and reflection.

It is important to utilize these insights, to "speak truth to power"—and more important, in a radical and revolutionary context, to the people.

The Centrality of Movements

The struggle for Black rights, in a nation predicated upon white supremacy, opened the door for various other social, cultural, gender, and ethnic movements to grow, coalesce, and flower. With the emergence of the Black freedom movement, the reigning ideology on Black rights, which extended to keep other social segments under its hegemony and domination, began to be chipped away. This historical footnote is added not to claim primacy over other movements, but to illustrate how interconnected seemingly disparate movements are, and how one movement can move other segments of society.

History, Marx teaches, is not an impassive, unconscious social phenomenon, but rather people in action against others. "History does nothing, it possesses no immense wealth, fights no battles. It is rather man, real living man, who does everything, who possesses and fights."[5]

Social movements give rise to other social movements, and open up social spaces for people who historically have been oppressed.

The Black Liberation Movement, most specifically the Black Panther Party, gave space in its national journal, *The Black Panther* newsweekly, to prison activists. It also covered and supported various prisoners' movements, such as those of New York's Martin Sostre, that of the Soledad Brothers, the international Angela Davis case, and that of the Party's most famous member, George L. Jackson. Indeed, Jackson was installed as a field marshal in the Black Panther Party's Central Committee, the only such prisoner so honored, which served to make him a larger target for the white nation.

The best impetus for successful jailhouse lawyering is a successful social movement to move the law and society beyond the barriers of the past. No movement can effectively exist in a vacuum; we are interconnected. Jailhouse lawyers must look beyond the state's imprisoning bars, brick, and cement to build relationships with others in the so-called "free" world to further and support social movements that spread liberating and progressive space within society.

AFTERWORD

Why, one wonders, would this book be written today?

It is written, we musn't forget, in the Prisonhouse of Nations—the United States of America. Here, there are more than 2.3 million men, women, and juveniles under lock and key. As the *New York Times* has recently reported, the U.S. has just under 5 percent of the world's population, yet it has a quarter of the world's prison population.[1] In the realm of imprisonment, the United States truly is Number one.

In such a milieu, it is not surprising that there are men and women who are called "jailhouse lawyers." With literally millions of persons so encaged, many of whom are illiterate, poor, and starkly isolated, why should we be surprised at the rise of jailhouse lawyers? The question should be, "Why are there not more?"

Much can be said of the fact that for many, many youth, the nation's educational system has failed dramatically. There are, of course, reasons for this. Nearly half a century after the landmark 1954 case *Brown v. Board of Education* theoretically outlawed school segregation, millions of children are still being miseducated in race- and class-segregated schools, where resources to provide a meaningful education are few and far between.[2] Such deficits in education almost guarantee that good jobs will bypass many who seek to climb their way out of America's burgeoning ghettoes. It should be added, parenthetically, that no federal constitutional right exists guaranteeing a citizen's right to education.

Indeed, for far too may people prison has become the educational system of last resort, for it is here that many people have learned not only to read and to reason, but also a smattering of history, politics, and law. The figure of Black revolutionary Malcolm X is instructive, for it was in the dim night-light under a cell door that his studies transformed him from criminal to committed social activist and revolutionary.[3]

Many jailhouse lawyers have spent many dreadful months and years in the hole reading nothing but law books (as much other reading material is severely restricted). Indeed, this was my own experience, which also featured long extended discussions with dudes like Steve Evans, "Chief Justice," and others. I am indebted to them for their insights.

Given these isolating conditions, usually under severe repression, jailhouse lawyers have climbed the redwoods of institutional grievances all the way to court filings, admittedly with mixed results.

Inasmuch as traditional career lawyers are rarely allowed to intervene in institutional hearings (states like Arizona are exceptional), prisoners are left to the winds of chance, as to which jailhouse lawyer they can find to render assistance.

Unless there is drastic social transformation of the sort that several commentators have suggested, in either bar membership or real confidentiality rules, the number of jailhouse lawyers (albeit of dubious quality) can only increase. For jailhouse lawyers are seeded by the weeds of systemic social injustice.

One may look long and exceedingly hard to find another book about jailhouse lawyers, for to the author's knowledge no other such work exists.

It has thus been an honor to engage in this act of underground reportage of a phenomenon that, while not new, has rarely received the kind of attention and detail that *Jailhouse Lawyers* aims to provide.

Men and women, often self-taught, have developed a tradition of selfless service and in some cases excellence, to serve the needs of society's dispossessed.

To be one of that number has been a challenge and an honor to this writer, who offers this reportage to illustrate what transpires in the depths of America, the Prisonhouse of Nations.

Mumia Abu-Jamal
Death Row
January 2009

APPENDIX A

APPENDIX B

ENDNOTES

INDEX

ABOUT THE AUTHORS

APPENDIX A

In The Supreme Court of The United States
Washington D.C.

Clarence Earl Gideon)
                Petitioner)
        vs.)
H.G. Cochran, Jr, as)
Director, Divisions)
of corrections State)
of Florida)

Petition for a writ
of Certiorari Directed
to The Supreme Court
State of Florida.

No. 890 Misc.

OCT. TERM 1961

U.S. Supreme Court

To: The Honorable Earl Warren, Chief
    Justice of the United States
        Comes now The petitioner, Clarence
Earl Gideon, a citizen of The United States
of America, in proper person, and appearing
as his own counsel. Who petitions this
Honorable Court for a Writ of Certiorari
directed to The Supreme Court of The State
of Florida. To review the order and Judge-
ment of the court below denying The
petitioner a writ of Habeus Corpus.
        Petitioner submits That The Supreme
Court of The United States has The authority
and jurisdiction to review the final Judge-
ment of The Supreme Court of The State
of Florida The highest court of The State
Under sec. 344 (B) Title 28 U.S.C.A. and
Because the "Due process clause" of the

255

fourteenth admendment of the constitution and the fifth and sixth articales of the Bill of rights has been violated. ~~Fith~~ Furthermore, the decision of the court below denying the petitioner a Writ of Habeus Corpus is also inconsistent and adverse to its own previous decisions in parelled cases.

Attached hereto, and made a part of this petition is a true copy of the petition for a Writ of Habeus Corpus as presented to the Florida Supreme Court, Petitioner asks this Honorable Court to consider the same arguments and authorities cited in the petition for Writ of Habeus Corpus before the Florida Supreme Court, In consideration of this petition for a Writ of Certiorari.

The Supreme Court of Florida did not write any opinion, Order of that court denying petition for Writ of Habeus Corpus dated October 30, 1961, are attached hereto and made a part of this petition.

Petitioner contends that he has been deprived of due process of law Habeus Corpus petition alleging that the lower state court has decided a

federal question of substance, in a way
not in accord with the applicable
decisions of this Honorable court. When
at the time of the petitioners trial.
He ask the lower court for the aid of
counsel. The court refused this aid
Petitioner told the court that this
court had made decision to the effect
that all citizens tried for a felony crime
should have aid of counsel. The lower
court ignored this plea.

Petitioner alleges that prior to
petitioners convictions and sentence
for Breaking and Entering with the intent
to commit petty Larceny. he had requested
aid of counsel, that, at the time of his
conviction and sentence, petitioner was
without aid of counsel. That the court
refused and did not appoint counsel, and
that he was incapable adequately of
making his own defense. In consequence
of which he was made to stand trial. Made
a Prima Facia showing of denial of
due process of law. (U.S.C.A. Const
Amend. 14) William V. Kaiser Vs.
State of Missouri 65 CT. 363
Counsel must be assigned to the
accused if he is unable to employ

DIVISION OF CORRECTIONS
CORRESPONDENCE REGULATIONS

MAIL WILL NOT BE DELIVERED WHICH DOES NOT CONFORM WITH THESE RULES

No. 1 -- Only 2 letters each week, not to exceed 2 sheets letter-size 8 1/2 x 11" and written *on one side only,* and if ruled paper, do not write between lines. *Your complete name* must be signed at the close of your letter. *Clippings, stamps, letters* from other people, *stationery or cash* must not be enclosed in your letters.

No. 2 -- All *letters* must be addressed in the *complete prison name* of the inmate. *Cell number,* where applicable, and *prison number* must be placed in lower left corner of envelope, with your complete name and address in the upper left corner.

No. 3 -- *Do not send any packages without a Package Permit.* Unauthorized *packages* will be destroyed.

No. 4 -- *Letters* must be written in English only.

No. 5 -- *Books, magazines, pamphlets,* and *newspapers* of reputable character will be delivered *only if* mailed direct from the publisher.

No. 6 -- *Money* must be sent in the form of *Postal Money Orders* only, in the inmate's complete prison name and prison number.

INSTITUTION _____ CELL NUMBER _____

NAME _____ NUMBER _____

one, and is incapable adequately of
making his own defense
Tomkins vs State missouri 65ct 370
on the 3rd June 1961 A.D. your
Petitioner was arrested for foresaid
crime and convicted for same, Petitioner
recieve Trial and sentence without aid
of counsel, your petitioner was deprived
Due process of law.
Petitioner was deprived of due
process of law in The court. Evidence
in The lower court did not show that a
crime of Breaking and Entering with
the intent to commit Petty Larceny had
been committed. Your petitioner
was compelled to make his own
defense, he was incapable
adequately of making his own defense
petitioner did not plead nolo contender
But That's what his trial amounted
to.

Wherefore the premises considered
it is respectfully contented that the
decision of the court below was in
error and the case should be
review by this court, accordingly the
writ prepared and prayed for should
be issue.

     It is respectfully submitted

     Clarence Earl Gideon
     Clarence Earl Gideon
     P.O. Box 221
State of Florida   Raiford Florida
county of union } ss

Petitioner, Clarence Earl Gideon,
personally appearing before me and
being duly sworn. Affirms, that
the foregoing petition and the facts
set forth in the petition are correct
and true

     Sworn and suberibed before me
this 5th. day of Jan 1962

     Laurence W. Dugger
     Notary Public
     My Commission Expires Aug. 19, 1962
     Bonded by American Surety Co. of N.Y.

APPENDIX B

The exhibits here show how one jailhouse lawyer designed and prepared forms for other prisoners to simply fill in and file, using language drawn from a state statute. On the one hand, the forms seem quite simple. Yet they have proved to be quite valuable to prisoners in Texas who were held in violation of the Texas penal codes.

Article 17.151, C.C.P, The Fast Track out of Texas Jails
  by Matthew T. Clarke, C.P.L.

While this article applies specifically to pre-trial detainees in Texas jails, the Academy prays it will act as a catalyst to prisoner-litigants as they research the fine points of law in their particular jurisdiction.

A little-known provision in the Texas Code of Criminal Procedure (C.C.P.) can result in the immediate release of many Texas jail pre-trial detainees. Article 17.151 was first passed by the Texas Legislature in 1977 and has remained unchanged since then. It provides for the release of a defendant who is being held in jail pending trial if the state is not ready for trial within the following time limits: a) 5 days if accused of a Class C misdemeanor; b) 15 days if accused of a Class B misdemeanor; c) 30 days if accused of a Class A misdemeanor; or d) 90 days if accused of a felony.

The time period starts with commencement of the detention and counts only for continuous detention. Release cannot be obtained if the person is being detained on another charge for which the time period has not elapsed, is serving a sentence, or is incompetent to stand trial. However, if the time period has elapsed, the person must be released on an affordable bond or a personal recognizance bond if no bond is affordable.

The provisions of Article 17.151 are mandatory and the reason for the delay is immaterial. Even if the accused caused the delay, he is entitled to release. *Rowe v. State*, 853 S.W.2d 581 (Tex.Cr.App. 1993).

After the Court of Criminal Appeals delivered its opinion in *Meshell v. State*, 739 S.W.2d 246 (Tex.Cr.App. 1987), which held that portions of the Texas Speedy Trial Act are unconstitutional, there was some doubt as to whether Article 17.151, which was also part of the Texas Speedy Trial Act, was also held to be unconstitutional. However, the Court of Criminal Appeals has specifically held that Article 17.151, Texas Code of Criminal Procedure, is constitutional despite *Meshell. Jones v. State*, 803 S.W.2d 712 (Tex. Cr.App. 1991). Unfortunately, often Texas detainees will be held long after they should have been released under Article 17.151. Then it is appropriate to file a pre-trial petition for a writ of habeas corpus. A sample petition is appended to this article. It has been this member's experience that approximately 20 percent of all inmates held in Texas jails are being held in violation of Article 17.151. This seems to reflect an attitude by the Texas prosecutors that excessive pre-trial detention acts to coerce some defendants into accepting unfavorable plea bargains just to get away from the jail.

The state may make out a prima facie case of being ready for trial by having declared itself ready within the time period. However, the defendant may rebut the state's case by showing that it could not possibly have been ready for trial (due to witnesses being out-of-state, or some other conditions). If the state has not declared itself ready within the time period, it will have the rebuttable initial burden of showing that it was in fact ready. If the state simply states that it has been ready, the defendant may again rebut that assertion by showing conditions which make it unlikely that the state could have proceeded to trial during the time period. (Jones, 803 S.W.2d at 718.)

This member has assisted over a dozen detainees in filing said petition for charges ranging from traffic tickets to capital murder and the success rate at achieving release has been very high. The only failures this member has observed have been when the defendant filing the petition was mistaken about when the state declared itself ready for trial and when the defendant voluntarily withdrew the petition following a threat by the state to proceed to trial immediately. Generally, release has followed within a week of filing the petition provided the defendant contacted the court coordinator and had a hearing scheduled at the next opening on the court's docket. In this regard, Article 11.11, C.C.P., is very helpful. It requires that petitions for a writ of habeas corpus be set for the earliest possible hearing.

Article 17.151, C.C.P., gives the member a rare tool which can result in immediate release for the person he is assisting. It would pay every member who is confined in a Texas jail to examine all of the inmates he can for eligibility for release under this Article. The look on a person's face, who a week before had no hope of release, after being told to "roll it up all the way," can be very rewarding.

NO._____

THE STATE OF TEXAS
IN THE DISTRICT COURT

_____   :

_____   :

                Petitioner   :

V.   :

_____ COUNTY, TEXAS   :   _____ JUDICIAL DISTRICT

PETITION FOR PRE-TRIAL WRIT OF HABEAS CORPUS PURSUANT TO ART. 17.151, C.C.P., FOR RELEASE DUE TO DELAY

TO THE HONORABLE JUDGE OF SAID COURT:

NOW COMES _____, Applicant in the above-entitled and numbered cause, and files this, Applicant's Petition for a Pre-Trial Writ of Habeas Corpus, Pursuant to Article 17.151, Texas Code of Criminal Procedure, for Release Due to Delay, and, in support thereof, would show the Court the following facts:

I.

APPLICANT ILLEGALLY RESTRAINED IN HER LIBERTY
Applicant is illegally confined in the _____
County Jail, in the custody of _____ _____, Sheriff of
_____ County, Texas.

II.

RELEVANT PROCEDURAL HISTORY
Applicant is confined pursuant to a criminal indictment, No.
_____, filed in the judicial District Court of _____ County,
Texas, on _____, 199___, charging Applicant with the felony offense of _____, a copy of which is attached to this petition.
Applicant was arrested for this offense on _____,
199___, and has been continuously confined on said charge since that date.

The State has yet to declare itself "ready" for trial. The State failed to
declare itself "ready" for trial within the ninety (90) day period prescribed
by Article 17.151, Texas Code of Criminal Procedure.

III.

ARTICLE 17.151. C.C.P. IS CONSTITUTIONAL
Applicant is well aware of the Court of Criminal Appeals' ruling in
Meshell v. State, 739 S.W.2d 246 (Tex.Cr.App. 1987), which held that por-
tions of the Texas Speedy Trial Act are unconstitutional. However, the
Court of Criminal Appeals has specifically held that Article 17.151, Texas
Code of Criminal Procedure, is constitutional despite *Meshell Jones v. State*,
803 S.W.2d 712 (Tex.Cr.App. 1991). There is no valid excuse for the
State's failing to be ready for trial within the ninety (90) day period which
would prevent Applicant from being eligible for release on a bond she can
make or personal bond. Even if the delay in the State's being ready is par-
tially attributable to the Applicant, release is still mandated after ninety (90)
days. *Rowe v. State*, 853 S.W.2d 581 (Tex.Cr.App. 1993).

IV.

APPLICANT IS ENTITLED TO RELIEF
Article 17.151, Texas Code of Criminal Procedure states the following
in relevant part:
Sec. 1. A defendant who is detained in jail pending trial of an accusation against him must be released either on personal bond or by reducing
the amount of bail required, if the State is not ready for trial of the criminal
action for which he is being detained within:
(1) 90 days from the commencement of his detention if he is accused
of a felony[.]

Applicant has been detained more than ninety (90) days without the State having been ready for trial. Therefore, Applicant is entitled to immediate release on personal bond or a bond she can afford.

V.
APPLICANT IS INDIGENT

Applicant is indigent and cannot afford to pay bail in this offense. Applicant has no significant cash reserves and no real or other valuable property she can sell in order to make bond. In this regard, Applicant requests that the Court take judicial notice of the fact that the Court has already appointed Applicant counsel due to her indigence.

WHEREFORE, PREMISES CONSIDERED, Applicant prays that the Court set this petition for immediate hearing upon its docket, as mandated by Articles 11.10 and 11.11, Texas Code of Criminal Procedure, and that a writ of habeas corpus issue to have Applicant brought before the Court for a hearing on this petition and that the Court, upon hearing this petition, order Applicant released pursuant to Article 17.151, Texas Code of Criminal Procedure.

Respectfully submitted,

_____

_____

Applicant, Pro Se Address

STATE OF TEXAS   :

COUNTY OF _____   :

VERIFICATION OF UNSWORN DECLARATION

I, _____, Applicant in this cause, state that, following under penalty of perjury: I am a prisoner, # _____, currently incarcerated at the _____ County Jail in _____ County, Texas. I am duly qualified and authorized in all respects to make this declaration. I have read the foregoing Petition for a Pre-Trial Writ of Habeas Corpus and that I have personal knowledge of the facts contained therein and said facts are true and correct.

EXECUTED in _____ County, Texas, pursuant to Article 132.001, et seq., Texas Civil Practice & Remedies Code, and 28 U.S.C. Section 1746, on this _____ day of _____, 199____.

_____

_____

Applicant, Pro Se Address

CERTIFICATE OF SERVICE

I, _____, hereby certify that a copy of the attached document was served on the State's Attorney by turning it over to _____ County Jail Personnel, first-class postage prepaid, addressed to: _____, District Attorney, _____,TX _____, for mailing via U.S. Mail on this _____ day of _____, 199____.

_____
_____
Applicant, Pro Se Address

ORDER GRANTING HEARING

On this _____ day of _____, 199____, came on for consideration the petition for pre-trial habeas corpus by Applicant, _____. The Court having considered same finds that said Applicant should be granted an evidentiary hearing.

It is therefore ORDERED that a hearing be set for the _____ day of _____, 199____, at _____ o'clock _____ in the _____ District Court of _____ County, Texas, for the purpose of applicant proving by a preponderance of the evidence that the facts alleged in her petition for a pre-trial writ of habeas corpus are true.

SIGNED this _____ day of _____, 199____.

_____
DISTRICT JUDGE PRESIDING

ORDER GRANTING PETITION

On this this _____ day of _____, 199____, came on to be heard the petition for pre-trial habeas corpus by applicant, _____, and the court having considered same, finds that said petition should be and is hereby GRANTED.

It is therefore ORDERED, ADJUDGED, and DECREED that Applicant be immediately released on personal bond.

SIGNED this _____ day of _____, 199____.

_____
DISTRICT JUDGE PRESIDING

ENDNOTES

In the summer of 2005, the author conducted a research survey that was circulated to jailhouse lawyers throughout the United States. The responses have been incorporated into this work and are referenced as "communication with author."

List of author's prison correspondence with dates:

Frank Atwood, August 28, 2005, Arizona State Prison, Eyman.

Amber Bray, August 21, 2005, Central California Women's Facility, Chowchilla, California.

George Rahsaan Brooks-Bey August 26, 2005, SCI Fayette, Pennsylvania.

Dejah Brown, July 19, 2005, Central California Women's Facility, Chowchilla, California.

Roger Buehl, July 7, 2005, SCI Albion, Albion, Pennsylvania.

Matthew Clarke, October 1, 2005, Ramsey One, Texas Department of Corrections, Rosharon, Texas.

Shaka Cinque aka Albert Woodfox, July 7, 2005, Angola State Penitentiary, Angola, Louisiana.

Anonymous, August 23, 2005, San Quentin, California.

Margeret "Midge" Deluca, July 29, 2005, Edna Mahan Correctional Facility for Women, Clinton, New Jersey; supplemental interview, March 7, 2007.

Jane Dorotik, July 18, 2005, April 2, 2007, CIW Corona, California.

Barry "Running Bear" Gibbs, September 24, 2005, Graterford, Pennsylvania.

Antoine Graham, August 8, 2005, New Jersey State Prison, Trenton, New Jersey.

Richard Mayberry, June 29, 2005, SCI Fayette, Pennsylvania.

Ed Mead, former prisoner, F.C.I. Marion, Illinois & Monroe Correctional Complex, Washington State, April 11, 2006.

Anonymous, September 9, 2005, Edna Mahan Correctional Facility for Women, Clinton, New Jersey.

David M. Reutter, August 31, 2005 Tomoka Correctional Institution, Daytona Beach, Florida.

Samuel C. Rutherford III, September 9, 2005, McNeil Island Correctional Center, Steilacoom, Washington.

Teresa Torricellas, August 2005, Central California Women's Facility, Chowchilla, California.

Iron Thunderhorse, August 22, 2005, Polunsky Unit, Livingston, Texas.

Charles "Dutchman" Van Dorsten, September 15, 2005, Muskegon Correctional Facility, Muskegon, Michigan.

Herman Joshua Wallace, July 5, 2008, Angola State Penitentiary, Angola, Louisiana.

Robert Williams, December 5, 2008, Fremont Correctional Facility, Colorado.

Ronald "Chief Justice Fat Burger" Williams, July 4, 2005, SCI Greene, Waynesburg, Pennsylvania.

Foreword from the U.K. Publisher

1. See: "USA: A life in the balance – the case of Mumia Abu-Jamal," http://www.amnesty.org/en/library/info/AMR51/001/2000
2. After a visit with Mumia in 2008, Archbishop Desmond Tutu wrote asking if handcuffs could be removed from prisoners during visits, and they were.
3. Legal Action for Women at the Crossroads Women's Centre (LAW). LAW has a sister organisation in San Francisco.
4. The implications are many. "The outpouring [of California's expenditure on prisons] has forced the state's governor . . . to slash other public services including schools with cuts that education leaders have warned could decimate the state's school system." ("U.S. prison population hits new high," *Guardian*, March 1, 2008.)

Preface

1. MOVE—which is not an acronym, but a term meaning to move, get active, resist, etc.—was a Philadelphia-based, multiracial, radical community known for its propensity for protest against various social forces and perceived injustices, from animal exploitation in zoos, to police brutality. As its protests grew, so too did the repression, and MOVE became increasingly blacker.

   On August 8, 1978, the Philadelphia Police Department attacked the West Philadelphia home and headquarters of the MOVE Organization firing thousands of shots into an occupied residence. A Philadelphia cop, James Ramp, was shot by friendly fire, yet nine MOVE members, men and women, were convicted of his murder on May 8, 1980. Philadelphia Common Pleas Court Judge Edwin Malmed sentenced Janine, Debbie, Janet, Merle, Delbert, Mike, Eddie, Phil, and Chuck Africa to thirty to 100 years for the third-degree murder of officer James Ramp.

Several days later Judge Malmed was a guest on the Frank Ford talk show on WWDB-FM radio, when I called in and asked him, "Who shot James Ramp?" Malmed replied, "I haven't the faintest idea." He later told other reporters, "I tried them as a family, and I sentenced them as a family." August 8, 2007, marked their thirtieth year in prison. Today they are eligible for parole, but police and corporate press are conspiring to block their releases. See: Mumia Abu-Jamal, *Live from Death Row*, pp. 188–189.

2. The term "hornbook" refers to a basic theory of law. *Black's Law Dictionary* gives the following definition: "The phrase 'horn-book law' is a colloquial designation of the rudiments or general principles of law." 5th ed., p. 664.

3. The First Amendment of the U.S. Constitution is the first of ten amendments referred to as the Bill of Rights. The First Amendment relates to freedoms of speech, religion, the press, and assembly.

1. Learning the Law

1. Warren Burger, then Chief Justice of the U.S. Supreme Court, quoted in *Time* magazine, June 27, 1977.

2. "Reports" and "reporters" are interchangeable; both refer to verbatim texts of opinions issued by courts.

3. *Santa Clara County v. Southern Pacific Railroad*, 118 U.S. 394, 6 S.Ct. 1132 30 L.Ed. 118 (1886). The case dealt with a county 5 percent tax on profits of Southern Pacific, which amounted to $13,366.53 for fiscal year 1882. Based on an opinion authored by J. Harlan, the assessment was declared "a nullity." Despite how the case has been used by later courts, it was decided based on California's constitution—hardly precedent for other states, much less the entire United States (p. 410).

4. *Black's Law Dictionary* defines headnotes as "a brief summary of a legal rule or significant facts in a case" (p. 48). In the case *U.S. v. Detroit Timber & Lumber Co.*, 200 U.S. 321, the court ruled that headnotes constitute no part of its opinion, and thus had no force of law. It is prepared by the Reporter of Decisions for the convenience of the reader. All U.S. Supreme Court opinions are published in at least three formats: the *Supreme Court Reporter*, a private publication of West Publishing Co.; *The United States Reports*, which is the official text of the Court itself; and *Lawyers Edition*, also published by a private company, which gives far more extensive coverage of such cases, as lawyers and law schools tend
to require references to appellate briefing data and other facets of cases. These reports are notated as S.C., U.S., and L.Ed., respectively.

5. *Santa Clara County v. Southern Pacific Railroad*, op. cit.

6. Edward Lazarus, *Closed Chambers: The Rise, Fall and Future of the Modern Supreme Court* (New York: Penguin, 1999), p. 29.
7. Raoul V. Mowatt, "Inmate wins his own acquittal in stabbing death at Holmesburg," *The Philadelphia Inquirer*, October 29, 1991, p. 6–8.
8. General Equivalency Diploma—a diploma certifying that one has attained high school–level learning.
9. *Johnson v. Avery*, 393 U.S. 483 (1969).
10. *Ayers v. Ciccone*, 303 F.Supp. 637 (W.D. Mo. 1969).
11. Mark S. Hamm et al., "The Myth of Humane Imprisonment: A Critical Analysis of Severe Discipline in Maximum Security Prisons, 1945–1990," in Michael Braswell, Steven Dillingham, and Reid Montgomery Jr., eds., *Prison Violence in America*, 2nd ed. (Ohio: Anderson, 1994), p. 188.
12. Mumia Abu-Jamal, *All Things Censored* (New York: Seven Stories, 2000), p. 240 (in text, not table form).
13. *Ruiz v. Estelle*, 503F.Supp. 1265 (S.D. Tex. 1980), pp. 1299–1300. See Ch. 7 on the *Ruiz* case and its impact on Texas.

2. What "the Law" Is

1. Will Durant, *The Story of Philosophy* (New York: Simon & Schuster, 1961), p. 7.
2. Karl Marx and Frederick Engels, *The Communist Manifesto* (Chicago: Kerr Publishing Co., 1998), p. 36. Originally published in 1848.
3. Emphasis added. Herbert Aptheker, *American Negro Slave Revolts* (International Publishers: New York, 1943), pp. 61–62.
4. Howard Zinn, *Declarations of Independence: Cross-Examining American Ideology* (New York: Harper Perennial, 1990), p. 158; fr. F. L. Meek, ed., *Lectures on Jurisprudence: Adam Smith* (Oxford: Oxford University Press, 1978).
5. Angela Y. Davis, "From the Prison of Slavery to the Slavery of Prison," in Joy James, ed. *The Angela Y. Davis Reader* (Malden, Mass.: Blackwell Publishers Inc.,1998), p. 76.
6. Durant, op. cit., p. 7.
7. Alexis De Tocqueville, *Democracy in America* (Bantam Classic: New York, 2004), pp. 303–304. Original published in 1835.
8. *Hobbs et al. against Fogg*, 6 Watts (PA.) 553 (1837), p. 554.
9. Ibid., 555–6.
10. Ibid., 556.
11. *Dred Scott v. Sandford*, 60 U.S. (19 How.) 393 (1857). The case was infamous for its finding that blacks "had no rights which the white men were bound to respect." It is generally regarded as a trigger for the U.S. Civil War.
12. *Hobbs v. Fogg*, 6 Watts (Pa.) p. 553 (1837).
13. John Africa, *The Judges Letter* (Philadelphia: n.p., ca. 1978).
14. *Fulwood v. Clemmer*, 206 F.Supp. 370 (D.D.C. 1962).

15. *Cruz v. Beto*, 405 U.S. 319 (1972).

16. *Africa v. Commonwealth of Pennsylvania*, 662 F.2d 1025 (3CA 1981).

17. E.g., *Colon v. Coughlin*, 58 F.3d 865, 872 (2nd Circ. 1995) (false charges claim); *Woods v. Smith*, 60 F.3d 1161 (5th Circ. 1995) (false charges claims); *Babcock v. White*, 102 F.3d 267 (7th Circ. 1996) (transfer); *Valandingham v. Bojorquez*, 866 F.2d 1135 (9th Circ. 1989) ("snitch" claim).

18. Zinn, *Declarations of Independence*, op. cit., p. 135.

19. Ibid., p. 135.

20. Ibid.

21. Cited in Howard Zinn, foreword to Peter Irons, *A People's History of the Supreme Court* (New York: Viking, 1999), p. vi.

22. Circuit Judge Newman's article has been published in a number of journals, including *The Correctional Professional* (January 1996), *Prison Legal News* (April 1996), and *62 Brooklyn Law Review* (1996).

23. U.S. Constitution, Eighth Amendment: "Excessive bail shall not be required, nor excessive fines imposed, nor cruel and unusual punishments inflicted."

24. *Prison Litigation Reform Act of 1996* (PLRA), Public Law 104–134, 110 Stat, 1321 (April 26, 1996).

25. Michael Meeropol, *Surrender: How the Clinton Administration Completed the Reagan Revolution* (Ann Arbor: University of Michigan Press, 1999). Cited in Gregory Albo, "Neo-Liberalism from Reagan to Clinton," *Monthly Review* (April 2001), pp. 81–89. Meeropol was born Michael Rosenberg, one of two sons of Ethel and Julius Rosenberg, who were targeted, convicted, and executed on June 19, 1953, by the U.S. government, ostensibly for spying for the Soviets. The case of the Rosenbergs became an international issue, with a great many people protesting the conviction. Years later, files became public revealing government and judicial collusion to ensure their convictions and execution, furthering government efforts to whip up a Red scare. See: Howard Zinn, *A People's History of the United States: 1492-Present* (New York: HarperCollins, 2005), p. 426; Mumia Abu-Jamal, *All Things Censored* (New York: Seven Stories, 2000), pp. 262–263. Indeed, a recent account in the *New York Times* (Sunday, September 14, 2008, p. 42) supports the claim that neither Rosenberg participated in atomic bomb secrets and that the prosecutors knew that Ethel Rosenberg was completely innocent, but thought by convicting her they would pressure Julius Rosenberg to confess to espionage.

26. Emphasis added. Michael Ratner and Ellen Ray, *Guantánamo: What the World Should Know* (White River Junction, Vt.: Chelsea Green, 2004), Appendix I, p. 110 (excerpt from Article I, "Convention Against Torture and Other Cruel, Inhumane or Degrading Treatment or Punishment," available at www.unhcr.ch/html/menu3/b/h_cat 39.htm).

27. *Ngo v. Woodford*, 403 F.3d 620 (9 CA 2005) n. 1.

28. See F.1, in *Ngo*, ibid.
29. *Siggers-El v. Barlow*, 433 F.Supp. 2d 811 (E.D. Mich. 2006) (cited in 18 *Prison Legal News* 34 [January 2007]).
30. "PLRA's Mental and Emotional Damage Award Ban Unconstitutional in $219,000 First Amendment Claim," 18 *Prison Legal News* 34.
31. Ibid.
32. 141 Congressional Record S14, 418 (daily ed. Sept. 27, 1995), Statement of Senator Hatch.

3. When Jailhouse Lawyers "Represent"

1. *Black's Law Dictionary*, p. 230.
2. In the United States, trials are usually handled by trial lawyers. On appeal to higher state or federal courts, one may hire appellate counsel or be granted or appointed such counsel.
3. *Commonwealth v. Billa*, 555 A.2d 835 (Pa. 1989), p. 842.
4. *Mills v. Maryland*, 486 U.S. 367 (1988), outlawed the requirement of unanimity in the finding of mitigating circumstances in death cases.
5. Emphasis added. *Com. v. Billa*, ibid., p. 181.
6. Civil rights actions have their impetus in the Civil Rights Acts, federal statutes enacted after the U.S. Civil War (1861–1865). They are known popularly as the Ku Klux Klan acts, for they were written in response to white terrorism against the newly freed captives in the South. Also called §1983 actions, under Tit. 42 U.S.C. §1983, which authorizes suits against state actors for violation of constitutional rights.
7. *Herron v. Harrison*, 203 F.3d 410 (6 CA [Tenn.] 2000), pp. 414–415.
8. *Thaddeus-X v. Blatter*, 175 F.3d 378 (6 CA 1999).
9. *Herron v. Harrison*, op. cit., pp. 414–15.
10. On May 13, 1985, the Philadelphia Police Department used a helicopter to drop a bomb on a residential building in which MOVE members were living. The bomb's blast resulted in the death of eleven people, including four children. Most of an entire city block burned down in the fire caused by the bomb.
11. Clark DeLeon, "MOVE: Blasting the media," *Philadelphia Inquirer*, January 24, 1981, 2-B.
12. Kitty Caparella, (untitled sidebar) *Philadelpia Daily News*, July 14, 1981.
13. Kitty Caparella, "Reunion: MOVE Leader Greets Accuser," *Philadelphia Daily News*, July 3, 1981.
14. A.W. Geiselman Jr., "Testimony of Witness Challenged," *The Bulletin*, July 9, 1981, Philadelphia edition.
15. Ibid.
16. Tom Masland, "Defense in MOVE Case Tells of Group's Power," *Philadelphia Inquirer*, July 14, 1981.
17. *The Guidelines* are a collection of John Africa's teachings, ideas, and outlook, many in typed, xeroxed, and handwritten form. From June 28

to July 29, 1975, the *Philadelphia Tribune*, a local Black biweekly, published a column titled "On the MOVE: The Writings of John Africa."

18. Trial transcript of *U.S. v. Africa*.

19. *United States v. Vincent Leaphart a/k/a John Africa, et al.*, #77-380 (E.D. Pa. 1981), N.T. (July 16, 1981), pp. 10.86–10.87

20. Ibid. Emphasis added.

21. Trial transcript of *U.S. v. Africa*.

22. Kitty Caparella, "Sobbing MOVE Chief Takes Case to Jury," *Philadelphia Daily News*, July 17, 1981.

23. Trial transcript of *U.S. v. Africa*.

24. Ibid.

25. *U.S. v. V. Leaphart*, op. cit., pp. 10.146–10.154.

26. Ibid. at 10.154.

27. Kitty Caparella, "No Hard Feelings, John Africa Says," *Philadelphia Daily News*, July 23, 1981.

28. Ibid.

29. Not being reduced to M-1 means that the charges were not reduced from felony to misdemeanor.

30. *Com. v. Janet Knighton*, M.C. 81-11-2088; *Com. v. Theresa Africa*, M.C. 81-11-2109; and *Com. v. Michael Jones, a/k/a Master Michael Africa*, M.C. 81-11-2206; 2207; 2208, Municipal Ct., City Hall, Philadelphia, Pa., March 15, 1982.

31. *Com. v. Knighton; Africa; Jones*, ibid.

32. *Faretta v. California*, 422 US 806 (1975).

33. Pennsylvania Constitution, Art. I; Sect. 9.

4. What about Street Lawyers?

1. *World Almanac and Book of Facts, 2008*, "Employed Persons in the U.S. by Occupation and Sex, 2005, 2006" (New York: World Almanac Books, 2008), p. 97.

2. Clarence Darrow, *Attorney for the Damned: Clarence Darrow in His Own Words*, Arthur Weinberg, foreword William O.Douglas. Also see: Darrow, Clarence, Crime and Criminals, Address to the Prisoners in the Cook County Jail, Simon and Schuster 1957

3. Howard Zinn, *A People's History of the United States, 1492–Present*, (New York: HarperCollins, 1980 [2003]) p. 367.

4. Clarence Darrow, *Crime and Criminals*, op. cit.

5. *Faretta v. California*, 886.

6. University of Chicago Web site: http://press-pubs.uchicago.edu/founders/print_documents/amendV-VI_criminal_processs2.html.

7. J.B. Bury, *History of the Later Roman Empire: From the Death of Theodosius to the Death of Justinian* [vol. I] (Mineola, N.Y.: Dover, 1958), p. 4.

8. Emphasis added. De Tocqueville, *Democracy in America*, op. cit., p. 323.

9. Ibid., pp. 321–22.

10. Jerry Fresia, *Toward an American Revolution: Exposing the Constitution &
    Other Illusions* (Boston: South End Press, 1988), pp. 1–2.
11. Ibid., p. 177.
12. Ibid., p. 20.
13. Ibid., p. 28.
14. 1 Pa. C.S.A. §1503 (a); (b). The Courts of Common Pleas, King's
    Bench and Exchequer were former superior and supreme courts of
    England prior to the Judicature Acts of the 1870s and '80s, which reor-
    ganized courts. The King's Bench, as the name suggests, was formerly
    a court presided over by the king (or queen) and dated from the reign
    of William the Conqueror, 1066 C.E.
15. 1 Pa. C.S. §1503 (a); (b).
16. Oliver C. Cox, *Caste Class & Race, A Study in Social Dynamics* (Monthly
    Review Press, New York 1948 [1970]), p. 318, fn.2; from J. G. Nicolay
    and John Hay, *Abraham Lincoln, Complete Works* Vol. 1 [1894], p. 105.
17. Zinn, *A People's History of the United States*, op. cit., pp. 260–61.
18. *Civil Rights Cases*, 109 U.S. 3 (1883), 25.
19. Ibid., p. 32.
20. Ibid., p. 62.
21. Irons, *A People's History of the Supreme Court*, op. cit., p. 214.
22. Howard Zinn, *Declarations of Independence: Cross-examining American
    Ideology* (New York: Harper Perennial, 1990), p. 156.
23. Mumia Abu-Jamal, "Defense Lawyer—For the Prosecution!" Novem-
    ber 29, 2000 (commentary), citing the *New York Times*, November, 24,
    2000.
24. Ibid.
25. *Strickland v. Washington*, 466 U.S. 668 (1984).
26. Roger Darloff, "Effective Assistance Ain't Much," *American Lawyer*
    (January–February 1993).
27. For the case in which the lawyer was high on heroin and cocaine dur-
    ing the trial, see Darloff, ibid.
28. *People v. Badia*, quoted by Roger Darloff, *Harper's magazine*, March
    1993.
29. Darloff, *American Lawyer*, op. cit.
30. *Vines v. United States*, 28 F.3d 1123 (11CA [Fla.] 1994), p. 1129.
31. Ibid., pp. 142–43.
32. *Johnson v. Norris*, 207 F.3d 515 (8CA 2000).
33. Ibid.
34. *The Concise Columbia Encyclopedia*, Third Edition (New York: Columbia
    University Press, 1983), p. 528.
35. *Rickman v. Bell*, 131 F.3d 1150, 1159 (6CA 1997).
36. *Rickman*, ibid., 1157.
37. William M. Kunstler, *The Emerging Police State* (Melbourne/New
    York: Ocean Press, 2004), p. 41.
38. MOVE members like Ramona Africa (survivor of the May 13 Mas-

sacre) continue to organize. She has spoken at Harvard, on numerous television shows, and frequently before international audiences in France, Germany, and beyond.

39. *Fontroy et al. v. Beard et al.*, 485 F.Supp. 2d 592 (E.D. Pa. 2007).
40. Ibid., pp. 597–598.
41. Ibid., p. 598.
42. Ibid.
43. Jerome F. Kramer, "Scholarship and Skills," *National Law Journal* (January 9, 1989), pp. 15–16.

5. The Jailhouse Lawyering of Mayberry

1. Literally, the Latin term means, "for himself," or one who appears or files papers in court, without benefit of a lawyer. Black's L Dict., 1099. In some jurisdictions, the term *pro per*—meaning "for himself"—or *in propria persona* is used to the same legal effect.
2. *Black's Law Dictionary* defines the "Court of Quarter Sessions" thus: "Formerly, a court of criminal jurisdiction in the state of Pennsylvania, having power to try misdemeanors, and exercising certain functions of an administrative nature" (pp. 324–325; 5th ed., 1979). Indeed, the formal title of the court was Court of Quarter Sessions of the Peace. The Court was established by the Pennsylvania constitution of 1776, and abolished in the Pennsylvania constitution of 1968, Art. V (Schedule); Sect. 4. The Clerk of Quarter Sessions now functions as the clerk of the courts for the Court of Common Pleas of the City of Philadelphia. Tit. 42 Pa. C.S. §2751.(c).
3. *Mayberry v. Pennsylvania*, 400 U.S. 455, 91 S.Ct. 499, 27 L.Ed.2d 532 (1971).
4. Ibid.
5. Ibid. pp. 500–501.
6. Ibid.
7. Jay Sterling Silver, "Equality of Arms and the Adversarial Process: A New Constitutional Right," 1990 *Wisconsin Law Review*, p. 1007.
8. Ibid., n. 1; citing Blackstone, *Commentaries*, p. 340.
9. *Mayberry v. Pennsylvania*, Ibid.
10. *Mayberry v. Pennsylvania*, p. 502.
11. Emphasis added. *Mayberry v. Weinrott*, 255 F.Supp. 80 (E.D. Pa. 1966), pp. 81–82.
12. Emphasis added. *Com. v. Langnes*, 434 Pa. 478, 255 A.2d 131, 136 (1969).
13. *Mayberry v. Frame*, 383 F.Supp. 212, 214 (W.D. Pa. 1974).
14. *I.C.U. v. Shapp*, 451 F.Supp. 893 (E.D. Pa. 1978); Dkt. No.: C.A. #70-3054, consent decree (ordered May 22, 1978).
15. Consent decrees are agreements made by both sides to an action, and sealed by a court. In a sense, it is a civil contract to which both sides are bound.

16. *Mayberry v. Maroney*, 529 F.2d 332, 336 (3CA 1976); Conover case: 477 F. Supp. 893 477 F.2d 1073 (3CA 1 973).
17. *Mayberry v. Maroney*, ibid., 336.
18. Communication with the author.
19. Ibid.
20. Ibid.

6. A Woman's Work in State Hell

1. Emphasis added. Angela Y. Davis, "Race and Criminalization: Black Americans in the Punishment Industry," *The Angela Y. Davis Reader*, ed. Joy James (Malden, Mass.: Blackwell Oxford, 1998), p. 66.
2. *Pro bono* is a Latin term meaning, literally, "for the good," and usually means the provision of legal services for free. *Black's Law Dictionary*, 1092. It is sometimes used in its fullest term: *pro bono publico*, L. "For the public good" (1083).
3. Communication with author.
4. Ibid.
5. A section of a state prison regulation that governs prison grievances that prisoners may file against staff, either individually or collectively.
6. A minute order is a brief excerpt of the court's order showing sentencing.
7. Communication with author.
8. Joy James, ed., *Shadow-Boxing: Representations of Black Feminist Politics* (New York: St. Martin's Press, 1999), pp. 28–29.
9. Ian F. Haney Lopez, *White By Law: The Legal Construction of Race* (New York: NYU Press, 1996), p. 44.
10. *U.S. v. Cruikshank*, 92 U.S. 542, 544–45 (1876).
11. *Fletcher v. Peck*, 6 Cranch 87. [10 U.S. 87, 3 L.Ed. 162 (1810)].
12. Ibid.
13. Richard Lawrence Miller, *Drug Warriors & Their Prey: From Police Power to Police State* (Westport, Conn.; Praeger, 1996).
14. Source: movementbuilding.org/prisonhealth/womens.html.
15. Communication with author.
16. Communication with author.
17. Ibid.
18. Sharon Schlegel, "Doing Doable Time," *Trenton Times*, October 5, 2004.
19. Ibid.
20. Communication with author.
21. Ibid.
22. Ibid.
23. Ibid.
24. Schlegel, "Doing Doable Time," op. cit.
25. Communication with the author.
26. The reference is to *Gilmore v. Lynch*, 319 F. Supp. 105 (N.D. Ca. 1970)

aff'd per curiam sub. nom. *Younger v. Gilmore*, 404 U.S. 15 (1971) which supports inmate assistance to file petitions and complaints to allow meaningful access to the courts.

27. Communication with author.
28. Ibid.

7. The Ruiz Effect: How One Jailhouse Lawyer Made Change in Texas

1. *Ruiz v. Estelle et al.*, 503 F.Supp. 1265 (S.D. Tex. 1989). W. J. Estelle, the first named defendant, was director, Texas Dept. of Corrections. Other source material for this chapter: Janet Elliot, "Inmate who fought for prison reform dies," *Houston Chronicle*, Nov. 15, 2005, pp. B1–B7.
2. *Ruiz v. Estelle*, ibid., p. 1281.
3. Ibid., p. 1295.
4. Ibid., p. 1369–70.
5. Ibid., pp. 1294–5.
6. Ibid., p. 1370.
7. Janet Elliot, op. cit.
8. Communication with the author.

8. From "Social Prisoner" to Jailhouse Lawyer to Revolutionary: Ed Mead's Journey

1. Communication with the author.
2. Ibid.
3. Ibid.
4. Ibid.
5. The White Panther Party, believed originally to have been formed in Ann Arbor, Michigan, functioned briefly as a radical support group for the Black Panther Party. Although it overtly emulated the Black Panthers in its mode of dress and rhetoric, its members went to jail on relatively minor weapons and drug charges. They did not engage in the level or frequency of conflicts faced by the Black Panthers, although they did experience police repression.
6. Communication with the author.
7. *Quotations of Chairman Mao Tse-Tung*. (Peking [Beijing]:Foreign Language Press, 1972).
8. Communication with the author.
9. *Jones v. North Carolina Prisoners' Labor Union*, 433 U.S. 119 (1977).
10. Communication with the author.
11. Ibid.

9. Jailhouse Lawyers on Jailhouse Lawyers

1. *Gideon v. Wainwright*, 372 U.S.335 (1963).

2. See www.ocpd.state.ct.us/images/Gideon%20Petition.gif.
3. Communication with the author.
4. Communication with the author.
5. Communication with the author.
6. Communication with the author.
7. Communication with the author.
8. Communication with the author.
9. Communication with the author.
10. Communication with the author.
11. A legendary lifer and denizen of the hole, Ben Porta, responded to the advertiser by hitting him the next morning with a milk carton full of piping-hot, watery feces. Not simply because he was an irritating jailhouse lawyer, but because he was loud and irritating, and dared to mention Porta's name.

10. The Best of the Best

1. Mark S. Hamm et al., in *Prison Violence in America*, op. cit., p. 188.
2. *Brooks v. Andolina*, 826 F.2d 1266 (3CA 1987).
3. National Association for the Advancement of Colored People.
4. After initial appeal, trial "resumed" in district court and there was still friction at the county jail.
5. Communication with the author.
6. *Furman v. Georgia*, 408 U.S. 238 (1972).
7. *Sostre v. McGinniss*, 442 F.2d 176 (2CA 1971), p. 189.
8. Communication with the author.
9. Communication with the author.
10. M. T. Clarke, "Article 17.151, C.C.P., the Fast Track Out of Texas Jails," *The Paralegal Bench*. This journal was published by NCOP/Academy for Paralegals, Inc., 2721 Merrick Way, Abingdon, Md. 21009-1162; (410) 569-9114. See appendix.
11. Communication with the author.
12. Communication with the author.
13. Communication with the author.
14. Communication with the author.
15. Communication with the author.

11. The Worst of the Worst

1. David Cole, "In Case of Emergency," *New York Review of Books*, July 13, 2006, p. 43.
2. Michael Ratner, "The Guantánamo Prisoners," in Rachel Meeropol, ed., *America's Disappeared: Detainees, Secret Imprisonment, and the "War on Terror"* (New York: Open Media/Seven Stories Press, 2005), p. 39. Newly elected President Barack Obama has issued an Executive Order

closing Guantanamo's detention center and forbidding torture. David Jackson and Richard Wolf, "Obama revamps rules on detainees," *USA TODAY*, January 23, 2009, p. 1A. However, there should be no question that torture remains, for Obama, as a member of the Illinois state legislature, surely knew of the torture that occurred, for decades, in the precincts of the Chicago Police Dept., especially under the command of then Lt. Jon Burge, who tortured people with abandon and expertise, and by so doing sending men like Aaron Patterson, Cortez Brown, and many other to Death Row. Glenn Allen, "Cortez Brown should be free." *Socialist Worker*, January 2, 2009, p. 13.

3. *McNeal v. State*, 551 So.2d 151, 158 n.2 (Miss. 1989).

4. *State [of Arizona] v. Melendez*, 172 Ariz. 68, 834 P.2d 154, 1992 Ariz. LEXUS 50 (1992).

5. Ibid., p. 71, where the court cited *Ohsrin v. Coulter* [142 Ariz. 109, 111, 688 P.2d 1001, 1003 (1984)], for the following definition of due process denials: "[T]he denial of due process is a denial of 'fundamental fairness, shocking to the universal sense of justice.' "

6. Ibid., p. 72.

7. Julie B. Nobel, "Ensuring Meaningful Jailhouse Legal Assistance: The Need for a Jailhouse Lawyer-Inmate Privilege," 18 *Cardozo Law Review* 1569 (1997); LEXC 18 *Cardozo Law Review* 1559, pp. 1585–1586. *Benedict v. State*, 11 N.E. 125 (Sup. Ct. Ohio, 1887).

8. 661 P.2d 1073 (Ca. 1983). Also see: *Woods v. New Jersey Dept. of Education*, 858 F.Supp. 51 (D.N.J. 1993), extending the attorney-client privilege to a lay advocate and the client she represented before the New Jersey Office of Administrative Law.

9. Julie B. Nobel, op. cit.

10. John E. Dannenberg, "Fahrenheit 451 on Cell Block D: [Certified Jailhouse Lawyer Program Proposed]," *Prison Legal News* (Mar. 2007), p. 30, citing Evan R. Seamone, *Yale Law & Policy Review* vol. 24, no.1 (2006), pp. 91–147.

11. David Kairys, "Legal Reasoning," in M.A. Foley, "Critical Legal Studies: New Wave Utopian Socialism," *Dickinson Legal Review* Vol. 91 (winter 1986), p. 473.

12. Andrew Z. Galarneau & Craig Pittman, "Jailhouse 'Lawyer' Works as Snitch," *St. Petersburg Times*, August 14, 1995, p. 6.; David Kocienieuski *et al.*, "FBI Coerced Nosair's Jail Friends," *Newsday*, April 14, 1993, p. 8.

13. *Dedeaux v. State*, 87 So. 605 (Miss. 1921) (citing *Wilson v. State*, 71 Miss. 880, 16 So. 304 1894).

14. *Crawford v. U.S.*, 212 U.S. 183, 204, 29 S.Ct. 260, 53 L.Ed. 465 (1909).

15. This war is eerily reminiscent of another so-called war, one just as dubious, and one that has left the social landscape strewn with destruction—the war on drugs.

12. The Social Role of Jailhouse Lawyers

1. *Brooks v. Andolina*, 826 F.2d 1266 (3CA 1987).
2. *Procunier v. Martinez*, 416 U.S. 396, 94 S.Ct. 1800 (1974).
3. Communication with the author.
4. As these words were written, Rehnquist the man was no more. None-theless, his judicial philosophy of antipathy towards the very notion of prisoners' rights is well known and continues to resonate within the court despite his passing.
5. From Karl Marx and Friedrich Engels, *Gesamtausgabe*, I, iii, 625; cited in E.H. Carr, *What is History?* (New York: Vintage, 1961), p. 60, n. 4.

Afterword

1. Adam Liptak, "Inmate Count in U.S. Dwarfs Other Nations," *New York Times*, April 23, 2008.
2. *Brown v. Board of Education*, 347 U.S. 483 (1954). In *Brown* the Court unanimously ruled that school segregation violated the Constitution's 14th Amendment under the equal protection clause. In doing so, it overruled a case precedent that had stood for over fifty years, *Plessy v. Ferguson*, 163 U.S. 537 (1896), which supported public segregation under the spurious, judge-created doctrine of "separate but equal." In fact, of course, African Americans suffered for over half a century under a system that was demonstrably "separate and quite unequal."
3. Alex Haley (coauthored with Malcolm X), *The Autobiography of Malcolm X* (New York: Ballantine Books, 1998), passim.

INDEX

"Passim" (literally "scattered") indicates intermittent discussion of a topic over a cluster of pages.

ACLU. *See* American Civil Liberties Union
Abu Ghraib prison, 14, 68, 233
accused terrorists, 234–35
Adams, John Quincy, 172
Adams, Niki, 21, 22
administrative segregation, 80, 188, 217, 225. *See also* behavioral adjustment units
Africa, Alphonso ("Mo"), 83–94 passim, 99–100
Africa, Delbert, 27–29
Africa, Ishongo, 87
Africa, Janine, 145
Africa, Jeanette, 101
Africa, Jeanne Champagne, 87
Africa, John, 58, 82–100, 114–115
Africa, Mike, 145
Africa, Phil, 88–89
Africa, Ramona, 115, 275n38
Africa, Theresa, 101–05 passim, 112, 115
Africa v. Pennsylvania, 59–60
African Americans. *See* Blacks
American Civil Liberties Union, 147, 149
 Prison Project, 224
American Revolution, 122–30 passim
Amnesty International, 21
anthrax, 149
Anti-Terrorist and Effective Death Penalty Act, 218
appellate counsel, 74, 76
appellate courts, 78–79
apprenticeship, 35–36
aristocracy, 124–28 passim, 133
Arizona, 250
 Supreme Court, 236–37
Armsberry, Chuck, 194–96 passim

attorneys. *See* lawyers
attorneys general, 63, 64
Ayers v. Ciccone, 47

Bagram, Afghanistan, 233
Bayou, Paul, 196
Bear, Running. *See* Gibbs, Barry "Running Bear"
Beard, Jeffrey A., 148, 149
behavioral adjustment units, 162
bench memos, 41
Billa case, 75–77, 211
bipolar disorder, 140–41
Black Codes, 17, 53, 72, 171–72
Black Muslims, 58–59, 222
Black Panthers, 23, 197, 209, 219, 222, 248, 277n5
Blacks, 25, 168
 civil rights, 130–33, 247–48, 280n2
 voting, 55–58 passim
Black's Law Dictionary, 211, 269n4
Blackstone Career Institute, 231
Blackstone, William, 155
books and reading, 43–44, 222
Boston massacre, 126
Bradley, Joseph, 131
breast cancer, 175, 177
bribery, 199
Britain. *See* Great Britain
Brooks, George Rahsaan, 218–25 passim
Brooks v. Andolina, 218–19, 243–44
Brown v. Board of Education, 280
Brownstein, Al, 224
Bryan, Robert R., 25
Buddhism and Buddhists, 59, 60
Buehl, Roger, 207–08, 215–16, 224–25
Buffalo, New York, 222
"building tenders," 16, 187–90 passim
Bureau of Alcohol, Tobacco, and Firearms, 85, 89, 114
Burger, Fat. *See* Williams, Ron
Bury, J. B., 123

California, 17. *See also* Central California Women's Facility; Corona Institution for Women; Valley State Prison for Women
California Prison Focus, 191
cancer, 175, 177
Carr, William, 100
censorship, 244
Central California Women's Facility, 168, 170, 174
certiorari, 206
Cheney, Dick, 234
"Chief Justice Fat Burger." *See* Williams, Ron
Church of God, 79
circuit courts, 78–79
City of Nightmares (Henderson), 45
civil disobedience, 61
The Civil Rights Cases (1883), 130–33 passim
Clarke, Matthew, 225–27, 258–60
class and law, 51, 52, 62, 73, 127, 133
    Clarence Darrow on, 118–21 passim
    Ed Mead on, 201
class and war: Eugene Debs on, 119
class consciousness, 203
client and lawyer, 73–74, 135–47 passim, 210, 236–39, 279n7
Clinton, Bill, 62, 66–67
closing arguments, 96–99
cocaine
    use by lawyers, 137, 145
    use by pregnant women, 175
Cold Creek Correctional Facility, 79
Cole, David, 234
colonial America, 121–22
Commentaries on the Laws of England (Blackstone), 155
Committee to Safeguard Prisoners' Rights, 223
communism, 203
confidentiality, 236–39
confiscation of belongings, 65

Conover v. Montamuro, 162
consent decrees, 161–62, 275n15
Constitution. *See* U.S. Constitution
Constitutional Convention, 1787, 127
contempt of court, 152–60 passim
Convention against Torture, 14, 69
convictions, wrongful. *See* judicial error
Corona Institution for Women (California), 179–83 passim
corporate personhood, 40
Court of Quarter Sessions (Pennsylvania), 152, 275n2
court reporters, 40
crack cocaine, 171
Cruz v. Beto, 59

Dalton, Roque, 44
Darrow, Clarence, 18–21
Davis, Angela Y., 53, 167, 248
Davis, J. C. Bancroft, 40–41
death penalty cases, 75–77, 135–36, 143, 230
death row, 13, 209
Debs, Eugene, 119
Declaration of Independence, 123, 132
Defenders Association of Philadelphia, 147
DeLuca, Midge, 174–79
Democracy in America (Toqueville), 54, 123–24
detainers, 42
Dickinson, James, 127
Diggs, Charles, 224–25
disciplinary action. *See* punishment
Dorotik, Jane, 168–74, passim, 215
double-celling, 16, 186
Dred Scott v. Sandford, 131–32, 270n11
drug offenses, 171
drug testing, 214
"drug war," 171–73 passim
drunk driving, 175
due process, 103, 279n5

Duncan, Taurus, 214–15
Durant, L. Marc, 100
Dye, Paul, 214

Edna Mahan Correctional Facility for Women, 175–79 passim, 229
education, 182–83, 249–50, 268n4. *See also* teaching
Eighth Amendment. *See* U.S. Constitution: Eighth Amendment
election law, 55
elections, 202
Ellsworth, Oliver, 61
England, 127–29 passim, 155–56, 244, 274n14
erroneous convictions. *See* judicial error
escapes and escape attempts, 148–49, 192–93
Evans, Steve, 37–43, 45

FBI, 240
Faretta v. California, 121–22
Fauntroy v. Beard, 148–49
Fayette state prison. *See* SCI-Fayette
Fifth Amendment. *See* U.S. Constitution: Fifth Amendment
First Amendment. *See* U.S. Constitution: First Amendment
Fogg, William, 55
Fonda, Jane, 198
Fontroy, Derrick Dale, 148
food, 64–66 passim
"Founding Fathers," 125–27
Fourteenth Amendment. *See* U.S. Constitution: Fourteenth Amendment
"freeman" (word), 57
Fresia, Jerry, 125
frivolous lawsuits (alleged), 17, 63–71 passim
Fulwood v. Clemmer, 59
Furman v. Georgia, 222

GED, 178–79, 214, 270n8
George Jackson Brigade, 200
Gibbs, Barry "Running Bear," 75–76, 210–12 passim, 229–30
Gibson, James, 56–57
Gibson, John Bannister, 56–57
Gideon, Clarence Earl, 206
Gideon v. Wainwright, 206–07
Glassey, Donald, 86–96 passim
Glover, Mary, 223
Glover v. Johnson, 223
Gorham, Nathan, 127
Graham, Antoine, 179, 213
Graner, Charles, 68
Graterford state prison. *See* SCI-Graterford
Great Britain, 127–29 passim. *See also* England
Green, Clifford Scott, 83
Greene state prison. *See* SCI-Greene
grievances, 181
Guantánamo Bay, Cuba, 233–35 passim
guards. *See* prison guards
The Guidelines (Africa), 90, 93–94, 272n17
Gulliver's Travels (Swift), 62

habeas corpus, 160, 195, 225, 260
Hamilton, Alexander, 127
Hamm, Mark S., 47
Hampton, Fred, 23
handcuffs, 268n2
Harlan, John, 131–34 passim
Hatch, Orrin, 63, 70–71
headnotes, 40
Henderson, Warren, 43–45
Herron, Isaac L., 78–81
Herron v. Harrison, 79
history: Marx on, 248
Hobbs v. Fogg, 58
"the hole." *See* administrative segregation
Holmesburg Prison, 27, 45, 219

hope, 179
"hornbook" (word), 269n2
Howard, Larry "Kareem," 219
hunger strikes, 84, 200
Huntingdon state prison. *See* SCI-
Huntingdon

*Imprisoned Citizens' Union (I. C. U.)
v. Shapp*, 18–19, 161–62
In Prison My Whole Life, 26
ineffective counsel, 135–46 passim
inequality, 52–53
informants. *See* snitches
International Covenant on Civil
and Political Rights, 14
Iraq, 233–34
Iron Thunderhorse. *See* Thunderhorse, Iron

Jackson, George, 248
Jackson, Ricardo, 101
Jackson, Robert, 41
Jailhouse Lawyer Bar Examination
(proposed), 239
"jailhouse lawyer" (term), 165, 205,
209
James, C. L. R., 21
James, Joy, 170
Johnson v. Avery, 46–47
Johnson v. Norris, 139–41
Johnson, William Samuel, 127–28
Jon, Abdul, 100–114
Jones, Damon, 212
*Jones v. North Carolina Prisoners'
Labor Union*, 201
Joyner, Robert, 219
judges, 60–61, 231–32
North Carolina, 51
Pennsylvania, 56–57, 76–77
on alleged flood of "crazy pris-
oner" lawsuits, 64
See also U.S. Supreme Court:
justices
judicial error, 174
Judicum Dei, 155

jury selection, 84–85
jury sequestration, 29, 30
Justice, William Wayne, 185–90
passim

Kairys, David, 240
Kerness, Bonnie, 178
Kramer, Jerome F., 150
"Ku Klux Klan acts," 272n6
Kunstler, William, 144

Larsen, Rolf, 76–77
law
definition of, 51–72
study and teaching, 35–49
See also election law; legal precedents
law clerks, 41, 42
law libraries, 166, 170, 176, 181,
183, 194, 226, 228
lawyers, 117–50
cocaine-using, 137, 145
John Africa on, 97–98
mentally ill, 140–41
self-representation and, 115
sleeping on the job, 137
Texas, 74
See also appellate counsel; attorneys general; client and
lawyer; ineffective counsel
lawsuits, prisoners'. *See* prisoners'
litigation
Lazarus, Edward, 41
Lee, Bob, 190
legal education. *See* law: study and
teaching
legal precedents, 62, 124
Lewisburg Federal Prison, 42
limiting instructions, 76–77
litigation, prisoners'. *See* prisoners'
litigation
*The Little Red Book. See Quotations of
Chairman Mao Tse-tung*, 200
Lincoln, Abraham, 35–36, 130
Lorde, Audre, 175–76

Luongo, Alfred I., 157–59 passim

mail, 146–49 passim
Malcolm X. *See* X, Malcolm
Malmed, Edwin, 268–69
manic depression. *See* bipolar disorder
Manville, Dan, 223, 224
Marion Control Unit. *See* U.S. Penitentiary, Marion, Illinois
marriage, 229
Marx, Karl, 51, 248
Marxism, 203
Massachusetts, 122
Mayberry, Richard, 18, 39, 151–66, 208, 216, 218
cited by others, 211–12, 223, 224
Mayberry v. Frame, 160–61
Mayberry v. Maroney, 162
Mayberry v. Myers, 166
Mayberry v. Pennsylvania, 153
Mayberry v. Weinrott, 157
McNeil Island Corrections Center, 193, 195
Mead, Ed, 191–204, 245
media, 68. *See also* television
medical care, 175–79 passim
Meeropol, Michael, 67, 271n25
Melendez, Ruben, 236–38 passim
Mencken, H. L., 60
mentally ill lawyers, 140–41
Meshell v. State [Texas], 259
Michigan Department of Corrections, 214
Miguel Mármol (Dalton), 44
Miller, Richard L., 171–73 passim
Mills v. Maryland, 272n4
miscarriage of justice. *See* judicial error
Mississippi: Supreme Court, 235, 241
Missouri Medical Center, 47
monarchy, 127
morality, 51
MOVE, 27, 59, 82–115, 145–46, 268, 272n10

Muhammad, Abu Bakr, 78
Muhammad, Gail, 178
"The Myth of Humane Imprisonment," 47–48, 80, 217

NAACP, 219
Nation of Islam members. *See* Black Muslims
National Association of Attorneys General, 64, 69
National Lawyers Guild, 22, 200, 223
Native Americans, 172
religious freedom, 58, 59
Nazis, 171
New York Times, 133
Newman, Jon O., 64, 69
Ngo v. Woodford, 69
Nobel, Julie B., 238–39
Norman trials, 155

O'Brien, Henry X., 159–60
outdoor exercise, 221
Owen, Richard Lee II, 223

Paralegal Bench, 226
paralegals, 35, 46, 179–83, 225–27, 231
Patrizio, Stephen, 83
peanut butter, 17, 63–66 passim, 201, 202
Pennsylvania, 18–19
Court of Quarter Sessions, 152, 275n2
Supreme Court, 30, 56–58, 76, 128–29, 152, 159–60, 230
See also Philadelphia; SCI-Fayette; SCI-Graterford; SCI-Greene; SCI-Huntingdon; SCI-Pittsburgh
Pennsylvania Institutional Law Project, 147
People v. Badia, 137
People v. Murphy, 137
People v. Tippins, 136

Pharmachem Sweat Patches, 214
Philadelphia
    police and MOVE, 82, 88,
        114–15, 268, 272n10
    trials, 82–115
Pittsburgh state prison. *See* SCI-
    Pittsburgh
plea bargains, 259
Plessy v. Ferguson, 280n2
Porta, Ben, 278n11
The Practical Stylist (Baker), 212
precedents. *See* legal precedents
presidents, 125–27
pretrial detention, 226–27, 258–66
prison discipline. *See* punishment
prison guards, 68, 70
Prison Law Monitor, 224
Prison Law Office, 17
Prison Legal News, 63–64, 191, 203,
    217
prison library assistants, 46
Prison Litigation Reform Act
    (PLRA), 14–17 passim, 62–63,
    66–71 passim, 161, 208, 244
Prison Radio Project, 23, 191–204
    passim
prisoners' litigation, 17, 60, 63–71
    passim, 161, 162, 185–90, 199, 227
    *Prisoners' Self-Help Litigation
        Manual*, 224
See also frivolous lawsuits (alleged);
    Prison Litigation Reform Act
pro se defense. *See* self-representa-
    tion
Procunier v. Martinez, 243
punishment, 15, 47–49
    civil rights suits and, 78–81

*Quotations of Chairman Mao Tse-
    tung*, 201

race relations, 163–65, 189
racism, 16–18 passim, 179, 272n6
    in education, 280n2
    in jury selection, 25
    in law, 53, 62, 130–134 passim,
        171–72
Ramp, James, 268–69
Ratner, Michael, 234
Read, George, 128
Rehnquist, William, 41, 279n4
religious freedom, 58–60 passim, 79
Renfroe, Adam, 101, 108–11 passim
restricted housing units, 221
retaliation, 47–49, 60
    civil rights suits and, 78–81,
        187–89 passim, 218–19
Reutter, David M., 212–13
revolution, 130. *See also* American
    Revolution
rich men, 125–27
Rickman v. Bell, 143–44
riders (legislation), 67, 72
Robinson, Alfredo, 214
Rosenberg, Ethel, 271n25
Rosenberg, Jerry, 222, 224
Rosenberg, Julius, 271n25
Rousseau, Jean-Jacques, 51
Ruffin, Thomas, 51
Ruiz, David, 16, 185–90
Ruiz v. Estelle, 16, 49, 185–90 passim
Running Bear. *See* Gibbs, Barry
    "Running Bear"
Rutherford, Sam, 230–32, 246–47

SCI-Fayette, 219
SCI-Graterford, 219
SCI-Greene, 68, 219
SCI-Huntingdon, 31, 38, 42, 161
SCI-Pittsburgh, 219, 221
salad bars, 64–66 passim
*Santa Clara County v. Southern Pa-
    cific Railroad*, 40, 269n3
Satanism, 59
Savage, Theodore, 148
Seamone, Evan R., 239
Seeger, Pete, 198
segregated schools, 249, 280n2
segregation, administrative. *See*
    administrative segregation

self-help legal services, 22
self-representation, 82–115 passim, 117–18, 151–66 passim, 206, 225
sentencing and sentences, 75, 77, 169–70, 225
sequestration of juries. *See* jury sequestration
sexual abuse, 171
Shoats, Russell "Maroon," 219
Siggers-El, Darrell, 70
Siggers-El v. Barlow, 70
Slaughter House Cases, 130
slavery, 17–18, 51, 53, 56
    influence on Texas prison organization, 188
    slave codes, 17, 53, 72
    slave owners, 125–27, 220
Smith, Adam, 52
Smith, David B., 135–36
Smith, Robert, 140
"snitch" (label), 60
snitches, 38, 86–87, 235–41
Snite, John, 83, 90–92 passim
socialists, 119
Society of Pediatric Research, 173
Soledad Brothers, 248
solidarity, 248
punishment for, 81
Sostre, Martin, 222–23, 248
Sostre v. McGinnis, 222
Sostre v. Otis, 222
Sostre v. Rockefeller, 222
South Africa, 171, 202
Southern Career Institute, 182
sovereign immunity, 244
Standard Minimum Rules for the Treatment of Prisoners, 14
Stanton Story, et al. v. William Robinson [Commissioner], et al., 219
State [Arizona] v. Melendez, 237
statistics, 25, 167, 171, 173, 205, 249
Steilacoom Support House, 195–96, 200
Story, Stanton, 219

Strickland v. Washington, 136–41 passim
strikes, 198, 219. *See also* hunger strikes
strip-searching, 221
suicide, 171
Supreme Court, U.S. *See* U.S. Supreme Court
Sunfighter Prisoner Newsletter, 200
Swift, Jonathan, 62

teaching, 209–210
television: on alleged flood of "crazy" prisoner lawsuits, 63, 64
Tennessee, 46, 79
terrorists, accused. *See* accused terrorists
Texas, 16, 74, 185–90, 225–27 passim
    legal forms, 258–66
Texas Speedy Trial Act, 259
Thaddeus-X v. Blatter, 79, 80
Thirteenth Amendment. *See* U.S. Constitution: Thirteenth Amendment
Thunderhorse, Iron, 223–24
Toqueville, Alexis de, 54–55, 123–24
Torricellas, Theresa, 179–83
torture, 68–69, 233–34
trial by ordeal. *See* Judicum Dei
triple-celling, 186
Tucker, Russell, 135–36
Turner v. Safley, 229
Tutu, Desmond, 268n2

UK. *See* Great Britain
U.S. appeals courts, 78–79
U.S. Bureau of Alcohol, Tobacco, and Firearms. *See* Bureau of Alcohol, Tobacco, and Firearms
U.S. Constitution
    First Amendment, 31, 60, 63, 70, 79, 80, 219, 243, 269n3

Fifth Amendment, 103
Sixth Amendment, 206
Eighth Amendment, 66, 271n23
  Thirteenth Amendment, 133, 160
  Fourteenth Amendment, 40, 130, 134, 280n2
U.S. Penitentiary, Marion, Illinois, 200, 233
U.S. Supreme Court, 25, 38–41 passim, 46, 134, 160, 161, 241, 245
  justices, 41, 61–62
publication of decisions, 269n4
  Faretta v. California, 121–22
  Fletcher v. Peck, 172
Furman v. Georgia, 222
Mayberry v. Pennsylvania, 153
Procunier v. Martinez, 243
Santa Clara v. Southern Pacific Railroad, 40
U.S. v. Cruikshank, 171–72
U.S. v. Detroit Timber & Lumber Co., 269
Uighurs, 234
United States Reports, 269n4

Vacco, Dennis, 65
Valley State Prison for Women, 168, 174
Van Dorsten, Charles, 213–15

Vasquez v. N.J. Dept. of Corrections, 229
Vietnam, 203
Vines, Miguel, 138–39
Vines v. U.S., 138–39

Washington State Penitentiary, Walla Walla, 200
Washington State Prisoners Labor Union, 200
Waynseburg, Pennsylvania, 68
wealthy men. *See* rich men
Weinrott, Leo, 152–57 passim
welfare, 17
Welfare Rights Organization v. Crisan, 238
Wheeler, Aaron C., 148
White Panthers, 194, 197, 277n5
Wicca, 59
Williams, Ron ("Chief Justice Fat Burger"), 209–211, 216, 229, 230
women prisoners, 167–83
work strikes. *See* strikes
Wright, Paul, 191, 217
writing, 212
wrongful convictions. *See* judicial error

X, Malcolm, 250

Zinn, Howard, 60–61, 130, 134

ABOUT THE AUTHORS

MUMIA ABU-JAMAL is an award-winning journalist and author of two bestselling books, *Live From Death Row* and *Death Blossoms*, which address prison life from critical and spiritual perspectives. In 1981 he was elected president of the Philadelphia chapter of Association of Black Journalists. His 1982 murder trial and subsequent conviction has raised considerable controversy and criticism for alleged constitutional violations and other improprieties. In spite of his more than two-decade-long imprisonment on death row, Abu-Jamal has fought for his freedom and for his profession. He holds a BA from Goddard College and an MA from California State University, Dominguez Hills.

ANGELA Y. DAVIS is Professor Emerita of History of Consciousness at the University of California and author of eight books. She is a member of the executive board of the Women of Color Resource Center, a San Francisco Bay Area organization that emphasizes popular education of and about women who live in conditions of poverty. Having helped to popularize the notion of a "prison-industrial complex," she now urges her audiences to think seriously about the future possibility of a world without prisons and to help forge a twenty-first-century abolitionist movement. Her most recent books are *Abolition Democracy* and *Are Prisons Obsolete?*, both published in the Open Media Series.